CONCORDIA

CONCORDIA

The Roots of European Thought

Comparative Studies in Vedic and Greek Ideas

Stephen R. Hill

Duckworth

First published in 1992 by
Gerald Duckworth & Co. Limited
The Old Piano Factory
48 Hoxton Square, London N1 6PB

ISBN 0 7156 2401 6

A catalogue record for this book is available
from the British Library

Photoset in North Wales by
Derek Doyle & Associates, Mold, Clwyd
Printed in Great Britain by
Redwood Press Ltd, Melksham

Contents

Acknowledgments

I am indebted to two friends for their wise advice and suggestions. First, my thanks go to Peter G. Harrison, co-author of *Dhātu-Pāṭha*: The Roots of Language, who has advised on many aspects of the Vedic tradition, including an original translation of Hymn to the Guru in Chapter Fourteen. Secondly, I am grateful to Dr Robert W. Sharples of University College London, for his suggestions on many aspects of the Greek tradition. Their assistance does not necessarily mean that they concur with all the ideas expressed in this volume.

Preface

A schoolboy's lot in post-war Britain was not a particularly enlightening one, not at least as I experienced it. The first cause of my lack of enlightenment was definitely Latin, and I suspect that many others suffered in exactly the same way. To sit indoors in serried ranks to learn Latin was not enjoyable, particularly when the sun was shining. One suspected that it was even unnecessary and probably pointless: no teacher had ever explained the purpose of the study and any objective it may have had, whereas there was clearly a point in learning French, as people living not far away actually spoke it.

To make matters worse, after laborious sessions learning by rote the verbal conjugations, declensions of substantives and numerals and some elementary syntax, sentences began to emerge. These early sentences were filled with gloom and they usually involved a general called Cotta, who led a laborious life crossing and recrossing rivers, taking and exchanging hostages, setting sieges, laying waste the countryside and being attacked by Barbarians. At the tender age of eight I began to harbour a sneaking respect for these Barbarians; they clearly did not want to learn Latin either, but were in the happier position of at least being able to do something about it. Even the introduction of the purpose clause failed to define the objective, although a new general, called Agricola, now appeared in sentences and was sent to Scotland in order to subdue the Scots. This also failed to attract: was Agricola a woman, I wondered, and did she wear a cloak?

As the Latin became harder, a tougher breed of general began to appear in even longer sentences – men such as Scipio, Hannibal and Caesar, who were harder to ignore, for they came with infantry and cavalry and tactics and strategy. Soon everyone in Europe was fighting and being conquered and having to learn Latin. My own future also took on a dismal hue: it would be necessary to be victorious at a Latin exam in four years' time to gain admittance to a public school, where advanced Latin would be taught so that you could pass the obligatory Latin examination to enter Oxford or Cambridge, those great universities, where people even spoke Latin on important occasions.

My Guardian Angel, however, had other plans and gradually

introduced me to rich pastures far away from the dry desert of the classroom, to the arts of music, painting, sculpture, architecture and literature, to Bach and Mozart, to Rembrandt and Renoir, Wren and Shakespeare. These works exuded a different quality altogether from Latin unseens. They called the mind on a hunt and 'real questions' were posed: 'Who am I?' 'What is this world?' 'What is the purpose of human life?' They were difficult, nagging questions that were strong because they were uncomfortable, insistent as they demanded answers. The campaigns of Cotta and Caesar wallowed in the mud of my unresponsive intellect, the doors of Oxford remained firmly closed to me and instead I searched to answer these fundamental questions, without which life held many enjoyable forms but little purpose.

If I have held your attention thus far, it is possibly on account of a growing satisfaction that your experiences were similar to mine and that you may be deriving some therapeutic benefit from our mutual and youthful detestation of Latin, and possibly classrooms in general. Be warned, however, for Guardian Angels can play tricks in order to set you on your way; for fifteen years after gleefully singing 'no more Latin, no more French, no more sitting on the old school bench', my Guardian Angel performed what in these days is called a 'U-turn' and much to my surprise took me back to school, at the less tender age of thirty-three, to read classics as a mature student at King's College, London.

During those intervening fifteen years I had been introduced to the great ideas of India and Ancient Greece and even to the Indo-European system of languages in which they were expressed. The discovery of the *Veda*, Upanishads, Greek philosophy and their related works and teachings revealed a unified whole, a great teaching and a common understanding reflected in the various cultures. In fact, it was possible to appreciate in the mind the unifying concept of 'One Man', for example where *Kṛishṇa* was Christ and vice-versa. The discovery that their names came from the same root, just as with *Īśā* and Jesus, was stimulating. The idea that true religions were in some way different and at odds with each other began to appear misleading and erroneous. The self-evident fact that there can only be 'One Truth' was borne out by the evidence from comparative studies in the language and key texts of the Indo-European cultures. It is the conviction that this approach can reveal meaning and understanding of the sacred teachings, with a little timely help from the Bard, that led me to write this book.

Perhaps two short examples of meaning and understanding, which may not in themselves be immediately obvious, may illuminate what I wish to convey. The traditional Homeric greeting to Odysseus from those he encountered on his journeys sounds reminiscent of that dreadful opening gambit at an English cocktail party: 'Who are you and whence do you come?' However, the sentence acquires a deeper meaning altogether when one realises that the Odyssey is a description of a spiritual journey and that it is those 'real questions' that are being posed at each encounter. Similarly, that repetitive introduction much favoured by the Gospellers, 'It came to pass', seems to have as much significance on a casual reading as 'Once upon a time', which means nothing whatsoever but is delightfully English. However, if the clause is expanded to 'It came in order to pass', we have miraculously a complete and accurate description of the entire phenomenal universe in one phrase. Like Odysseus, we must all pass through this physical world and, through guidance from the 'real questions', come to realise that this insubstantial passing pageant is here to teach us the eternal verities. We may then begin the return journey to the Self and whence we came.

Finally, I would not wish to appear in more mature years as an ignorant denigrator of Latin. Latin is not just the language of Cotta and his military escapades, but is also the language of devotion; no one can hear a sung mass in Latin without feeling its force. In my next incarnation, however, I would prefer to start with the great ideas expressed in Greek, so as to experience conscious ideas in a young mind, rather than mere military, logical and historical matters. Even better would be an introduction to comparative alphabets, the parts of speech and grammar based on the Sanskrit system which expresses the natural laws of Creation, so that this approach imbued the other systems with its intelligence and universality. Then one could in one's early teens appreciate, for example, *Śaṅkara's* authoritative commentaries on the Upanishads. This possibility need not be considered as a distant aim, for it is only a change of mind, rather than some over-exertion of mind, that is required. The question that demands an answer is therefore: why teach young minds about military campaigns, invasions, subjections and their supposed attendant benefits, when the blessings of the greatest teachings of mankind are also available? The idea that history is determined by military might and political acumen is but one side of the coin; on the other lies history seen from the standpoint of consciousness and human development.

In this book, I wish to chart a course, however rough and ready, to illuminate the potential benefits of an approach based on comparative studies in Indo-European Thought. It sets out to formulate some first thoughts on a possible new approach. It does not aim to be an exhaustive enquiry into any of the subjects touched upon, for that would defeat its object, which is to stimulate enquiry. Rather, it is a general survey giving the lie of the land; any attempt to make such a work complete and comprehensive would probably be impossible and certainly unhelpful. It is more in the nature of an historical meditation or play on Indian and Greek themes and so interpretations drawn are for the purpose of this comparative approach rather than seeking to enter into a debate on the historically most probable interpretation within either tradition. This book may generate interest in exploring the possibilities and even encourage an examination of the wealth of material that is already available, as I seek to demonstrate that such a study does have a beginning, a middle and an end.

S.R.H.

Introduction

> The Lord, whose being is ever in his own
> Self, turned the senses outwards.
> Therefore, a man's senses turn outwards
> and not to the inner Self.
> A few men of discrimination cognise the
> indwelling Self,
> By turning away from sense objects and
> desiring immortality.
>
> *Kaṭha* Upanishad, Ch.II, Canto 1, v.1

The starting point for this book is the expansion of pure consciousness into Creation as an act of Love. The Creation Myths, the ensuing cosmologies and the appearance of epic, philosophical and literary writings are examined and some commonly held beliefs disappear: the idea that civilisation is built up over centuries in a linear progression, with a gradual expansion of knowledge and learning on the back of the triumph of good over evil, is tidy but not necessarily correct. The Universal Mind, it seems, is not given to straight lines but rather to circles. In fact, according to some interpretations, in the age in which we live, civilisation is actually declining: the growth of learned books, which is assumed to indicate progress, is actually the result of a distinct loss of memory, as the oral traditions die out. And all this is apparently in accordance with the laws of universal dissolution, which is rather alarming, as the notion that Mankind is in some way progressing and living a fuller life is a commonly held belief.

It is true that scientific breakthroughs in the twentieth century have transformed our physical lives in such basic fields as medicine, transport, communications and home comforts, but these are material advances, and belonging to the physical world of becoming do not exist in the spiritual world of being. A society comprising inventive technocrats lacking spirituality would be as useless as one made up entirely of sages who lacked practical ability. In our technological society, science thinks it sees ever further into an improving future, but Man seeking true knowledge must research the roots of his culture, which lie in the past, and rediscover their essence by returning to traditional classical texts, reinterpreting them afresh and representing them in a true and appropriate form for the new millennium. To begin this odyssey, let us summon up our English bard, Will Shakespeare, to speak of universal and eternal verities in timeless poetry.

When I consider every thing that grows
Holds in perfection but a little moment,
That this huge stage presenteth naught but shows
Whereon the stars in secret influence comment;
When I perceive that men as plants increase,
Cheered and checked even by the selfsame sky;
Vaunt in their youthful sap, at height decrease,
And wear their brave state out of memory:
Then the conceit of this inconstant stay
Sets you most rich in youth before my sight,
Where wasteful time debateth with decay
To change your day of youth to sullied night;
    And all in war with time for love of you,
    As he takes from you, I engraft you new.

Shakespeare, Sonnet 15

PART I

Creation, Roots & Gods

1

Birth of Creation

The universe was created by sound. The sound was causal and belonged to the language of Gods rather than men. It was causal in the sense that 'the Word' spoke everything into existence. In the Vedic tradition, this sound is known as *praṇava śabda*, meaning 'ever present and ever new', with the prefix *pra-* meaning 'beyond', implying 'beyond Creation'.[1] The *praṇava* is *sat*, meaning 'that which cannot be broken'. This sound is '*AUM*', which is a *mantra* rather than a spoken word: being in the *mantra* system of language as opposed to the *vyākaraṇa* or vernacular system, it is beyond the reach of the senses and the mind, beyond being and non-being, for as the Vedic Creation Hymn describes the unborn condition:

> Then that which is was not.
> That which is not was not.
>
> *Ṛigveda*, 10,127,1

AUM is 'the sacred syllable' and implies assent to the expanding Creation, carrying the meaning of 'Amen, so be it':

> Verily, this syllable is assent:
> for whenever a man assents to anything,
> he says simply *AUM*.
> This indeed is a realisation;
> that is, assent is.
>
> *Chāndogya* Upanishad, Ch.1, Canto 1, v.8

'*AUM* is all that which has been, that which is and is to be; that all is *AUM*, only *AUM*. Literally analysed, *AUM* is made up of three letters; the letter "A" is *Vaiśvānara*, the spirit of waking Souls in the waking world; "U" is *taijasa*, the spirit of dreaming Souls in the "world of dreams"; and "M" is *Prajñā*, the spirit of sleeping and undreaming Souls; and the whole *AUM* is said to be unknowable, unspeakable, into which the whole world passes away, blessed above duality'.[2] The first and purest sound to arise from *AUM* is *aham*. This sound can only be heard by the Creator or *Ātman*, for it is only less than *AUM* in that it arises out of it. *Aham* is called *nāda śabda*, meaning the imperceptible 'roar',[3] which is the sounding Will of the Creator.

In the Judaeo-Christian tradition, the same idea is expressed in the opening words of St John's Gospel: 'In the beginning was the Word' or '*Logos*'. The Gospeller has carefully used the historic imperfect tense 'was': the historic expresses the idea that 'the Word' existed before the beginning and the imperfect that it continues to exist; this echoes the meaning of *praṇava* in the Vedic tradition. The Gospeller rightly states that 'the Word was God' for the *praṇava śabda*, *nāda śabda* and *aham* are the '*Logos*' and in their purity are one and the same. The Creator then entered into every part of Creation when 'the Spirit of God moved upon the face of the waters'.[4] The Self saw its own reflection in the water, could not resist identifying with the vision, and so plunged into the ocean of immortal bliss. This description is reminiscent of the descent of the Soul in the third-century A.D. writings of Plotinos, where the Soul 'plunges in an excessive zeal to the very midst of its own chosen sphere'.[5] The unembodied Self became embodied in order to experience Itself, but with this desire, however, the possibility of subject and object became endemic in the embodied being.

It is clear that the two accounts are essentially similar but they are somewhat cryptic: what is 'the Word' or '*Logos*' and how exactly does it work? Most would accept the idea that sound is at least contiguous with Creation: you cannot dissociate in your mind the waves breaking on the shore from the actual roar of the sea and its groundswell. Audible sound travels at sea level and in clear air at 1,100 feet per second. Visible light on the other hand travels at 186,000 miles per second in all conditions, which is accepted as infinite speed. As the eye is always receiving sensory impressions ahead of the ear, the conditioned mind automatically and mistakenly believes that sound is the effect and not the cause. In fact, the unmanifest sound that emanates from the pure consciousness as *aham* resounds throughout Creation and is experienced as the unceasing feeling of existence. This is the meaning of the Vedic sutra *Bhū Sattāyām*,[6] which proclaims that 'being' is ever present in 'existence'.

Thus Creation is spoken into existence in a truly scientific way by a *mantra* system of causal language, which is imperceptible and of necessity in existence before the beginning. This language of the Creator was existing in the undifferentiated and unmanifest consciousness: '*prajñā*, consciousness, is *pratiṣṭhā*, the support of the whole universe'.[7] In order to manifest, however, the imperceptible 'roar' was required to produce a vibration. This vibration was necessary to differentiate the pure consciousness into the manifold aspects of Creation: for in order for God to create, he clearly had to create something apart from Himself. This significant phase in the expansion of Creation is referred to in the Vedic version as *edha*, meaning 'increase, extension, prosperity and happiness',[8] and the activity takes place through the agency of *spadi*, meaning 'vibration'.[9]

The opinion of the wisest commentator on Vedic literature is instructive, for *Śṛī Ādi Śaṅkara*, (*c*. A.D. 788-820), the founder of the *Advaita* doctrine of 'Non-duality', warns that the necessary vibration in the expansion of Creation is even less than the most minute oscillation: in fact 'It vibrates, that is, it appears to vibrate'.[10] Behind this subtle commentary stands a mighty theme, that the Creator appeared to create duality, in the sense of the Creator and his Creation, but in actual fact this vibration is the pure magic of the Creator at work. This subtle and necessary trick of Creation, whereby the absolute *Brahman* is manifested as the relative world, is beyond logical formulation and is referred to as *māyā* in the *Veda*. *Śaṅkara* adds that 'the vibration of consciousness, as it were, is set in motion by ignorance, for the unmoving consciousness can have no vibration'.[11] Thus, he concludes, consciousness, or what may be called spirit, is unborn and immovable.

This philosophic stance lies at the heart of the Vedic tradition and is called *Advaita*, meaning literally 'Not Two' and is referred to as 'Non-duality'. Non-duality means 'the joy arising from a knowledge of the identity of the universe and the Supreme Spirit',[12] which is none other than the knowledge that the inner world which is the cause of the manifest Creation and the outer world of beautiful forms are in fact one. For it is the Self Itself, while remaining in the inner world, which at the same time projects Itself, by the apparent minutest and imperceptible oscillation in consciousness, as the ever changing outer world of beautiful manifest forms in time and space. The essence of *Advaita* is that the Creation in all its varied manifestations is nothing but a projection of one's own Self, or pure consciousness.

The manifest world in which we 'live, move and have our being'[13] is only temporary. In fact, it is almost not there at all; when you are absent from your study, the study and its books are no longer present, and just as that which is in presence cannot be denied, so absence cannot be experienced even as non-presence. The manifest world only comes into being because the inner world is there to project it. When it appears beautiful, the ordinary mind's activity has stepped aside to reveal the beauty of the playful projection of the Self. The joy in the moment of the Self discovering the Self through the Creation, which Creation is in turn its very own projection, is reflected in the *Vedic* tradition in this statement by the Lord *Śṛī Kṛishṇa*:

> My womb is the great *Brahman*,
> in that I create and sustain the seed.

Thence O *Bhārata* [*Arjuna*]! the simultaneous generation of all created beings.

Gītā, Ch.14, v.3

The simple structure is 'as above, so below'. The individual Soul is of the same consciousness as the *Brahman*; the physical body is of the same substance as the universe. However, the introduction of *spadi* or vibration causes *sparddha* or an element of friction to enter into Creation.[14] In the Vedic tradition, *Prajāpati*, the Lord of all created beings, 'projected all the organs of action; these, being projected, contended with one another'.[15] The result of this rivalry is that 'the generations of *Prajāpati* are twofold, the Godly and the Ungodly, and they contended with each other for these worlds'.[16] With the duality, however, jealousy, envy and desire entered Creation, for the illusion of *māyā* is fundamental to both the human sleeping and waking conditions: 'As in dream the mind vibrates by the instrumentality of *māyā*, presenting an appearance of duality, so also in the waking state, the mind vibrates by the instrumentality of *māyā*, presenting an appearance of duality'.[17]

The above Vedic description is most closely reflected in a brief statement by Plato: 'Clearly, all things are created when the first principle receives increase and attains to the second dimension, and from this arrives at the one which is neighbour to this, and after reaching the third becomes perceptible to sense. Everything which is thus changing and moving is in process of generation; only when at rest has it real existence, but when passing into another state it is destroyed utterly'.[18] Plato is here referring to the *aham* or creative principle, the *edha* or expansion and the *vyakta* or manifest Creation. Plato equates the creative principle with the Soul as the 'Self-moving' principle in Creation, which is unmoved by anything else:

> The Soul through all her being is immortal, for that which is ever in motion is immortal; but that which moves another and is moved by another, in ceasing to move ceases also to live. Only the Self-moving, never leaving Itself, never ceases to move, and is the fountain and beginning of motion to all that moves besides. Now the beginning is unbegotten, for that which is begotten has a beginning; but the beginning is begotten of nothing, for if it were begotten of something, then the begotten would not come from a beginning. But if unbegotten, it must also be indestructible; for if beginning were destroyed, there could be no beginning out of anything, nor anything out of a beginning; and all things must have a beginning. And therefore the Self-moving is the beginning of motion; and this can neither be destroyed nor begotten, else the whole heavens and all Creation would collapse and stand still, and never again have motion or birth. But if the Self-moving is proved to be immortal, he who affirms that Self-motion is the very idea and essence of

the Soul will not be put to confusion. For the body which is moved from without is soulless; but that which is moved from within has a Soul, for such is the nature of the Soul. But if this be true, must not the Soul be the Self-moving, and therefore of necessity unbegotten and immortal?

Phaidros, 245C-246A

The first meaning of English 'kinetic' (from Greek '*kinēsis*', which is the word Plato uses here for 'movement'), is 'producing and causing motion'.[19] The word *kinēsis* or 'movement' is used by Plato to describe the Soul's attribute in the sense of 'the dance' of Creation and of the Soul's property to 'set the process in motion',[20] whereby Creation is made manifest at the appointed time. For as it is written in the Upanishads, 'the Self has duly allotted the respective duties to the eternal years',[21] meaning the Self has allotted them to the *Prajāpatis* or Creators called 'the eternal years'.

2

Dhātu and *Stoicheion*

Dhātava (the plural of *dhātu*) and *stoicheia* are the unmanifest and universal roots of all constituent matter and of language; this is logical, as matter arises from sound. Everything in Creation begins as *dhātu* or 'seeds' which are held in the *avyakta prakṛiti* or 'unmanifest nature', until in due season they are sent forth by the sounding Will of the Creator to cause manifestation in Creation. *AUM* is the *dhātu* of *dhātu* or seed of seeds; the *dhātu* arise out of *aham*, but they cannot be pronounced as they are in the *mantra* system. For the purposes of the *vyākaraṇa* system, meaning 'differentiating the expansion of Creation in manifest speech', the ancient grammarians formulated sounds which are called *dhātu* but they are only gross sounds in the vernacular; the true *dhātu,* which can only be heard by the *Ātman* in the Spiritual World, are in fact the seed forms for the entire Creation.

The *dhātu* reside in unmanifest nature until activated by the operation of *sphoṭa*, which is an explosion in consciousness, like a conception, where everything is gathered for the purpose of expansion. The *sphoṭa* is a point with no dimension where cause, action and effect are already present, including the law governing the movement of cause, through action, into effect, as required by the creative will. A definition of *sphoṭa* is 'bursting, opening, expansion, roar; in philosophy, sound conceived as eternal, indivisible and creative; the eternal and imperceptible element of sounds and words and the real vehicle of the idea which bursts or flashes on the mind when a sound is uttered'[1]. The greatest expansion of a *sphoṭa* is a whole universe. This happens in an instant and the imperceptible 'roar' rumbles on; while it continues to roar, Creation exists, but when it ceases, Creation is no more. The same process is behind each word that we utter; the *dhātu* is activated by the *sphoṭa* instantaneously and 'bursts or flashes on the mind', which instantly interprets the action into language, whether as speaker or listener. (This is an elaborate process involving more than just the strictly mental apparatus.) Likewise, each human embodiment is a *dhātu* activated by a *sphoṭa*, an explosion which rises and falls, just as the bursting of a bud leads to flower and bloom, forming a new seed in the process.

Plato gives a description of how the men of old first formulated the *stoicheia* of language and refers to the need to analyse language back to its roots in order to obtain proper understanding:

> And we shall make roots [*stoicheia*] for the expression of actions [*ta pragmata*], either one letter [*sumpolla*] added to one letter, as seems appropriate, or to several letters, thereby producing syllables as they are called, and from combinations of syllables [*sullabas*], compose nouns [*onomata*] and verbs [*rēmata*], and in turn from the combinations of nouns and verbs we shall create language, large and fair and whole... Whereas the men of old put language together in this way, so we must take it apart in like manner, if we are really to know how to investigate the whole subject in a workmanlike manner.
>
> *Kratylos*, 424E-425E

There is happily a text from the *Vedāṅga* or 'limb of the *Veda*' called *Dhātu-Pāṭha* through which the meaning of key words may be investigated (see Appendix III). Certain ancient grammarians indentified the root sounds, which are verbally based, of the Indo-European system of languages, and these were handed down as part of the oral tradition of India as *Dhātu-Pāṭha*, literally 'a recital of roots'. It is important to appreciate that although these roots in the *Dhātu-Pāṭha* are expressed in Sanskrit, they are the essential roots of the Indo-European languages and most certainly are not roots exclusive to the Sanskrit language. This is an important distinction, as otherwise an incorrect assumption might be made that certain words in other languages are based on Sanskrit roots; rather, it is that words in many languages derive from a common root sound expressed in the natural alphabet.

The *Dhātu-Pāṭha* gives for each *dhātu* or root a *dhātvartha*, meaning the *artha* of a *dhātu* or the 'indication of meaning' of 'a root', which is a word or compound which describes the activity in which the use of that particular root may be found; for as roots are always verbal, they always appear in activity and consequently the *dhātvartha* is always expressed in the seventh case, namely the locative. Thus the first sutra of the *Dhātu-Pāṭha*, namely *Bhū Sattāyām* referred to above, means 'you will find the use of root *bhū* in [the activities of] *sattā*'.[2] The locative ending is *–āyām*, which has been removed to leave the word *sattā* as it will appear in a dictionary. Now root *bhū* means 'to become' or 'to be', and English 'to be' is directly from this root; *sattā* means 'pure consciousness, reality, existence'. So the sutra means 'you will find the use of the root meaning "being" in [the activity of] "pure consciousness".' This is the first sutra in the *Dhātu-Pāṭha* as it is the first state in Creation and all activities are dependent on it. In fact, it stands on its own at the start of the *Dhātu-Pāṭha* as it cannot accurately be described as 'in the activity of', as there is no activity at this level of Creation; hence these words are shown above in parenthesis. The *dhātvartha sattā* is further informing that the substratum of everything in Creation is existing in a pure state at its respective level. Finally, it is possible that the *Dhātu-Pāṭha* follows the steps in the expansion of Creation in its ordering of the *dhātu* and also in its division of *dhātu* into ten *gaṇa* or 'categories or families'.[3]

In the expansion of Creation, 'the Word' or '*Logos*' is the instrument of the creative principle, in the sense that the universe is spoken into existence. *Logos* means 'the word or outward form by which the inner thought is expressed and the inward thought itself – so that *Logos* comprehends both *ratio* and *oratio*',[4] meaning the intelligence of the creative principle on the one hand and the speech by which it is manifested on the other. The *dhātu* of '*Logos*' is *lokṛi*,[5] which has two *dhātvartha*; the first states that the use of *lokṛi* will be found in the activity of *darśana*, meaning 'seeing, intelligence, becoming visible and therefore known',[6] and in *bhāshārtha* or 'speech'[7]. The *darśana* equates to the *ratio* and the *bhāshārtha* is the *oratio* as the Creation is spoken into existence. The *Dhātu-Pāṭha* also provides a telling insight into the meaning of the root *hu*, from which English 'God' is derived,[8] for there was originally an 'Indo-Germanic type *ghutom*, perhaps meaning the being who is worshipped',[9] which was phonetically like 'ghost'. The *dhātvartha* compound for *hu* is *dānādanayoḥ*, which refers to the gift of the outward thrust of Creation and then the return as food for the Gods, in the form of worship, praise and sacrifice.[10] For the Gods exist as universal forces and are strengthened or weakened by the respects paid to them.

Whereas it was only the ancient Aryan grammarians who bequeathed an actual text of linguistic roots to subsequent generations, the ancient Greeks also subscribed to a similar concept, namely *stoicheion* meaning 'element or root', which can be said to have formed an important and central part of Greek thinking, which was fundamental not only to the science of language, but also to the sciences of physics, mathematics and epistemology. Indeed, in both traditions, the idea of elements or roots assumed far wider connotations: the Sanskrit dictionary definition for *dhātu* includes 'layer, stratum, constituent part, ingredient, element, primitive matter, a constituent element or essential ingredient of the body, the five organs of sense, element of words, grammatical or verbal root or stem'[11]. Hesiod referred to the '*rhizai*' or 'roots of the earth and restless sea',[12] which were above Tartaros, and where 'there were shining gates and an immoveable threshold of bronze, with unbroken roots, self-grown'.[13] The fifth-century philosopher Empedokles of Akragas defined four real *rhizōmata* or 'roots', namely the elements earth, air, fire and water, which are the ultimate, exclusive, and eternal constituents which combine in different ratios to form the universe. They are not generated and do not perish and are 'the seed from which comes all that has been, all that is, and all that will be', not only of mortal things, but also 'the long-lived Gods, high in Honour'.[14] His contemporary, the Ionian Anaxagoras of Klazomenae, however, accepted the principle that there could be no coming into being of what was not but did not agree that the elements alone caused the visible things of the world, for he maintained that every type of material was fundamental. This logical impasse led him to formulate the concept of *spermata* or 'seeds', which closely resembles the wider concept of *dhātu*. Anaxagoras maintained that in the beginning the world was a mixture of an infinite number of seeds, which took their quality after their prevailing component, whether it was of colour, taste or any natural substance, and the seeds also contained their own nutrition for growth. This is significant, for the *dhātu* of the word *dhātu* is root *dhā*, which has the *dhātvartha* compound of *dhāraṇaposhaṇayoḥ*, meaning 'holding, bearing, keeping in remembrance' and 'the act of nourishing, fostering, and supporting'.[15]

Plato was the first to name Empedokles' elements as *stoicheia*, but he himself held that the geometric figures constituting them are the genuine physical elements[16] and that the One and the Dyad are the *stoicheia* of the Forms. Aristotle defined and classified the usage of *stoicheia*, including the elementary demonstrations inherent in all mathematical and logical proof, whence Euklid's 'Elements'.[17] He defined *stoicheion* as 'the primary immanent thing, formally indivisible into another form, of which something is composed. For example, the elements of a sound are the parts of which that sound is composed and into which it is ultimately divisible, and which are not further divisible into other sounds formally different from themselves',[18] which is an accurate definition of the structure of a *dhātu*, but it does not address its key attribute of meaning, for he regarded all words as mere convention. It was not until the Stoics in the Hellenistic Age made systematic studies of the structure of language and they held that 'the primary sounds imitate things'.[19] The Stoics' interest in etymology and meaning is well recorded by later grammarians and philosophers, but unfortunately there is no extant list of these 'primary sounds'. The *Dhātu-Pāṭha* is the only comprehensive list of roots that has survived from antiquity, borne on the strength of the Vedic oral tradition.

3

'Only the *Guṇāḥ* Act'

All the possibilities for Creation are held in the *avyakta prakṛiti* or 'unmanifest nature', whole and entire, in the form of *dhātava* or 'seeds'. For Creation to manifest, a vibration is required in the pure consciousness which leads to the *sphoṭa* or 'explosion in consciousness' acting on the *dhātava*.

Standing in the *avyakta prakṛiti* are also to be found the three *Guṇāḥ*, namely *Sattva*, *Rajas* and *Tamas*. They are in fact the three mighty Gods that govern everything in Creation and hence, when used in this sense, the initial consonant is given in upper case. In fact they are representative of the threefold force of the *praṇava śabda* of *AUM*, which creates, sustains and dissolves the Creation. *Sattva* is the creative force and represents the letter 'A'; *Rajas* is the energy force and represents the expansion in the letter 'U'; and *Tamas* is the force of regulation and dissolution in the letter 'M'. In the manifest Creation, the three *Guṇāḥ* pervade all phenomena as 'a quality, characteristic or property of all substances. They are a constituent of nature, any one of the three properties belonging to all created things'[1] and they act together as the law of three forces.

Sattva carries 'the quality of purity and goodness'.[2] *Rajas* is 'active, urgent and variable, predominating in air, light, day and the world'[3] and is the 'cause of the great activity seen in creatures'.[4] *Tamas* is 'the gloom or darkness of hell'[5] and the 'cause of heaviness, ignorance, illusion, lust, anger, pride, sorrow, dullness and stolidity'.[6] *Sattva* predominates in Gods, *Rajas* in men and *Tamas* in demons. 'Take but good note', remarks the Bard on the play of the *Guṇāḥ*, 'and you shall see the triple pillar of the world transformed into a strumpet's fool.' The 'triple pillar of the world' is the *prakṛiti* or 'nature' which manifests in *sattva*, *rajas* and *tamas* in the three worlds of causal, subtle and gross.

The meaning of the *dhātu* or 'root' of each of the *Guṇa* is instructive. *Sattva* is from *dhātu sat*, which means 'being';[7] *sat* itself is from *dhātu asa*,[8] (or *as* when the grammatical indicatory suffix is removed), which has *dhātvartha bhūvi* (or *bhū* when the locative case ending is removed), meaning 'being';[9] *dhātu as* also has a compound *dhātvartha* of *gatidīptyādāneshu*,[10] comprising *gati*, *dīpti* and *ādāna*, with plural ending *–eshu*. This is a subtle compound meaning the 'state or condition, with motion implied', of 'the light' of the *Ātman* 'being received or drawn towards the Self',[11] which indeed is a state of supreme satisfaction, that is only possible in a *sāttvika* state; in a *tāmasika* quality of this state there is the possibility of attachment and identification to the light, which may take the form, for example, of identification with the living body, for identification with the light that shines from its skin leads to the belief that the body is the Self! *Rajas* is from *dhātu rañja*, meaning 'to be excited or glad',[12] which has *dhātvartha rāge*,[13] meaning the colour 'red' and 'feeling or passion, affection, vehement desire'.[14] *Tamas* is from *dhātu tamu* meaning 'to choke, be exhausted, perish, perplexed, become immoveable or stiff',[15] which has *dhātvartha kaṅkshāyām*,[16] meaning 'wish or desire';[17] this is an unexpected indicatory meaning of the *dhātu*, but it may indicate the bondage that is caused by desires, which arise from the impurities of heart and mind.

The *sphoṭa* or 'explosion in consciousness' is sattvic or *sāttvika* and it sets the *dhātu* or seed in motion by upsetting the equal balance of the *Guṇāḥ*, imbuing it with the activity and energy for growth. The expansion is promoted by the *rājasika* quality and when the time comes for Creation to be dissolved, the *tāmasika* quality presides over the mighty triumvirate. Thus the *Guṇāḥ* truly govern Creation. When the Lord *Śrī Kṛishṇa* was explaining Creation to *Arjuna*, he stated that man does not do anything whatsoever, for 'only the *Guṇāḥ* act'.[18] *Śaṅkara* in his commentary states that 'it is by the *Guṇāḥ*, manifesting themselves as the body and the senses, that all our actions, conducive to temporal and spiritual ends, are done. The man is variously deluded by egotism, identifying the aggregate of the body and the senses with the Self [called the state of *ahaṅkāra*, or the *aham* in *kāra* or "activity"]; he, through ignorance, sees actions in himself: as regards every action, he thinks "I am the doer".' In fact, the *ahaṅkāra* is lit with the light reflected by *citta*, the conscious aspect of mind, but it identifies with that light and with what is lit. The Lord *Śrī Kṛishṇa* expands this statement with a description of each *guṇa* in relation to *buddhi*, the discriminatory function of the mind, which is lit by the reflected light from *citta*, as follows:

> The *buddhi* [understanding] which knows action
> and non-action,
> What ought to be done and what ought not to be done,
> What is to be feared and what is not to be feared,
> What binds and what frees the Soul,
> That *buddhi*, O *Arjuna*, is of the nature of *sattva*.

That by which one knows in a mistaken way the
right and wrong,
What ought to be done and what ought not to be done,
That *buddhi*, O *Arjuna*, is of the nature of *rajas*.

That which, shrouded in ignorance, conceives as
right what is wrong,
And sees all things contrary,
That *buddhi*, O *Arjuna*, is of the nature of *tamas*.

Gītā, Ch.18, vv.30-32

There is no exact replication of the concept of the three *Guṇāḥ* in the Greek tradition, but just as the *Guṇāḥ* operate as the law of three forces throughout Creation, so in the Greek tradition the Olympian Gods appear in triads as three forces, as do the Fates, the Seasons, the Graces, the Furies and the Muses.

Hence, it was a traditional approach that Plato adopted when he described the three principles at the birth of Creation, namely the universal concepts or Forms, the Receptacle and the Demiurge,[19] and which also appear in the Judaeo-Christian teaching as The Holy Trinity of God, the Son and the Paraclete. The concept of triads recurs throughout Neo-Platonic teachings, such as in Proklos' metaphysical principles, which are multiplied by each possessing Being, Life (or Power) and Thought.

The absence of the concept of *Guṇāḥ* in the Greek tradition left a potential vacuum in the attempt to explain the qualities in nature and the motive force in the composition and combination of the elements. Nevertheless, Plato formulated an ingenious solution based on his skill as a geometrician. For the quintessential symbol of the law of three forces is the ubiquitous triangle, the plural of which in Greek is *ta trigona*; the Greek is almost trying to say '*tri guṇāḥ*'! but such a notion would be misplaced. In fact, *trigonon* in Greek is a noun derived from *gignomai* meaning 'I become', which is in turn derived from *dhātu janī*[20] which has *dhātvartha* compound *prādurbhāve*, meaning 'manifesting, becoming, appearing'[21] which is the result of the alleged action of the triangles. *Guṇāḥ*, however, is from *dhātu gañj* and is shown, as a result of a grammatical rule change, as *dhātu guji* in the *Dhātu-Pāṭha*,[22] which has a *dhātvartha* compound of *avyakte śabde* meaning 'unmanifest speech', for the *Guṇāḥ* arise from *AUM*.

Plato maintains that the triangles appear in 'all manifest bodies', for being composed of the elements they are solid, and every solid must necessarily be contained in planes, and every plane rectilinear figure is composed of triangles'.[23] Plato reasons that there are three types of triangle: first is the right-angled isosceles, which has one form only, and then the right-angled scalene (unequal-sided) triangle which has infinite forms; from these two he takes the right-angled isosceles (with angles 45, 45 and 90 degrees) and 'the most beautiful of which the double forms a third triangle, which is the equilateral triangle',[24] that is he takes the half-equilateral form of the scalene right-angled triangle (with angles 30, 60 and 90 degrees), from which the square faces of the cube and the equilateral faces of the four, eight and twenty-hedra are formed respectively. These two forms of elementary triangle are different or unequal, and their 'inequality is the cause of the nature which is wanting in uniformity' and this 'generates an inequality which is always maintained and is continually creating a perpetual motion of the elements in all time'.[25] Thus Plato sought to explain the fundamental attribute of the ever-changing phenomenal world by the inequality of the triangles. Yet he had admitted that it would be an 'unaccustomed argument which I am compelled to use' and that if anyone could point out from the infinite number of forms a more beautiful form than the equilateral triangle for the construction of the elements, then he 'shall carry off the palm, not as an enemy, but as a friend'.[26]

The Vedic concept of action and non-action, of 'only the *Guṇāḥ* act' and its inescapable corollary of 'I am not the doer', is clear and unambiguous. In the early Greek tradition, this powerful idea found no such simple expression, but the concept was latent in many other guises, such as in the action of Gods, Spirits and Fates, which caused men to act or react or suffer at the hand of forces beyond their control, which is repeated in the Judaeo-Christian thinking in the phrase *deo volente*, or 'Thy Will be done'. In the classical period, Plato's concept of 'Self-moving Soul' which 'is the fountain and beginning of motion' was the nearest a Greek idea came to 'only the *Guṇāḥ* act'.

4

The Traditional Indian and Vedic Gods

In the *praṇava śabda* of *AUM*, beyond Creation, resides *Māyā*, the Goddess of the Undifferentiated, and the three *Guṇāḥ*, namely *Sattva*, *Rajas* and *Tamas*, the three mighty Gods who regulate the entire Creation and every animate and inanimate body in it. The first three male Gods in the traditional Indian philosophy emerge in Creation as the forceful and take three wives, who are the force of the forceful, making six Gods at the outset of Creation. From *Sattva* in the letter 'A' arises *Vishṇu*, the upholder and preserver of all being, whose spouse is *Lakshmī* and they preside over the universe and wealth and power in all their forms; from *Rajas* in the letter 'U' arises *Brahmā*, the deified personification of *Brahman*, whose spouse is *Sarasvatī* and they preside over knowledge, and she in particular is the Goddess of Language and mother of the *Vedas*; from *Tamas* in the letter 'M' arises *Ṡiva* or *Māheṡa* whose spouse is *Pārvāti* or *Kali*; he is everthing and presides over the laws governing life and death and she is the Goddess of learning and sciences. *Ṡiva* is the fearful and auspicious God of destruction, for he is death and also the dissolver of *ahaṅkāra*, or the destroyer of physical existence and of the subtle bonds of ignorance; ultimately, *Ṡiva* as the lord of death is therefore also the death of death. *Kali* is the Goddess of Time, in which both disintegration and liberation take place.

Vishṇu is the Supreme Being and is often identified with *Nārāyaṇa*, the personified *purusha* or primeval living spirit. When Creation is unmanifest, he moves on the face of the waters or the ocean of milk, reclining on *Ṡesha*, the thousand-headed serpent of infinity known as 'the remainder'.[1] The Ocean of Milk is the seeds of past action, and the ocean is of milk as these seeds are stored as energy, for water on its own would not offer nutrition. Another name of *Vishṇu* and *Ṡesha* is *Ananta*, meaning 'timeless'[2] for when the time for Creation to manifest comes around, the God *Brahmā* emerges from a lotus growing from *Vishṇu's* navel.[3] *Brahmā* looks all around him and is therefore depicted with four heads, but he sees only the Ocean of Milk; he is bound to create, but what should be create? He meditates and then knows he only has to do what he has done countless times before; out of his navel is born *Sarasvatī*, whose name means 'the ever-flowing utterance of creative speech',[4] for she chants Creation into existence.

As *Śiva* is everything, he is the most important deity and has many images, the most common of which is the male phallus inserted in the *yoni* or 'female emblem' which appears in every one of his temples, for he is the God of *liṅga* or 'gender'. *Śiva* has three eyes with the crescent moon on his brow. The Ganges flows down his matted hair as an emblem of purity and is therefore as white as milk. His arms are strong and smooth like the trunk of an elephant; he is smeared with ashes and adorned with shining armlets. A garland of pearls and a snake surround his neck and he wears a tiger skin. Two of his hands hold a trident and an axe; the other two of his hands show the gesture of granting boons and removing fears. *Śiva* is often shown seated on a white bull, carrying a white banner with his body as white as camphor. The colour white is a symbol of purity, yet *Śiva* is the lord of death and is all *tamas*, whereas *Vishṇu* is all *sattva* and is shown outwardly black; the explanation for this apparent juxtaposition is that darkness is surrounded by light and light is enveloped in darkness, or because white is the basis of all colours, all other colours are superimposed on white, yet it exists before and after all other colours. The three eyes of *Śiva* represent the sun, the moon and fire; the middle eye is pure perception, from which a single glance burned *Kāma*, the lord of lust, to ashes. The moon is placed above the third eye and represents the power of procreation co-existent with the power of destruction; the moon is also the cup of offering and the measure of time, while the serpent represents the cycle of years. The tiger skin is the power of nature and as *Śiva* is beyond nature and is its master he wears the tiger skin as a trophy. His four arms represent universal power, the three-pronged trident represents the three *Guṇāḥ*, the spear and axe are his weapons of destruction. The ashes are from the periodic universal conflagration that destroys all the Gods, including *Vishṇu* and *Brahmā* and the whole of Creation. Finally, the vehicle of *Śiva* is a white bull which represents the natural instincts that govern men; *Śiva* climbs onto the bull by stepping on *Kumbhodara*, the pot-bellied lion who represents greed and lust for food, but *Śiva* as the master of lust rides on the bull.

The name of the God *Vishṇu* is from *dhātu vishu*,[5] which has *dhātvartha secane*, meaning 'pouring out, emitting, sprinkling or watering, a shower bath'.[6] *Brahmā* is from *dhātu bṛihi* meaning 'to roar'.[7] *Śiva* is from *dhātu śvidi*,[8] which has *dhātvartha śvaitye* meaning 'white, brilliant as the dawn'.[9] *Lakshmī* is from *dhātu laksha*,[10] which has the *dhātvarthas darśana, aṅkana* and *ālocana*, meaning 'seeing and presence', 'marking and writing' and 'perceiving and reflecting', respectively.[11] *Sarasvatī*'s name is from the word *saras* meaning 'anything flowing' and therefore 'speech';[12] this word is from *dhātu śṛi*[13] which has *dhātvartha gatau* denoting 'movement' in all its forms.[14] Finally, *Kali* is from *dhātu kāla*,[15] which has the *dhātvartha* compound *lavanapavanayoḥ*, where *lavana* means 'reaping' and 'a sickle' and *pavana* means 'purifying',[16] two very appropriate activities for the Goddess of death and liberation.

These six Gods are called the 'traditional' Gods of Indian philosophy, for they do not appear in the *Veda*. These three pairs of forces are the embodiment of *ahaṅkāra*, *citta*, and *buddhi*: *ahaṅkāra* is *aham* in *kāra* or 'activity' which is experienced as the constant feeling of existence; *citta* is the conscious aspect of mind and *buddhi* is the discriminatory aspect; and these three pervade Creation. *Citta* is *Vishṇu*, *buddhi* is *Brahmā* and *ahaṅkāra* is *Śiva*. From these three Gods is created *manas*, who is called the God *Indra*, who is the messenger for *Brahmā*, the presiding deity of a single universe and there are millions of universes in the unmanifest, but likewise there are many *Indras*. From *Indra*, who is the first of the Vedic Gods, come all the *Indriya*, which means the five senses of knowledge and the five organs of action. Then from the mind of *Brahmā* is created Man who is known as *Manu*. His wife is *Śatarūpā*, meaning 'truly formed' and they are the primordial human beings, known as *ādi purusha*, from whom all the generations of mortal human beings are descended, as in the Christian tradition of 'the only begotten Son of God', or Christ, who is the *Prajāpati*. As everything begins in *AUM*, it is truly said that there is one family of Gods and that all mankind is also one family.

In the *Dhātu-Pāṭha*, the root *mana*, or *man* when the final suffix is removed, from which *manas* and *manu* are derived, is one of the most important roots with a very wide range of meaning; in Greek, for example, it branches into five distinct meanings.[17] The infinitive *man* in Sanskrit means 'to think' and in English the root developes into 'mind' and 'man'. The Roman God of Wisdom, Minerva, is from this root. There is a closely related root, namely *manu*,[18] from which are derived the Greek *manthanō* meaning 'I learn' and therefore also *ta mathēmatika* or 'mathematics', meaning literally 'the things that are known'. Man, however, suffers loss of memory and forgets the knowledge that is freely available to him and falls prey to the demon *Apasmāra*, meaning 'loss of memory', who spreads a veil of darkness over Creation and the bliss of Creation turns to misery. The Great Lord *Māheśa* took compassion on Creation and in the form of Lord *Śiva*, took up his drum called *Ḍamaru* and began to dance in order to dispel the darkness of the demon *Apasmāra*. The measured beating of his drum produced all the rhythms of Creation and especially the fourteen *māheśvarāṇi sūtrāṇi*, which retraced the steps by which this Creation of sound evolved from the sounding Will of the Creator; these fourteen *sūtrāṇi*, together with their latent forty-two *pratyāhara* or sequential combinations of vowels, are also the key to *Pāṇini's* 'Eight Meditations' on grammar and much else besides.

Indra is 'the Lord of Gods, the God of rain'[19] and of the 'firmament'. He is inferior to the triad of *Vishṇu*, *Brahmā* and *Śiva*, but in the *Veda* he is placed in 'the first rank of the other Gods, yet he is not regarded as an uncreated being, and is spoken of as "being born", and as having a father and a mother ... He is of a ruddy or golden colour and can assume any form at will. He rides in a bright golden chariot drawn by two tawny horses. His most famous weapon is the thunderbolt, which he uses with deadly effect in his warfare with the *rakshasas* or 'demons of darkness', with drought and inclement weather ... He is thus the Lord of the Atmosphere, the dispenser of rain and governor of the weather ... The *soma* juice is his favourite drink and under its exhilarating influence he performs great achievements and pleases his devout worshippers who are said to invite the God to drink the juice ... He richly rewards his adorers, particularly those who bring him libations of *soma*, and he is supplicated for all sorts of temporal blessings, as cows, horses, chariots, health, intelligence, prosperous days, long life and victory in war.'[20]

Kaśyapa was the son of *Brahmā* and had two wives, *Diti* and *Aditi*, from whom two streams of beings were born. *Diti* gave birth to every animal, vegetable and mineral on land, in sea and air; *Aditi* gave birth to the higher beings of the spiritual generations of Gods. *Kaśyapa* 'was thus the father of Gods, demons, men, beasts, birds and reptiles, in fact of all living beings. He is therefore often called *Prajāpati*'.[21] *Aditi* means 'not tied', implying boundless freedom. She is the Goddess of the vast heavens, of the immensity of the boundless expanse beyond earth, beyond the clouds and beyond the sky and of inexhaustible abundance of all created forms.[22] *Diti*, however, is not given any distinct character in the *Veda*.[23]

The next most prominent deity of the *Ṛigveda* is *Agni*,[24] the God of Fire. 'He is an immortal and has taken up his abode among mortals as their guest; he is the domestic priest, the successful accomplisher and protector of all ceremonies; he is also the religious leader and preceptor of the Gods, a swift messenger employed to announce to the immortals the hymns and to convey to them the obligations of the worshippers and to bring them down from the sky to the place of sacrifice. He is sometimes regarded as the mouth and the tongue through which both Gods and men participate in the sacrifices.[25] He is the Lord, protector and leader of people, monarch of men and the Lord of the house, friendly to mankind and like a father, mother, brother and sister. He is represented as being produced by the attrition of two pieces of fuel which are regarded as husband and wife ... He is said to have four horns, three feet, two heads and seven hands. The highest divine functions are ascribed to *Agni*. He is said to have spread out the two worlds and produced them, to have supported heaven, formed the mundane regions and luminaries of heaven, to have begotten *Mitra* and caused the sun to ascend the sky. He is the head and summit of the sky and the centre of the earth. Earth, Heaven and all beings obey his commands. He knows and sees all worlds or creatures and witnesses all their actions[26] ... He is the guardian of immortality. He is like a water trough in a desert and all blessings issue from him ...'.[27]

Mitra, the son of *Agni*, is a Sun-God. His name implies friendship[28] and he is associated in the *Veda* with *Varuṇa*, the 'regent of the ocean and of the western quarter, represented with a noose in his hand'.[29] Whereas *Mitra* is a God of day and conscious forces, *Varuṇa* is a God of night and unconscious forces. *Marut* or *Vāyu* is the God of Wind, who is the regent of the north-west quarter'[30] and who presides over the five *praṇa* or vital airs which sustain life, and hence he is considered as the God of inexhaustible energy in Creation, amongst his many functions. *Rudra* is the God of destruction, who 'is said to have sprung from *Brahmā*'s forehead and to have separated himself afterwards into a figure half male and half female, like a Greek hermaphrodite, the former portion separating again into the eleven *Rudras*, hence these later *Rudras* are sometimes regarded as inferior manifestations of *Ṡiva*'.[31] *Sūrya* is the principal Sun-God, the fire of the heavenly sphere which illumines the World, and he is therefore the God of the Intellect; *Savitṛi*, another Sun-God, is known as 'the stimulator, rouser and vivifier'[32] and is but one of many Gods emphasising the creative aspect of the universe.

Finally, no account of the Vedic and traditional Gods of Indian philosophy, however brief, could be complete without a description of the Greek equivalent of Athene, the Goddess of Wisdom. *Gaṇeṡa* or *Gaṇapati*, the God of Wisdom and remover of obstacles, is the son of *Ṡiva* and *Pārvāti*. The *gaṇa* in his name means 'categories' or the collections of related orders of things in Creation, and he is known as the 'ruler of all categories'. He is therefore worshipped at the commencement of every important undertaking. He is represented as a short, fat man with a protuberant belly, for his belly is said to contain all universes and manifestations, and he is usually riding on a mouse and has the head of an elephant.[33] The explanation for this extraordinary symbol is explained by various myths, but perhaps his head represents the elephantine power of memory, in his case the power to memorise the entire *Veda*, and the mouse represents the *Ātman*; for just as a mouse can disappear down a tiny hole in the wainscot, so in the *Veda* the return to the Self is by a most minute and secret hole or empty space in the heart. In this empty space, the light of the *Ātman* reflects itself; whereas *Ātman* is everywhere, it is in this space where its light is reflected. This space where the *Ātman* reflects Itself is called *citta*, it is a part of the cosmic *purusha* or 'soul or spirit', whence comes the expansion of Creation and whither it is withdrawn. The God of Wisdom is the deity to be invoked by the enquirer that would find this space.

The mouse, however, is also a thief, for he steals cheese and other victuals from the larder. The Sanskrit word for a mouse is *musha* from root *musa*,[34] which has *dhatvartha khaṇḍane*, meaning 'dividing, reducing to pieces, removing, cheating and deceiving'.[35] The point of this indication of meaning is that the *Ātman* dwelling in the heart is the real enjoyer of the sensations and pleasures of all creatures, for just as the mouse steals the cheese unnoticed, so the *Ātman* 'steals' all that people think they possess, for it hides behind all the manifestations of Creation and is the real enjoyer. For the *Ātman*, being the cause of everything, is the one who does enjoy every aspect of Creation. The individual believes the *ahaṅkāra* is the enjoyer, unaware that the indwelling *Ātman* is the real thief that steals all the joy of his own Creation, unnoticed like the mouse.

Gaṇapati is also shown with his trunk bent to one side, signifying that while *idam* or 'everything else in Creation other than *aham*' appears intelligible to mind and can be described by speech, *aham* or the Self cannot be directly understood by ordinary intelligence or portrayed in speech and is therefore said to be crooked; thus *Gaṇapati's* trunk is bent to symbolise the elephant's habit of removing obstacles out of his path with his trunk. *Gaṇapati* has only one tusk for One is the symbol of illusion or *māyā* from which everything is sprung; and he has only one tooth to symbolise that this *māyā* is supported by the *Ātman*, the One without a second. Finally, *Gaṇeśa's* ears resemble winnowing fans which winnow the words that are addressed to him: his ears separate the wheat from the chaff and virtue from vice, for the God of Wisdom has no need to hear the words of the unwise, still less to hear report of their actions.

5

The Select Band of Olympian Gods

Whereas there are the six traditional Indian Gods and thirty-three Vedic Gods, or thirty-nine Gods in total, there were only twelve Olympian Gods. The supreme contribution of Homer and Hesiod was their codification of the deeds of the select band of the twelve Olympian Gods, and their relationships with each other and with men, descriptions that were to define for all subsequent European generations the celestial hierarchy, so that human consciousness at the creation of the Greek nation could evolve its appreciation of the divine, for each God represented a particular universal force. Thus the whole family of twelve Gods represented for the Greeks the consciousness of the entire universe. Herodotos, praising the superiority and greater antiquity of Egyptian culture over the Greek, wrote:

> But it was only, if I may so put it, the day before yesterday that the Greeks came to know the origin and form of the various Gods, and whether or not all of them had always existed. For Homer and Hesiod are the poets who composed our Theogonies and described the Gods for us giving them all their appropriate titles, offices and powers …
>
> Herodotos, Book II, ll.53ff.

Hesiod's and Homer's Gods were the divine element of a much larger tapestry that engendered the cult of hero and warrior, kingship, aristocracy and honour, and the ideals of womanhood, and also defined the first concepts of justice, chivalry, service, manners, and much else. And yet it was clearly the Gods and 'their appropriate titles, offices and powers' that Herodotos considered to be the most important bequest of the epic poets.

Hesiod's *Theogony* describes three generations of Gods who ruled in succession: Uranos and Gaia, Kronos and Rheia, and finally Zeus and Hera. The Gods of the first generation were the creators of the Solar system, for out of Chaos is born Gaia, Mother of the Earth, together with Tartaros and Eros. Gaia united herself with Uranos, Heaven, whom she brought to birth and with whom she built a cosmic unity. Uranos and Gaia created the Titans, and in the expansion of Creation the Titans were the agents for the differentiation of the cosmic forces. Thus, the number twelve is often linked with the appearance of space, and from the Titans and their various unions and marriages, the stars and the elements appear in their due order. Through the union of Okeanos with Thetis arose the realm of Water, and the Okeanides were born. The offspring of the Titans, Orios and Phoibe, were Leto the Night and Asteria the Starry Sky. The children of the Titans, Hyperion and Theia, were Selene the Moon, Helios the Sun, and Heos the Dawn. For the ancient Greeks, the Winds, the Dawn, the Night, the Sea and the Rain, and all the Heavenly Bodies, were living and divine Beings, and thus they personalised them as Leto and so on.

The age of the rule of Uranos and Gaia and the twelve Titans signified a particular stage in the earth's evolution connected with the first epochs of the creation of the planet earth. These spiritual beings wished to preserve their consciousness according to the earliest stage of earth's evolution. This caused the opposition of the younger generation, and Kronos, Uranos' youngest son, overcame his Father with the help of Gaia and succeeded him, just as Lemuria followed Hyperborea. Kronos and Rheia were considered a single spiritual unit and together with their six children, Hestia, Demeter, Hera, Hades, Poseidon and Zeus were always linked with the number Seven.

Kronos' youngest son, Zeus, in turn rebelled and took over the Divine Kingship, just as Atlantis followed Lemuria, whose volcanic forces and earthquakes and cataclysms finally subsided and were chained when he threw the Titans and Cyclops into Tartaros. Just as the first generation of Gods ruled over the earliest stages of the earth's development as forces in a cosmology, the second generation of Gods represented a theogony, and finally Zeus and the Olympians became figures of mythology. The Olympians everywhere appeared as a triad: thus, Zeus governed the sky, Poseidon governed the Sea, and Hades governed beneath the Earth; the three leading divinities were Zeus, his son Apollo, and his daughter Athene; three further sons of Zeus were Hermes, Ares, and Hephaistos, and his three other daughters were Aphrodite, Artemis and Hestia. The Olympians were accompanied by three *Moirae* or 'Fates', three *Hōrae* or 'Seasons' and three *Kharitae* or 'Graces'; there were three *Erinuēs* or 'Furies', namely Megara, Alekto and Tisiphone; and finally nine (three times three) Muses surrounding Apollo on Mount Parnassos. Thus the law of three forces was deified forever in the Greek mind.

The essential root of the name of the father of the Gods, Zeus, is from *dhātu dyuta*, which has *dhātvartha dīptau*, meaning 'shining'.[1] The Greek word for God is *theos*, which derives from *dhātu divu*, or actual root *div*, which means: 'The Sky: brightness, sheen, glow'.[2] The root *dyuta* is also the source for the Latin Jupiter and Juno (derived from *Diu-Pater* and *Diu-no*), and for English 'divine', whereas root *divu* is also the root for Latin *deus* and English 'deity'. The root *divu* has for its *dhātvartha* the following lengthy compound:[3]

> Krīḍā-Vijigīshā-Vyavahāra-Dyuti-Stuti-Moda-Mada-Svapna-Kānti-Gatishu

Clearly, a message of considerable import is intended; beginning at the end, the *–shu* ending in *–gatishu* indicates the locative case of *gati* and is applied to this final *dhātvartha* in the compound in order to provide the sense that 'you will find the use of *dhātu div* in the "state or condition" of all the compounds previously given'.

In order to demonstrate in a practical way the correspondences between the *dhātvartha* meanings and Homer's depiction of the Gods, a direct comparison between the activities of these *dhātvartha* and the events of *Iliad* Book XIV will be drawn as an example. Book XIV shows Zeus distracted from the battle between the Greeks and the Trojans with the result that his plan for defeat of the Greeks is thwarted; in particular, his wife Hera seduces him into making love, while the Greeks, with Poseidon's help, drive the Trojans back and achieve victory. The book conveniently falls into three sections: first, a meeting between Nestor and the three major wounded heroes: Agamemnon, Diomedes and Odysseus;[4] then the seduction of Zeus by Hera;[5] and finally the Greek Victory.[6]

Krīḍā is the first word in this long *dhātvartha* compound and is found in 'playing, sporting (said of winds), playing about in water, working miracles for one's amusement, a playground'.[7] Book XIV of the *Iliad* opens with a description of Nestor in two minds as to which way to join the battle and his indecision is portrayed by means of a simile of the play of wind on sea and the will of Zeus: 'As when the open sea is deeply stirred to the groundswell but stays in one place and waits the rapid onset of tearing gusts, nor rolls its surf onward in either direction until from Zeus the wind is driven down to decide it.'

Vyavahāra is demonstrated in 'conduct, practices of law and kingly government, administration of justice, punishment ...'.[8] Back to the next action in the battle, Nestor meets Agamemnon who informs him that the wall with which the Greeks sought to protect their ships has been destroyed by the Trojans, and Agamemnon's opinion on this major setback is: 'Such is the way it must be pleasing to Zeus, who is too strong, that the Akhaians must die here forgotten and far from Argos.'

Moda is expressed in 'joy, delight, gladness, pleasure, fragrance, perfume'.[9] At this moment in the battle Hera embarks on her plan to seduce Zeus, and before going to see Aphrodite she prepares herself for the role of seductress: 'entering she drew shut the leaves of the shining door, then first from her adorable body washed away all stains with ambrosia, and next anointed herself with ambrosial sweet olive oil, which stood there in its fragrance beside her and from which, stirred in the house of Zeus by the golden pavement a fragrance was shaken forever forth, on earth and in heaven'.

Vijigīshā is found in being 'desirous of victory, emulous, desire to conquer or overcome or subdue'.[10] It is not difficult to imagine the thoughts running through Hera's mind as she approaches Aphrodite to seek her help as she asks: 'Give me loveliness and desirability, graces with which you overwhelm mortal men, and all the immortals.'

Kānti is in the actions of 'desire, wish, loveliness, beauty, splendour, female beauty, personal decoration or embellishment ... Beauty enhanced by love, a lovely or a desirable woman personified as wife of the Moon'.[11] It is not surprising that Zeus is overcome by Hera, for Aphrodite had given her a special zone, or belt: 'She spoke, and from her breasts unbound the elaborate, pattern-pierced zone, and on it are figured all beguilements, and loveliness is figured upon it, and passion of sex is there, and the whispered endearment that steals the heart away even from the thoughtful.'

Stuti is in 'praise, eulogy, panegyric, commendation, adulation'.[12] As Zeus prepares to make love to Hera, he recites, in a Figaresque manner, a long list of his previous conquests, but finally admits: 'for never before has love for any goddess or woman so melted the heart inside, broken it to submission, as now ... so much as I now love you, and the sweet passion has taken hold of me.'

Mada is experienced in 'hilarity, rapture, inspiration, intoxication, sexual desire or enjoyment, lust, presumption, conceit, spiritous liquor, wine, *soma*, honey, intoxication or insanity personified'.[13] Zeus and Hera then make miraculous love: 'So speaking, the son of Kronos caught his wife in his arms. There underneath them the divine earth broke into young fresh grass, and into dewy clover, crocus and hyacinth so thick and soft it held the hard ground deep away from them. There they lay down together and drew about them a golden wonderful cloud, and from it the glimmering dew descended.'

Svapna is found in 'sleep, drowsiness and dreaming'.[14] After making love, Zeus adopts a rather usual male reaction: 'So the father slept unshaken on the peak of Gargaron with his wife in his arms, when sleep and passion had stilled him; but gently Sleep went on the run to the ships of the Akhaeans with a message ...' Hera had certainly achieved a significant victory, albeit temporary, for Hupnos, the God of Sleep, had previously stated: 'But Zeus, a son of Kronos, would I not approach, nor send to sleep, except that he himself so bid me.' *Svapna* and the Greek God of Sleep, Hupnos, both derive from the *dhātu* [*ñi*]shvap,[15] which has *dhātvartha śaye*, meaning simply 'lying, sleeping, resting'.[16]

Dyuti is manifest in 'Splendour, brightness, lustre, majesty, dignity and a threatening attitude'.[17] Sleep has run to Poseidon to tell him of Zeus' slumber; then the latter rouses the Greeks and himself leads them gloriously into battle: 'Then when in the shining bronze they had shrouded their bodies they went forward, and Poseidon the shaker of the earth led them, holding in his heavy hand the stark sword with the thin edge glittering, as glitters the thunderflash none may close with by right in sorrowful division, but fear holds all men back.'

Finally *Gati* is 'motion in general, arriving at, obtaining ... state, condition, situation and metempsychosis'.[18] As the battle commences, the blood-letting ensues, and amongst those who fall is Prothoenor, hit in the shoulder by a spear: 'Poulydamos vaunted terribly over him, calling in a great voice: I think this javelin leaping from the heavy hand of Panthoos' high-hearted son was not thrown away in a vain cast. Rather some Argive caught it in his skin. I think he has got it for a stick to lean on as he trudges down into Death's house.' *Gati* is the most common *dhātvartha* in the *Dhātu-Pāṭha* and it is mostly used to denote 'movement'. However, this *dhātvartha* is used in this instance to signify 'state, condition or mode of existence' as described by the previous *dhātvartha*, as the particular state of any being is the result of movement in one of the three worlds; hence 'metempsychosis' is given as a suitable meaning in this context, as Prothoenor's death is an example of *gati*, being the law of movement and modification of mind and matter at the time of death.

While considering the etymology of the names of the Olympians, it is useful to note the aptness of Homer's epithets. One of the epithets for Zeus describes him as 'the Cloud-Gatherer' (or possibly 'Cloud-Compeller'), which is a straightforward enough description of a God of consciousness, for to make the sun shine it is only necessary for the God to take all the clouds to one side. However, it is not so obvious to see why Zeus should also 'delight in thunderbolts', a pastime he shared with the Vedic God *Indra*: however, it is interesting to note that in the Vedic tradition the Lord *Śrī Kṛishṇa* says to *Arjuṇa*:

> 'All this creation owes life and movement to the
> supreme *Brahman*.
> *Brahman* strikes terror, like an uplifted thunderbolt;
> find it, find immortality'.
>
> *Kaṭha* Upanishad, Ch.2, Canto III, v.2

And in the Greek tradition, there is the statement of Herakleitos: 'Thunderbolt steers all things'.[19]

The origins and etymology of Poseidon, the God of the Sea, are obscure. His name appears to be linked to the Greek word *posis* for which the original form was *potis*, meaning 'lord, master, or husband'. The root for *posis* is *pā*, which appears twice in the *Dhātu-Pāṭha*:[20] the first *dhātvartha* is *pāne*, meaning 'drinking, kissing'[21] or to do with liquid or watery substances; and the second is *rakshaṇe*, meaning 'guarding, watching, protecting, tending, preserving'.[22] His foremost domain of the Sea extended over all waters and life-giving moistures, including saliva, sap and semen. In early legends he was also 'HORSE', an untameable stallion, whose hooves thundered across the wide plains of Greece, thereby discovering springs of water, or sometimes releasing them with a blow of his trident. In the list of his own attributes, the Lord *Śrī Kṛishṇa* also states: 'Know me among horses as *Uccaisravas*';[23] this was the name of the kingly horse which was born in the ocean when it was churned for the Ambrosia. The God was therefore also a symbol of fertility, power and men.

Poseidon's power was reflected in Homer's epithet of 'earth-shaker' for he was the God that caused earthquakes, as the early Greeks believed that they were in some way linked to massive movements of water beneath the earth. However, perhaps this power was of a subtler kind, for another Homeric epithet is 'earth-holder', and indeed the sea holds the earth. Contrary to outward appearances, whereby the sea in its rages appears to be attacking the shoreline and gradually eroding it, in actual fact it is this very clashing of the seas that creates the earth. This process is connected with the name of Zeus' daughter, Aphrodite, meaning 'born on the foam'; for the waves of the sea create the foam and it is with the sun's action on the foam that the elements combine for a due course of time, during millennia, to produce the firm earth. The *Dhātu-Pāṭha* gives for root *aplṛi*, the root for *aphros* meaning foam, the *dhātvartha lambhane*,[24] which has amongst its meanings 'the act of obtaining or attaining, causing to get and procuring'.[25] In short, Aphrodite and Poseidon play the major roles in the expansion of Creation and in forming the earth. As this expansion of Creation is essentially joyous and an act of love, so the Homeric epithet for Aphrodite is 'laughter-loving' and she takes her place as the Goddess of Love, for the entire Creation arises from the ocean of immortal bliss.

Hades, brother of Zeus and Poseidon, ruled beneath the earth as King of the Underworld, the home of all the 'perished dead'. The etymology of Hades' name derives from Greek root *Fid*, where the initial digamma was pronounced as a labial, giving phonetically the root *vid*. This root also forms *oida*, which is one of only three Greek verbs having a perfect form and a present meaning, for *oida* means 'I have seen', but always carries the present meaning that therefore 'I know'.[26] This is an important root which appears in Latin as *video*, 'I see', and in English as *wit* (Anglo-Saxon *witan*) and is also the source of the Sanskrit word *Veda*. The word *oida* has lost its original digamma or initial labial, and in its original form of *Foida* (phonetically *voida*) was very close to *Veda*, whereas Latin retained the labial to produce *video*. Now the form 'Hades' includes a negative prefix 'a-' added to the stem of *oida*, producing *A-idēs*; so Hades' name means 'no knowledge, no vision', an appropriate title for the God of the Underworld. The root *vid* appears five times in the *Dhātu-Pāṭha*.[27] The *dhātvartha* and their meanings are;[28] *jnane* – 'knowledge'; *sattāyām* – 'being'; *vicāraṇe* – 'reflection'; the compound *cetanākhyānanivāseshu*, where the meanings are *cetana* – 'consciousness'; *ākhyāna* – 'communication'; *nivāseshu* – 'residing in'; and finally *lābhe* – 'attaining'. The initial negative in the God's name indicates that none of these states or activities was possible in the domain of Hades.

Hades was the mythological son-in-law of Demeter for he wedded her daughter Persephone, and the story is incorporated as a myth in the Homeric Hymn to Demeter. For Hades stole Persephone and took her to the Underworld and Demeter, suffering in her heart bitter pains for her lost daughter, wandered over the earth in search of her, until Helios, the Sun God who sees everything, informed her of her daughter's whereabouts. Zeus eventually sent Hermes, the swift-footed Messenger of the Gods, to the Underworld with the command to bring Persephone up to earth again so that mother and daughter might be reunited. However, Persephone had eaten some pomegranate seeds in the Underworld and could not return to live on earth for the whole year, but was required to divide her time between living on earth and beneath the earth. Demeter, the Goddess who governed the fruits of the earth, especially corn, could not cause the earth to bring forth fruit for the half year that Persephone was in the Underworld; thus Demeter became the Goddess of seasons and of the light and dark halves of the year. Indeed, the last two syllables of her name – *mētēr*, are from the root *mā*, and the *Dhātu-Pāṭha* gives *dhātvartha mane*,[29] the essential meaning of which is 'measure'.[30] Demeter is the Goddess who provides measure to mother earth and organic life through her control of the seasons, and *mētēr* in Greek (*mater* in Latin) also means 'mother'.

In the Myth of Persephone, it was seen that Zeus sent Hermes to Hades on behalf of Demeter. Hermes' principal function was messenger to the Gods, but he also acted as a guide to travellers and conducted Souls of the dead down to the Underworld. The origin of his name may well come from *hermai*, meaning 'stone heaps', which were the guide to travellers on the roads of ancient Greece. However, in the *Iliad*, Hermes also becomes a divine guide to the living, often acting in consort with Athene, the Goddess of Wisdom. In the *Odyssey*, Hermes has already begun to conduct Souls on their last journey, but never appears as a messenger in the *Iliad*, for that role was undertaken by Iris.

While the origin of the name Athene is totally obscure, that of her brother, Hephaistos, the noble Craftsman-God, who represented the subtleties of universal consciousness by means of his cunningly contrived artifacts wrought from metal in the heat of the fire, which is *aithos* in Greek, comes from root *indhī*. Curtius links Greek *aithos* and Latin *aestus* meaning 'burning' and 'fire' to Sanskrit root *indhe*, which is shown in the *Dhātu-Pāṭha* as [*ñi*]*indhī*.[31] The *Dhātu-Pāṭha* gives *dhātvartha dīptau*, meaning 'brightness, light, splendour and beauty',[32] which adequately reflects the divine conscious source of Hephaistos' creations. This root also forms *aithō* and *aither* in Greek, which appear in English as 'ether', the foremost element in which all manifest Creation has its being,[33] and Hephaistos made use of all the elements.

The origins of Apollo and his sister Artemis, the huntress, who both delighted in music and dance, are obscure. However, Apollo, who was also the God most clearly manifesting the health and gaiety of youth, respect for law and love of moderation, was linked by several ancient commentators with the Greek verb *apollumi*, meaning 'to kill or slay or destroy utterly', and hence his Homeric epithet of the 'far-worker', because as the God most closely involved with precision, he was also the God of the bow and arrow which brought death from a distance. Finally, baneful Ares, the God of War, Hestia, the Goddess of the Hearth, and Hera, which is the feminine form of Hero, an appropriate title for the wife of Zeus, complete the select band of Olympian Gods.

The Vedic, Indian and Greek traditions are polytheistic, a concept which is unsettling for monotheists. However, polytheism is essentially the differentiation of the concept of God into various powers, which are then ordered into a hierarchy:

> All the Gods are this One Soul,
> and all dwell in the Soul.
>
> *Manu-Smṛiti*, 12,119,13

The universal and individual Soul is the sum of all the Gods, and all the Gods are therefore nothing other than the expression of the single Godhead.

6

The Five Vedic Elements and the Goddess *Māyā*

The Vedic system of astronomy is called *Jyotisha* and is one of the six *Vedāṅga*, or 'limbs of the *Veda*' (see Appendix III). This system depends upon the number nine, which is interpreted as the limit of Creation, and it therefore represents the fully manifest *praṇava śabda* or *AUM*. The number nine has the inherent capacity to remain as nine in multiplication, as in the expansion of Creation (see Appendix I), for example:

3 x 9 = 27; 2 + 7 = 9
9 x 9 = 81; 8 + 1 = 9

The number nine is therefore the limit of manifest Creation.

With the sounding Will of the Creator arising from *AUM*, the *Brahman* at number one as *sat* steps into Creation in the *avyakta prakṛiti* at number two, where the three *Guṇāḥ* and all the forms and laws for the Creation are stored in the form of *dhātu* or seeds. At this point the sounding Will or imperceptible 'roar' of the *nāda śabda* is called *aham*, which is the name of all creatures. Duality has entered the play and thus *aham* is the name of the unity, standing as consciousness and observing everything else, and *idam* now becomes the name of 'everything else' that is in the great universal storehouse.

The meaning of *aham* is extremely subtle: 'emulation, competition, assertion of superiority; as *ahaṅkāra*: egotism, sense of self, self-love considered as an *avidyā* [or spiritual nescience] in *Vedaṅta* philosophy; pride; self-conceit *i.e.* the conceit or conception of individuality',[1] but *aham* is also known as the *mahat-tattva*, 'the great that thou' or 'the great principle, the intellect',[2] which is the cosmic *ahaṅkāra* meaning 'thou art that *Brahman*'. It is truly an extraordinary fact that with the manifestation of the great intellect also comes duality.

Then the *sphoṭa* or 'explosion in consciousness' upsets the balance of the *guṇāḥ* or 'qualities in nature' that cause the *dhātu* to expand into *vyakta prakṛiti* or 'manifest Creation' at number three, just as described by Plato's three principles. In fact these are the first three points in an enneagram or 'circle of nine points', which itself arises as Creation expands and 'as imagination bodies forth the forms of things unknown'.

It now falls to describe the remaining six points of the circle and then the number ten (see Appendix I). The sound of *aham* pervades and persists for the duration of Creation as the unceasing feeling of existence. The force of *sphoṭa* at number three has of necessity to be experienced by a conscious party at level four in order to become manifest. It is experienced at level four as the *ahaṅkāra*, or *aham* in *kāra*, 'the Creation'. (The *m* of *aham* has become the nasal *ṅ* or the *anusvāra* under the laws of *sandhi* or crasis.) '*Aham*' is 'the name of all creatures' as every being is aware of the unceasing feeling of existence. It comes down into English as 'I am', which is why when someone asks you your name, you usually reply 'I am ....' and you then give your name.[3]

This conscious reflector at four must now be given a location in which to experience, or as the Bard put it, give to 'airy nothing a local habitation and a name', so that the experiencer can assume the faculties with which to experience. The *ahaṅkāra* is composed of three constituents, which may be considered together as the flywheel of the now conscious experiencer. They are *citta*, *buddhi* and *manas* and are both for the *samashṭi* or 'universal', and for the *vyashṭi* or 'individual'. *Citta* cognises the experience in consciousness and reflects it to *buddhi*, which has the power to judge or form conceptions or notions and ascribe values to the experience, whilst *manas* is the faculty or instrument that is the agent for the interpretation of the experience. These four act together in a moment: after a deep sleep, a man awakes in a strange room; the first experience is one of 'I am' or *ahaṅkāra*; then *citta* cognises the strange room with its colours, furniture and curtains and the local sounds; the cognition causes values, attributes and desires to be formed in *buddhi*; with the desires, various actions and reactions are instantly formulated as *manas* goes into action as the interpreter or discursive mind. The whole process is over in a flash, for pure *citta* reflects whatever is presented to it at the speed of light.

Ākāśa or 'ether' stands at number five; it is the crossroads or halfway house on the way to number nine. Before it stands the world of subtle and causal nature and after it stands the gross physical manifestation. It acts as the connector between these worlds, transforming the subtle energy into physical energy. From the ether, *vāyu* or air arises at six and gives the sensation of touch and also carries the sound of ether. From air, *tejas* or fire arises at seven and gives heat and light, as well as the touch of air and sound of ether. Heat is only created when there is some movement or vibration, so it can only come after there is the air in which to vibrate and in this way the whole process is induced and drawn forward. From fire, *jala* or water arises at eight and gives the taste and bonding power, as well as the heat and light of fire, touch of air and sound of ether. Finally, comes the *pṛithivī* or earth at number nine which is the full and final glorious manifestation of the Creator. It is the perfect medium to reflect all the five qualities of the elements, for it has smell and crystalline form of its own, the taste and bonding power of water, the heat and light of fire, the touch of air and the sound of ether.

The causal form of each element is the one before it. Thus the earth particles are caused by a combination of the other four; the causal form of water is the three elements before it and so on. The empirical evidence is straightforward: an ounce of earth mixed with water, when boiled by fire, disappears as steam in the air, and the causal form of air is ether. Anything in the manifest Creation contains all five elements, whether it be animal, vegetable or mineral. This is because each element contains one half of its own element and one half mixed from the other elements. This is known as the *pañcīkaraṇa* system, meaning 'making fivefold',[4] or the interpenetration of the five causal elements (see Appendix II). Taking the whole of manifest Creation, since everything is created out of ether, then everything will be found in it; in air, the other four elements will be present and so on. Thus the qualities of sound, touch, light, taste and smell penetrate downwards and the substances of earth, water, fire (as form also) and air penetrate upwards into the ether, to imbue all Creation with the joy of the qualities and to render the substances into subtler expressions.

Everything in Creation comprises the five elements through the *pañcīkaraṇa* system, whereby the mixture is created for the formation of the worlds and 'all that is therein'. All physical forms of animal, mineral or vegetable are created by the interpenetration of the five elements. In the Vedic system there are eight million, four hundred thousand types of living species, which are divided into four groups: mammals are womb-born, birds and reptiles are egg-born, other creatures are earth-born and yet others, such as germs, are sweat-born, arising out of moisture. They all contain varying proportions of the five elements and all manifest out of the glorious earth at number nine. For as Plato stated, 'when the time came that the mortal creatures should also be created, the Gods fashioned them out of earth and fire and various mixtures of both elements in the interior of the earth'.[5]

The three mighty *Guṇāḥ* permeate and pervade all Creation and they manifest in the qualities of the elements. For example, *Sāttvika* air is fresh and carries the fine scent of earth, the *rājasika* air is the wind and *tāmasika* air is stale air, as in an unventilated room. *Sāttvika* fire is the light of consciousness or knowledge, *rājasika* fire is in the celestial lights such as the sun, moon, stars and lightning, and *tāmasika* fire is the reduced lights on earth found in fire and emanating from candles and light bulbs.[6] *Sāttvika* water is the universal water from which oceans are created; the River Ganges is said to be *sāttvika* as according to tradition it is never polluted. The *rājasika* water is in the constant movement of the climatic system, running as rivers, rising as mist, forming clouds and then raining down to provide water for daily use. *Tāmasika* water is polluted water which is not fit for use. Finally, *sāttvika* earth is in the lush, green pastures and beautiful forms, *rājasika* earth is in all the moving embodiments and *tāmasika* earth is ground which is sterile and useless. Hence the three mighty *Guṇāḥ* govern every particle and event in Creation.

The *Guṇāḥ* are qualities in nature, whether in bodies, actions or the play of the elements. Let us summon up the Bard to give a more revealing account of these qualities and one with some art to it too: air is sattvic when filled with 'sounds and sweet airs that give delight'; rajasic when 'the bawdy wind, that kisses all it meets' blows strong; and tamasic when filled with 'foul words' that 'are but foul wind, and foul wind is but foul breath, and foul breath is noisome'. The sattvic form of fire brings Self-knowledge, for 'even so my sun one early morn did shine with all triumphant splendour on my brow', whereas rajasic fire is a common visitor, for 'full many a glorious morning have I seen flatter the mountain tops with sovereign eye'; and the tamasic form of fire shines not in the heavens but on earth, as when 'the glow-worm shows the matin to be near, and gins to pale his uneffectual fire'. Water is sattvic when 'love's fire heats water, water cools not love'; rajasic when 'it droppeth as the gentle rain from heaven', whereas tamasic 'water is a sore decayer of your whoreson dead body'. The sattvic form of earth is bountiful and nourishes 'the vine, the merry cheerer of the heart' and 'the even mead, that erst brought sweetly forth the freckled cowslip, burnet, and green clover'; the rajasic form has an altogether different quality, as in a 'rage like an angry boar chafed with sweat'; and tamasic earth is experienced when body is heavy and mind dull, and 'duller shouldst thou be than the fat weed that rots in ease on Lethe wharf'.

This law of three is also reflected in the structure of the enneagram in the three sets of three measures: first one to three, which contains the creative process; then four to six, which contains the elements for expansion and sustenance; and thirdly seven to nine, which are for the complete fulfilment of Creation. Thus the enneagram displays both the law of three and the law of seven at work in the Creation.

The expansion of the elements as an act of Love is all a result of the *māyā* or divine magical play, as when the waves of the sea are driven by the wind and come rushing in with the surf that sparkles brilliantly in the sunlight to pound upon the shore, producing particles of fiery sand that are the earth particles themselves. The five senses are also an integral part of this magical play, for without sound, touch, sight, taste and smell, the play could not be appreciated: sound is the play of ether, touch is the play of air, sight is the play of light or fire, taste is the play of water and smell is the play of earth. Manifest Creation is all a play of the *Guṇāḥ*,[7] the play of the Creator through the power of *Māyā*. 'Such tricks', said the Bard, 'hath strong imagination that if it would but apprehend some joy, it comprehends some bringer of that joy; or in the night, imagining some fear, how easy is a bush supposed a bear'. For the *Veda* state that the world is an illusion, which is not to say that it does not exist; it has existence in time and space, but it is termed an illusion as it has no independent existence. When the *Veda* state that the *Brahman* exists, it means that the *Brahman* exists independently without any assistance, for it exists by Itself and is Self-sustaining, eternal and all-powerful, whereas the world is totally dependent on and sustained by the *Brahman*.

Māyā is the Goddess of the Undifferentiated, meaning the undifferentiated power of *Brahman*, which has no beginning. She is also called the Goddess of Illusion, in the sense that she conjures the relative out of the absolute. She is composed of the three *Guṇāḥ*, but is superior to their effects and, being the very midwife of relative Creation, is therefore their cause and origin. She is in very fact the compound of the three *Guṇāḥ* and the causal body of the Soul. She neither exists nor does not exist; she has neither the qualities, character or attributes of existence nor of non-existence; she is not constituted of elements or parts nor does she constitute an indivisible whole. Her wonder and her magic are ineffable. She is neither mortal nor immortal, but she can be 'destroyed' – but there is nothing of her that can be destroyed – by the realisation of the pure *Brahman*, the one without a second, just as the mistaken idea of a snake (or a bear) is extinguished by the grateful realisation that it is a rope (or a bush). *Māyā* is the 'dark lady' who alone is worthy of the constant adulation and praise recorded in the Bard's sonnets.[8] She is described as 'Beauty Itself, In Itself, with Itself' by Plato; she exists in 'the realm of love':

> He who has been led by his teacher in the matters of love to this point, correctly observing step by step the objects of beauty, when approaching his final goal will of a sudden catch sight of a nature of amazing beauty, and this, Sokrates, is indeed the cause of all his former efforts. This nature is in the first place for all time, neither coming into being nor passing into dissolution, neither growing nor decaying; secondly, it is not beautiful in one part or at one time, but ugly in another part or at another time, nor beautiful towards one thing, but ugly towards another, nor beautiful here and ugly there, as if beautiful to some, but ugly to others; again this beauty will not appear to him as partaking of the level of beauty of the human face or hands or any other part of the body,

neither of any kind of reason nor any branch of science, nor existing in any other being, such as in a living creature, or in earth, or in heaven or in anything else, but only in the ever present unity of Beauty Itself, in Itself, with Itself, from which all other beautiful things are derived, but in such a manner that these others come into being and pass into dissolution, but it experiences no expansion nor contraction nor suffers any change.

Symposium, 210E-211A

The *dhātu* of *māyā* is *mā*, which means 'to measure, mete out, mark off; measure out, apportion, grant; arrange, fashion, form; show, display, exhibit; to cause to be measured out or built'.[9] The words *mātrā*, meaning 'measure of any kind',[10] and *mātri*, meaning 'mother'[11] are from the same root. The *dhātvartha* for *dhātu mā* is *māna*,[12] which means 'measure, form, appearance, proof';[13] and the *dhātu* of *māna* is, not surprisingly, *mā*. This key root pervades Greek, Latin and English as *metreō*, *metior* and measure, and it also produces *mimos*, *mimicus* and mimic or imitation.[14] An imitation certainly has a mother, namely the original, and an exact copy, such as produced by a mirror, is based upon exact measurements, and this is why the three concepts of mother, measure and mime arise from the same root *mā*, which is itself found in the activity of 'measuring'. It is appropriate that the name of the Goddess of the Undifferentiated and of Illusion, *Māyā*, is derived from this very root, for she is the Mother of the Creation, she measures out the immeasurable so as to prove it by its own appearance, and thereby she mimics what is absolute in a relative form. This is expressed in the *Veda* in many ways, as for example:

He was the model for each and every form,
that form of His is for the purpose of
His manifestations.

Ṛigveda, 6,47,18

Śaṅkara's commentary on this verse is that 'had name and form not been manifest, then the transcendent formless nature of the Self, being an undifferentiated mass of consciousness, could not be known', which is why *Māyā* is called the Goddess of the Undifferentiated and she makes it known through a myriad of forms.[15] The body, organs, *praṇas* or 'life-breaths', *manas*, *ahaṅkāra*, all modifications, the sense objects, pleasure and pain, the five gross elements, in fact the whole universe up to the Undifferentiated, all this is the Non-Self. From *Mahat* down to the gross body, everything is the effect of *Māyā*; all these and *Māyā* herself are there to be known as the Non-Self, and therefore unreal, like a mirage.

Finally, the circle of nine points may also be expressed with *Brahman* as *sat* at number nine and with earth at number one. When taken in this sequence, *prakṛiti* is at number seven, which is the number of perpetual motion, for one over seven produces the constantly recurring 1428571~, or the number of natural perpetuation. This pattern provides a different interpretative sequence (see Appendix I); for example, the *sat* at one feels the consciousness of the emerging Creation at number four in the *ahaṅkāra*, draws on the forms in the *avyakta prakṛiti* at number two, and as the manifesting 'spirit moved over the face of the waters' at number eight, it necessarily finds manifestation through ether at number five, with the agency of form-giving fire at number seven, in order to experience itself, and return to itself at number one, from which everything began and from which it will proceed again in due season.

7

The Greek Creation Myths and the Four Elements

There were many parallels for the early Greek myths, namely the *Ṛigveda* from India, the 'Book of the Dead' from Egypt and the 'Poem of Creation' from Mesopotamia. Although there are broad similarities between these pre-Hellenic myths and those elaborated by Hesiod, Pherekudes and the Orphic teachers, there is no exact evidence to link them, although considerable correspondance does exist and Scandinavian and Polynesian myths repeat similar themes too. Some myths emphasise the place of a Creator God, acting as an artisan to form the world, either on his own or with the help of other beings created from him; he may bring the universe forth from nothing or more usually from some pre-existing, primordial substance. Other myths depict the origin as an emanation or as a spontaneous hatching. Very often, the phenomenal world is connected in its origin with a primeval Chaos, which is often personified as having a nature that opposes the creating and ordering process. The Chaos remains active in the universe and reveals its presence at the human level, of man torn between Good and Evil, and at the divine level, where dualistic systems can operate. The alternative theories of an egg, atomic, chaotic or time-born Creation are not in themselves untrue as far as they go, but they show only a limited and partial view and their aim was often to demonstrate the illusory nature of the universe rather than to explain its origins.

Hesiod's Theogony describes the beginning of Creation and its development from *Khaos* or 'Chaos'. The exact meaning of Chaos is obscure; Aristotle's opinion that it was space is possibly incorrect, as this was an idea that developed later. The Stoics' view that it was either water or disordered, shapeless matter, not dissimilar to the Undifferentiated of the Vedic tradition, are also later developments. Greek *khaos* and *khaskō* are derived from *dhātu khanu*, which has *dhātvartha avadāraṇe*, meaning 'breaking open, bursting open'.[1] The phrase '*Khaos genet*' ' implies that the first stage in the differentiation of Creation was the production of a vast gap between sky and earth;[2] from this gap Erebos or 'darkness' and Night were born; then Night gave birth to Ether or 'the upper air' and Day, whose father was Erebos. Earth in her turn gave birth first to the Starry Sky, Uranos, 'equal to her, that he may cover her altogether', and then to the Great Mountains and the Sea or Pontos, 'without any desired love'. Lastly, of her union with the sky the river Ocean was born. Kronos and Rheia, the children of Earth and Sky, were the parents of Zeus; the Olympian Gods were born therefore after the powers which they controlled had already come into existence.

The same characteristics and general order are evident in the two main other sources of early Greek cosmogony, namely Pherekudes and the Orphic myths, who introduced certain innovations. Pherekudes introduces Zas (*i.e.* Zeus), the principle of Life, the organiser and craftsman of the universe above Khthonie or 'earth' and above Kronos or the 'lower part of the sky' here, although all three always existed. Zas changes into Eros, who spreads a nuptial veil at his marriage to Khthonie, on which he will embroider the earth and ocean; next, the veil is then somehow borne on a winged oak, presumably symbolising the foundations and substructures of the earth. At some point, Kronos makes fire, wind and water out of his own seed, which are then disposed of in five recesses or nooks, which produce other generations of Gods. Finally, Zas must triumph over evil, and the gods fight a battle against the serpent Ophioneus and his army; the victorious Gods take over the sky and the monsters are hurled into the ocean.

The Orphics believed man is a divine immortal spirit. There are four main Orphic Creation myths and in the Hieronimos/Hellanikos version, for example, the earth comes from matter and is mixed with water. The union of earth and water produced a monster, Kronos or Herades, unageing time, to whom is added Adrasteia or Necessity, which is incorporeal. Then Kronos manufactures an enormous egg, the two halves of which are Sky and Earth. There is also reference to a first-born God, Protogonos, or Zeus or Pan, who orders all things, and in another version recorded by Damaskios, a God called Phanes, the Luminous God, or sometimes Metis, Intelligence. Another myth relates how Dionysos, son of Zeus, was lured away by the Titans, who ate him. Zeus burnt the Titans with a thunderbolt and from the ashes Man was born. The Titans were evil and earthbound, but the divine spark from Dionysos' ashes is in Man too, and the spark will eventually rejoin the ethereal fire.

In these myths the universal powers are personified, and although there is some distinction between the personifications and the actual forces, scientific analysis is not attempted. There is however a sense of an ordered and well regulated development, beginning with a common source and developing through an ordered relationship of the various levels of Creation, each of which is real and an ultimate descendant of that same source. Myth claims recognition by the faithful and does not pretend to justify itself to the critical; Aristotle's description of their authors as '*muthikōs sophizomenoi*', or 'wise old myth merchants' is apt. However, these attempts to organise the forces of Creation into a system of stable relationships where they might retain their inherited properties was also the aim of the rational thinkers; indeed the myths were the seed or germ for the scientific and philosophic enquiries, and the mythopoeic cosmogonies not only survived but lived by the side of science and philosophy, and Plato and the Stoics did not hesitate to draw on their rich store of symbolic representations.

Thales and the first Ionian philosophers abandoned mythopoeic modes of thought, of personification and anthropomorphic, theistic explanations and they attempted to explain the manifest Creation in terms of its observable constituents. This was an obvious way for Thales, Anaximander and Anaximenes to proceed, for they were practical astronomers, land-surveyors and geographers, amongst other activities. Their cosmogony postulated as the first reality a single living substance, from which everything developed; hence they were called Hylozoists. Thales called it *to hugron*, 'the moist', Anaximander called it *to apeiron*, 'the indefinite' or 'unbounded' and Anaximenes called it *to aēr*, or 'the vapour'; hence they identified the elements of water, possibly of ether and also of air as being universal. They regarded this primordial substance as divine, being eternal, and Anaximander considered it as surrounding and governing the innumerable worlds.

But the Milesian scientists/philosophers have clearly developed a long way from the Cosmogonists. Aristotle comments on their expansion into rational thought as follows: they 'thought that principles in the form of matter were the only principles in the form of all things: for the original source of all existing things, that from which a thing first comes into being and into which it is finally destroyed, the substance persisting but changing in its qualities, this they declare is the element and first principle of existing things, and for this reason they consider that there is no absolute coming-to-be or passing away, on the ground that such a nature is always preserved ... for there must be some natural substance, either one or more than one, from which the other things come into being, while it is preserved'.[3]

Plato treats space as a nature distinct in its own right from the other four elements, and 'it is eternal and indestructible and provides a home for all created things'.[4] Plato subscribed to a system of interpenetration of the elements which was very similar to the Vedic *pañcīkaraṇa* system, except that it was only four elements that co-mingled within space, whose function was to include everything in and leave nothing of the four elements on the outside. Plato treated fire and earth as the first elements for the body of the universe. The bonding agent was 'proportion' and God placed water and air as the two means between fire and earth, and made them to have the same proportion as far as was possible, that is as fire is to air so is air to water, and as air is to water so is water to earth (*cf.* Appendix II). Plato's order of the elements, fire, air, water, earth, puts fire before air, for he considered it as less solid and finer than air. The effect of the interpenetration process is given by Plato in the form of a mathematical equation: 'for whenever in any three numbers, there is a mean, which is to the last term what the first term is to it; and again, when the mean is to the first term as the last term is to the mean, then the mean becoming first and last, and the first and last both becoming means, they will all of them of necessity come to be the same, and having become the same with one another will be all one'.[5] Plato further states that the revolutions of the universe generate a centrifugal force which compresses the elements and allows no void. So fire, being the finest element, penetrates everything and makes everything visible; air follows next, then water and then earth, which is the densest element, with the least rarity. Now 'those things which are composed of the largest particles have the largest void left in their compositions, and those which are composed of the smallest particles have the least. And the concentration caused by the compression thrusts the smaller particles into the interstices of the larger',[6] and in this way the Creator 'framed the universe, putting intelligence in Soul, and Soul in body, that he might be the Creator of a work which was by nature fairest and best'.[7]

It is fitting to end this chapter with the Sokratic eulogy to the earth, that full and final glorious manifestation of the Creation from which all visible and beautiful bodies and objects are derived:

> In the first place, the earth, when looked at from above is in appearance streaked like one of those balls which have leather coverings in twelve pieces, and is decked with various colours, of which the colours used by painters on earth are in a manner samples. But there the whole earth is made up of them, and they are brighter far and clearer than ours; there is a purple of wonderful lustre, also the radiance of gold, and the white which is in the earth is whiter than any chalk or snow. Of these and other colours the earth is made up, and they are more in number and fairer than the eye of man has ever seen; the very hollows (of which I was speaking) filled with air and water have a colour of their own, and are seen like light gleaming amid the diversity of the other colours, so that the whole presents a single continuous appearance of variety in unity. And in this fair region everything that grows – trees, and flowers, and fruits – are in a like degree fairer than any here; and there are hills, having stones in them in a like degree smoother, and more transparent, and fairer in colour than our highly-valued emeralds and sardonyxes and jaspers, and other gems, which are but minute fragments of them: for there all the stones are like our precious stones, and fairer still. The reason is that they are pure, and not like our precious stones, infected or

corroded by the corrupt briny elements which coagulate among us, and which breed foulness and disease both in earth and stones, as well as in animals and plants. They are the jewels of the upper earth, which also shines with gold and silver and the like, and they are set in the light of day and are large and abundant and in all places, making the earth a sight to gladden the beholder's eye. And there are animals and men, some in a middle region, others dwelling about the air as we dwell about the sea; others in islands which the air flows around, near the continents; and in a word the air is used by them as the water and the sea by us, and the ether is to them what the air is to us.

Moreover, the temperament of their seasons is such that they have no disease, and live much longer than we do, and have sight and hearing and smell, and all the other senses, in far greater perfection, in the same proportion that air is purer than water or the ether than air. Also they have temples and sacred places in which the gods really dwell, and they hear their voices and receive their answers, and are conscious of them and hold converse with them; and they see the sun, moon, and stars as they truly are, and their other blessedness is of a piece with this'.

Phaido, 110B-111B

Sokrates says he is describing 'the upper earth which is under the heaven' rather than our 'spoilt and corroded earth'; however, this is Plato's literary signature for describing the metaphysical Forms or models on which the physical world is based.

Hamlet: O God, I could be bounded in a nutshell,
And count myself a king of infinite space,
Were it not that I have bad dreams.
Guildenstern: Which dreams, indeed, are ambition;
For the very substance of the ambitious
Is merely the shadow of a dream.
Hamlet: A dream itself is but a shadow.
Rosencrantz: Truly, and I hold ambition
Of so airy and light a quality,
That it is but a shadow's shadow.
Hamlet: Then are our beggars bodies,
And our monarchs and outstretched heroes
The beggars' shadows.

Shakespeare, *Hamlet*, Act 2, Scene 2.

PART II

Words, Seers, Bards & Heroes

8

The Gift of Language

In the Vedic tradition, the Sanskrit alphabet and grammar necessarily came with the Creation. Hence the *praṇava śabda* sound of *AUM,* the Supreme Spirit and the Sanskrit alphabet are all termed *akshara*, meaning 'indestructible'. Sokrates describes this natural alphabet and its formation thus:

> Some God or divine man, who in the Egyptian legend is said to have been Theuth, observing that the human voice was infinite, first distinguished in this infinity a certain number of vowels, and then other letters which had sound but were not pure vowels [i.e. the semi-vowels]; these too exist in a definite number; and lastly he distinguished a third class of letters which we now call mutes, without voice and without sound [i.e. consonants, which cannot be sounded on their own without a vowel], and divided these, and likewise the two other classes of vowels and semi-vowels, into the individual sounds, and told the number of them, and gave to each and all of them the name of letters.
>
> *Philēbos*, 18B-C

This remarkable analysis of the natural alphabet is an accurate description of the Sanskrit system, which contains sixteen vowels, five semi-vowels and twenty-eight consonants, including the three sibilants.

Saṃskṛita, a name which means 'that which is perfectly formed', is the true science of language. It is indeed 'perfectly formed' and its classification of the alphabet into the five places of utterance takes its order from the natural human capacity for the production of guttural, cerebral, palatal, dental and labial sound: the pure vowels, semi-vowels and their dependent consonants enable the Sanskrit language to express a full range of human sound, which is the very basis of 'the natural language'. Consequently, Sanskrit possesses the power to express the complete system of grammar, as evidenced by *Pāṇini's* 'Eight Meditations' on grammar, and its attendant root system. There is nothing accidental either in this system of language or in the capacity of the human vocal mechanism, that together may be truly classified as the oral manifestation of a natural science. Consequently, two unique features of the Sanskrit language are that it has experienced no evolution or modification over the centuries and there are no textual disputes over the key Vedic texts, which is a remarkable phenomenon when compared with the scholastic efforts that have been and continue to be spent on Greek textual emendations.

The *mantra* system of sounds, which is beyond Creation and which can only be heard in the Spiritual World, starts the process of Creation by appearing to cause a vibration in the pure and undifferentiated conscious substance, which is Love. For the expansion of Creation as the first act of Love, the differentiation of the consciousness necessarily creates subject, verb and object; for just as the Creation is spoken into existence by the *mantra* system, there must be a natural alphabet and a system of attendant grammar in Creation so that sentences can be formulated to describe the universal laws, the relationship between the *vyashṭi* or the 'individual' and the *samashṭi* or the 'universal', and the *avyakta* or the 'unmanifest' and the *vyakta* or the 'manifest'. Sokrates stated this relationship succinctly when he said: 'the Gods gave the first names, and therefore they are right'.[1]

Each word arises when a *sphoṭa* activates a *dhātu* and causes *vṛiddhi*, meaning 'expansion or development'. At this point, the emerging word is held in its *pratipadika* or 'uninflected' form. Then the *Guṇāḥ* act in a specific way on the vowel sounds, which bring out the quality of the *dhātu* by means of the addition of another short measure of *a*. Thus *a*, *i*, *u*, *ṛi* and *lṛi* become *ā*, *e*, *o*, *ar* and *al*, or *ā*, *ai*, *au*, *ār* and *āl*, by the addition of one and then two short measures of *a*; so *cit*, for example, becomes *cet* with the additional measure of *a*, and with the addition of another (and final) short measure of *a* becomes *cait*. At this point the process of *vibhakti* shares out the substance of the Self to enable the act of Creation to take place; *vibhakti* means 'expansion in Love', where *vi-* means 'expansion' and *bhakta* means 'Love'.[2] A technical definition is: 'partition; a portion or share of inheritance; inflection of nouns, a case or a case termination'.[3] It now requires the necessary conjugation, declension, or adjectival or adverbial suffix or prefix to take its place in a sentence; this stage is called *pratyaya*, meaning 'certainty and conviction', and the *pratyaya* endings express *vibhakti* in the fully formed *pada* or word, which is now manifest and is ready to take its part in the sentence.

For a sentence to be formed, the grammarians defined the six *kārakāṇi* or six 'cases', which describe the six relationships in an action. The first *kāraka* is defined as *druvamapāye-pādānam,* which means 'the eternal unmoving, from which all movement comes, is *apādāna*',[4] which closely resembles Plato's Self-mover. The second *kāraka* is defined as *karmanā yamabhipraiti sa sampradānam*; this means 'that for which the action is intended as an offering or gift, is *sampradāna*'.[5] The third *kāraka* is *sadhakatamam kāraṇam*, meaning 'that which is most propitious, for the accomplishment of the action, is the instrument'.[6] The action takes place in *ādhāro-dhikaraṇam*, where 'the substance of the Creator is the location'.[7] Pausing at this point, the play of Creation can be expressed thus:

> From the eternal unmoving from which all movement comes, an action is intended as an offering or as a gift, and is accomplished by the most auspicious instrument, and takes place in the substance of the *Brahman*.

The next *kāraka* to appear is *karturīpsitatamam karma*, when 'that which is most beloved by the actor is the action'.[8] And the actor is *svatantraḥ karttā*, 'he who has the system within himself is the agent of the *Ātman* for the action'.[9] So now we have the following description for all the relationships in an action or *kāraka*:

> The actor, as the agent for the *Ātman*, moved by the eternal unmoving from which all movement comes, has the system within himself for the action, which is most beloved and is intended as an offering or as a gift, and is accomplished by the most auspicious instrument in the substance of the *Brahman*.

The six *kārakāṇi* are the six possible relationships in an action; they are the fully perfected manifestation of *vibhakti* in the 'expansion of Creation as an act of Love'. This outward thrust of Creation is a manifestation of love into the various physical forms and the return to the source is also within this act of love, experienced as an inward movement back to the cause. All desires experienced by the *karttā* or 'actor' arise from this love; if the *sampradāna* or 'the intention' is towards the cause, then it is expansion into subtler levels, towards 'the most beloved', which is the cause; but if the intention is towards repeating experience related to physical forms and beauty, then the *Vibhakti* or 'expansion of love' suffers distortion and loss of power.

With the Creation of man and the living creatures came birth and death and procreation, and the undifferentiated consciousness was necessarily divided into three *liṅga* or genders. *Liṅga* means 'a mark, sign, badge, characteristic; any assumed or false badge or mark; the sign of gender or sex or organ of generation, the male organ or Phallus, especially that of *Śiva* worshipped in the form of a stone or marble column which generally rises out of a *yoni*'.[10] The *dhātu* of *liṅga* is *likha*, which has *dhātvartha aksharavinyāse*,[11] which is a compound of *akshara*, the name of the alphabet and also 'a syllable or sound; The Imperishable, The Supreme Spirit',[12] and *vinyāsa* meaning 'arrangement, disposition, putting together, composing and displaying'.[13] Hence gender is the 'false badge or mark' that disguises The Supreme

Spirit in its endless ability to express Itself in countless forms through procreation and gender, although 'it remains the One and Unchanging Supreme Spirit'.[14] Thus *punliṅga* is the masculine force, *strīliṅga* is the feminine force of the forceful and *napunsakaliṅga* is the neutralising force that contains the other two; they pervade the Indo-European languages and they manifest throughout the living creatures as the law of three in endless procreation and differentiation. In this process of expansion there is of necessity the concept of *vacana* or 'speaking and counting', as one, two or plurality; there are three *kāla* or 'times', past present and future; and there are three aspects of an action, in terms of relation to the Self within, to the Self in another or to the Self in all.

Sir Monier Monier-Williams, the nineteenth-century Oxford lexicographer, wrote that Sanskrit is 'the best guide to the structure of Greek as well as of every other member of the Aryan or Indo-European family – a language in short which is the very key-stone of the science of comparative philology',[15] and he calls it 'the eldest sister of these languages',[16] no doubt in due deference to the sacred syllable *AUM*, from which all *dhātu*-based languages arise. In fact, Sanskrit is the model for the regulations governing persons, numbers, genders, conjugations, declensions, pronouns and numerals for the Indo-European family of languages. As the younger languages developed from their 'eldest sister', it was inevitable, with the action of the *Guṇāḥ* over the centuries, that the original purity of Sanskrit would be corrupted and the elegance of its grammar and syntax would be gradually reduced. The first attrition was experienced by the pure vowels; by the time Homer's songs were committed to writing, the only pure vowels left in Greek were Iota (*i*) and Upsilon (*u*). Alpha (*a*), Epsilon (*e*), Eta (*ē*), Omicron (*o*) and Omega (*ō*) had all become hard, while Epsilon and Eta had effectively become diphthongs. The consonants also suffered as the palatals merged with the gutturals and the distinction between cerebrals and dentals was dropped, while the distinctively sibilant Greek double consonants of *Dzēta*, *Ksi* and *Psi* appeared in later Greek writings.

Similarly with the *kārakāṇi*, the English names reduce their significant meaning: *karttā* is now called the nominative, *karma* is accusative, *sampradāna* is dative, *apādāna* is ablative and *adhikaraṇa* is locative; these names do not fully express the subtle aspects of the relationships. *Karaṇa* as instrumental is dropped and the ablative is allowed to take over this function in Latin and English, while Greek drops the ablative altogether; the *adhikaraṇa* is merged with the dative; the *sambodhaṇa* in Sanskrit, which is not *kāraka*, is allowed to become a vocative case; and finally the *sambandha* in Sanskrit, which is not *kāraka* as it expresses the relationship between two nouns and not between a noun and a verb, becomes a genitive case. These distortions of the *kārakāṇi* were the indirect cause that led Middle Platonic writers in the first two centuries A.D. to develop what has been called the 'metaphysics of prepositions',[17] as they struggled to define the true relationship of actions, agencies and instruments. For Varro, heaven became the 'by which', earth the 'from which', and the Ideas 'according to which'.[18] For Potamo of Alexandria, the efficient cause is 'by which', matter 'from which', quality 'with which' (*i.e.* instrumental dative) and place the 'in which'.[19] Seneca, in the course of an argument to show that there is only one cause in the strict sense, namely God, formulated that matter is the 'from which' and that the efficient cause, namely *Logos* or *Ratio* or the Demiurge, is the 'by which', enmattered form is the 'in which', paradigmatic form is the 'to which' and the final cause is 'for the sake of which'.[20] For Potamo, intellect is 'by which', and 'the most accurate presentation' is the 'through which'.[21] For Sextos Empirikos, the human agent is the 'by which' and sensation and reason are the 'through which'.[22]

For Ptolemy, intellect is *krinon* or 'what judges', sensation is 'through which' and reason is the 'with which'.[23] The arena for conflicting prepositional usage grows larger with each addition, but the elegance and precision of the original system of *kārakāṇi* has been lost sight of. Other distortions appear of varying effect, as when Latin, for example, dropped the dual number (apart from the dual *–o* ending in *duo* or 'two' and *ambo* or 'both'), and Greek also eventually dropped the use of the dual altogether.

The classical and modern languages, however, still have the power to explain the great traditions, but as they are copies, or even copies of copies, they cannot retain the subtle sound of the *Vedas* and cannot express them in their pure form; and this is a result of the lawful play of the *Guṇāḥ*, although some would say it is the result of the work of inferior grammarians, armed with reckless ambition, seeking improvements.

The gift of language is the principal factor that elevates man above the animal kingdom, for animals cannot produce consonants and thus cannot formulate sentences to express thoughts and communicate them; speech enables mankind to seek and communicate knowledge, which is a divine gift that lends intelligence to human life. This chapter must, however, end on a note of serious caution as regards the limitations of language. Sokrates discourses with Phaidros on the shortcomings of language in relation to its ability to help men to remember the truth. He recites a tale concerning the old Egyptian God called Theuth, an inventor who Sokrates alleged was the discoverer of the use of letters. Theuth went to show his discovery to the God Thamus, whose reaction to the invention took Theuth by surprise:

'O most ingenious Theuth, the parent or inventor of an art is not always the best judge of the utility or inutility of his own inventions to the users of them. And in this instance, you who are the father of letters, from a paternal love of your own children have been led to attribute to them a quality which they cannot have; for this discovery of yours will create forgetfulness in the learners' Souls, because they will not use their memories; they will trust to the external written characters and not remember of themselves. The specific which you have discovered is an aid not to memory, but to reminiscence, and you give your disciples not truth, but only the semblance of truth; they will be hearers of many things and will have learned nothing; they will appear to be omniscient and will generally know nothing; they will be tiresome company, having the show of wisdom without the reality.'

Phaidros, 274E-275B

The grammar of language also contains the concept of duality, namely the division of activity into subject and object, where the *karttā* or 'actor' forgets he is 'the agent of the *Ātman*' and believes 'I am the doer'. This mistake, taking the 'I' as having a real and independent existence, is at the very root of ignorance; this 'I' invokes the possessive pronoun 'mine' and the desire to claim for itself all numbers of things and attributes, which are contrary to the true nature of man and Creation. The daily use of language and the structure of grammar serves to reinforce this duality, so that it becomes second nature for man to think in terms of 'me' and 'mine'. The purest word from *AUM* is *Aham*, but in the science of language 'me' and 'mine' become substitutes for *Aham*; in the *Gītā*, Lord *Śṛī Kṛishṇa* says 'mine' many times, but he means the *Ātman* and not the body, *manas*, *buddhi* or *ahaṅkāra*. Man must avoid the twin pitfalls of identification and attachment which is unfortunately reinforced by the daily use of language, for the truth is that the Creation, Creator and Self are one, for *Aham* is *Ātman*, which is *Brahman*.

The idea that daily use of language, even or especially in its correct grammatical form, can directly reinforce philosophical nescience is a fact that is not easily acceptable at first. One of the great Advaitist philosophers of the twentieth century, however, His Holiness *Jagadguru Śaṅkarācārya Śṛī Bharati Kṛishṇa Mahārāj*, known as the '*Śaṅkarācārya of Puri*' (1884-1960), was also a leading scholar in his own right, particularly of Sanskrit; in 1904 he passed the Master of Arts examination at the American College of Sciences, Rochester, New York, in seven subjects simultaneously. He stated clearly that correct grammatical usage is for the unconscious individual 'mere custom, mere thoughtless custom' and is 'incorrect from the standpoint of real philosophical thinking' and he continued by analysing the simple sentence, 'I see an object':

> 'I' is the subject of the sentence. 'See' is the predicate, and the object is such and such a thing; similarly, 'I hear'. What is it that I hear? All that can be said is, 'The sound comes into the ear'. I cannot say 'I hear'. There is no such action as hearing [by the subject, the 'I']. If the obstacle to vision is removed, then automatically the seeing begins. And who is the Seer? No one can say, because there is no action which I have, as an active agent or subject of the predicate, actually performed ... Actually, there is no such action as 'seeing'; 'being seen' [the passive mood], even that is not there. All that can be said is, 'something has come into view' [into the viewing]. I am not the actor. I am not the active performer of any deed. How can I say, 'I see', 'I hear', 'I smell', 'I taste' [or 'I smell']. The sound comes into the ear and I claim the credit for having heard something. What have I done? If there is something preventing my hearing, if there is cotton wool placed in the ear and I remove it, even then I am not doing an active action of 'hearing'. All that I am doing is, I have removed the obstruction in the way of the sound coming into the ear.
>
> *Sanātana Dharma*, Ch.XIX, 182 ff.

This is a true example of the application of the principle expounded in the *Gītā*, namely 'I am not the doer'. There is no seer or hearer, there is only seeing, seeing, seeing and there is only hearing, hearing, hearing, for they are universal activities, like living and being, that have no need of a subject. It is not by chance that the *Dhātu-Pāṭha* sets out the root structure of the Indo-European languages as being entirely verbal, for verbs express activities and it is in activities themselves that the play of creation is manifest. The principle 'I am not the doer' now means that there is 'No one to do anything in the first place'; it is for this reason that Lord *Ṡṛī Kṛishṇa* takes the precaution of advising Prince *Arjuna* that the philosophy of non-action is not a philosophy of inaction, for non-action can only be learnt in action:

> No man can attain freedom from activity by refraining from action;
> nor can he reach perfection by merely refusing to act.
>
> *Gītā*, Ch.III, v.4

The wise men who know they are not the doer do not claim anything, but those who labour under the idea that they are a specific someone have not the slightest idea which specific person composed the *Vedas*, the epics, the myths, the psalms or the Bard's plays or sonnets; for who, recognising and expressing his own Self in such great works, would need recognition in return from that which does not exist? The comedy of errors is that the 'I that believes it does exist' will not exist for long anyway, so it is far wiser to acknowledge that it does not exist while it is apparently in existence, for after the death of that which does not exist, there can be no acknowledgment of its non-existence, for even the dead live on in their ignorance.

For the living there are 'words, words, words' for the artful and joyful communication of aspects of the relative world that really do exist: 'old men have grey beards, their faces are wrinkled, their eyes purging thick amber or plum tree gum, and they have a plentiful lack of wit, together with most weak hams'; and the living enjoy grammar and syntax for the logical analysis of that which relatively is and conditionally might be, as in this amusingly tautological example of the apodosis and protasis of a remote, unfulfilled, future conditional: 'for you yourself, sir, should be as old as I am, if, like a crab, you could go backward.' The real 'I am' is of course ageless; the false 'I am' thinks that it ages, so such deluded Souls are deprecatingly referred to by the Bard as 'tedious old fools'.

9

The Great Ages, Conflagrations and Floods

Sokrates is speculating with Hermogenes on the early Greek deities and is considering Hesiod's use of the word *daimon*:

> You know how Hesiod uses the word? ... Do you not remember that he speaks of a golden race of men who came first ... He says of them:
>
> But now that fate has closed over this race
> They are holy demons upon the earth,
> Beneficent, averters of ills, guardians
> of mortal men. [*Works and Days*, ll.120-3]
>
> ... What is the inference? Why, I suppose that he means by the golden men, not men literally made of gold, but good and noble; and I am convinced of this, because he further says that we are the iron race ... and therefore I have the most entire conviction that he called them demons, because they were *daemones* (knowing or wise) and in our older Attic dialect the word itself occurs. Now he and other poets say truly, that when a good man dies he has honour and a mighty portion among the dead, and becomes a demon; which is a name given to him signifying wisdom. And I say too, that every wise man who happens to be a good man is more than human both in life and death, and is rightly called a demon.
>
> *Kratylos*, 397 ff.

Hermogenes then asks about the meaning of the word 'hero', and Sokrates replies that the name signifies 'that they were born of love. Do you not know that the heroes are demi-Gods? All of them sprang either from love of a God for a mortal woman, or of a mortal man for a Goddess.'

Plato further draws a direct comparison between the life of mankind in the golden age and the iron age, as follows:

> In those days God himself was man's shepherd, and ruled over them, just as man, who is by comparison a divine being, still rules over the lower animals. Under him there were no forms of government or separate possession of women and children; for all men rose again from the earth,

having no memory of the past. And although they had nothing of this sort, the earth gave them fruits in abundance, which grew on trees and shrubs unbidden, and were not planted by the hand of man. And they dwelt naked, and mostly in the open air, for the temperature of their seasons was mild; and they had no beds, but lay on soft couches of grass, which grew plentifully out of the earth. Such was the life of man in the days of Kronos, Sokrates; the character of our present life, which is said to be under Zeus, you know from your own experience. Can you, and will you, determine which of them you deem happier?

Politikos, 271E-272B

In these passages Sokrates hints at the reduced power of men in the successive gold, silver and bronze ages, until men of the iron age have become far removed from the direct experience of the Gods: spiritual blindness is the hallmark of the iron age, while the Heroic Age that preceded it contained beings begotten partly of divine parentage. Yet even in the iron age, the ancient Greeks, through the Eleusinian mysteries and the schools of philosophy, kept alive the divine search for evolution of the Gods within the human Soul. The Seers and initiates of this continuous mystical process revealed the Gods, and the master teachers of the classical period did the same for their disciples. The inference of Plato's speculation is that the Gods were considered by the early Greeks to be projections of macro-cosmic forces, in light and fire, water and earth, lightning and thunder; for the Gods who inhabited the macrocosm also inhabited the microcosm, and hence Hesiod's and Homer's songs show the close interaction and interdependence of the life of Gods through constant sacrifice and obedience to their commands; during his long journey home, Odysseus is constantly referred to in the discussions of the Gods as being particularly meritorious for having constantly sacrificed to them throughout the siege of Troy. In fact, the Gods, or divine forces as we may consider them in the context of an interpretation assuming a spiritual allegory, are only too eager to help such a one on the return journey; and though at times Odysseus' courage, conviction and intelligence are severely tested, yet the Gods also help the hero to surmount difficulties, and apparently opposing forces, for example Poseidon, actually come to his help by creating the very obstructions that the hero must overcome.[1]

These forces of the Cosmos also had their counterpart within man as the microcosm, and this fact was considered very practical and even obvious: for example, the sensory organs of knowledge and the organs of action are themselves the embodiment of divine forces, just as in the Vedic tradition they belong to the God *Indra*. The eyes embody the Sun and Moon, for as Sokrates said to Hermogenes, these were probably the only Gods known to the aboriginal Hellenes, for quite simply without their help nothing can be seen. The Sun is a God of the divine world and also resides in the eye and the mind, which are necessary for seeing; thus the Gods continually serve both the spirit and the form. Even in the iron age, the mystic could become initiated into the secrets of the sanctuaries of a divinity when he cognised the God within his own Soul and thus achieved perfection in relation to that particular force.

The Pythagoreans in the fifth century B.C. may have held notions of a cyclical view of the cosmos, but added a new element: the human Soul was subject to continual reincarnation, so that a Soul would be re-embodied in each succeeding age. They held a notion of the Great Year, or astronomical year, an idea that was to be taken up by Plato and Aristotle. Empedokles also held the view that by means of purification a Soul could be released from further incarnation. He propounded the view that forces of Love and Strife opposed each other, so Strife undid the work of Love. At a physical level this meant that the elements, formerly fused together, gradually broke apart under the influence of Strife; then Love in turn fused them together again, and it was in this process when Love was ascendant, that Creation, including Man, came into being. Empedokles' Strife and Love are motive forces as distinct from the material elements, at least according to Aristotle. This pattern is repeated at the human level too, so that the earliest age of man was an age of Love in comparison with his own age, for in that earlier age men had not learnt to shed blood and eat flesh, and trees kept their leaves the whole year round, producing fruit without stint. The similarities with Hesiod's golden age are obvious, and as the peripatetic Dikaearchos stated in the fourth century, as the art of agriculture was unknown in that former age, the earth must have produced food of itself. Empedokles' concept of the dualistic forces of Love and Strife resembles an alternative Vedic philosophic system comprising a duality of forces: in this system, *Agni* is the god of fire and *Soma* is the god of water and they oppose each other in the Creation. *Agni*, for example, is the eater and *Soma* is the eaten. They constantly subdue each other, for the rule is that the eater is always eaten.

Four of the five ages of Hesiod (the Heroic Age being solely a Greek concept), are prefigured in many ancient writings of India; for example, a full description is given in the *Ṡṛīmad Bhāgavata* by the sage *Maitreya* in answer to a question from *Vidura*. He gives the duration of the four *yuga* or 'ages' as 4,320,000 human years or 12,000 celestial years; 10,000 celestial years relate to the duration of the *yuga* proper and 2,000 represent the intervening periods between the *yuga*. In each *yuga*, a special *dharma* or 'virtue or code of conduct' is prescribed for men. In the *kṛitayuga* or 'golden age', *dharma* consists of austerity, purity, charity and truthfulness; with each succeeding *yuga*, one of these four limbs of *dharma* is removed. Hence in the transition to the *dvāparayuga* or 'silver age', doubt removes austerity; in the transition to the *tretayuga* or 'bronze age', attachment removes purity; and in the transition to *kaliyuga* or 'iron age', pride removes charity. Thus only truthfulness enters the iron age and in that age this last remaining limb of *dharma* is itself threatened with destruction.

There is a close parallel here to the descriptions of the ages by Hesiod. In the transition to the silver age, he refers to the loss of austerity as follows:

> they recklessly
> Injured each other and forsook the Gods;
> They did not sacrifice, as all tribes must,
> But left the holy altars bare.
>
> *Works and Days*, ll.134-6

Of the men of the bronze age, Hesiod states that 'men loved the groan and violence of war'[2] and as regards the loss of charity in the iron age, he states that 'the brother-love of past days will be gone'.[3]

Maitreya stated that 1,000 revolutions of the four *yuga*, together with an equal period when Creation is withdrawn, constitute a day and a night in the life of *Brahmā*, the Supreme Lord of the Universe, and there are three hundred and sixty such days in a year. *Brahmā's* life lasts for one hundred years and then *Brahmā* himself ceases to exist. This *mahāyuga* or 'great age' of 311,140,000,000,000 human years is governed by fourteen *Manu*, meaning 'Man par excellence or the representative man and father of the human race',[4] and consists of seventy-one and six fourteenths' revolutions of the four *yuga*; each has a particular *Manu*, with his descendants, particular groups of seven *Ṛishis* and Gods and particular *Indras*, meaning 'rulers of the three worlds': namely, *bhūḥ* or 'earth',[5] *bhūvaḥ* or 'atmosphere',[6] and *svaḥ* or 'heaven',[7] and their *gandharva* or 'attendants'. Into this Creation of *Brahmā* are born the sub-human creatures, human beings, manes and gods, according to their respective *karma*, meaning 'received office or obligation as determined by past actions'.[8] At the close of the universal day, *Brahmā* assumes an iota of *tamoguṇa*, the 'quality in nature of *tamas*', meaning 'inertia, decay, rest and darkness'[9] and dissolving all activity, retires for the universal night, as all Creation, including the moon and the sun and all the three worlds, are withdrawn into him by force of Time. *Maitreya* continues by describing this process of the withdrawal of Creation, termed *pralaya* in the Vedic tradition:

> When the three worlds are being consumed by the divine energy in the form of fire emitted by the mouth of Lord *Saṅkarśaṇa*, the serpent – god, the *Bhṛigu*, 'a mythical race of beings who find fire and bring it to men'[10]

> and six others who have their abode in *maharloka*, 'the fourth of the seven worlds ... the abode of those saints who survive a destruction of the world',[11] feel oppressed by the heat of that conflagration and ascend from the *maharloka* to the *janaloka*, 'the fifth of the seven worlds'.[12] Meanwhile, the seven oceans exceed their bounds at the approach of universal destruction. Their waters get unusually swollen and with their waves tossed by boisterous and fearful gusts of wind they submerge the three worlds in no time.
>
> *Śṛīmad Bhāgavata*, Bk.III, Disc.11, vv.29, 30

The passage is also reminiscent of aspects of Plato's story of an imagined conversation between his forebear Solon and a certain very old Egyptian priest. The priest stated as follows:

> '... There have been, and will be hereafter, many and divers destructions of mankind, the greatest by fire and water, though other lesser ones are due to countless other causes ... but the truth is that there is a destruction, occurring at long intervals, of things on earth by a great conflagration ... and sometimes the Gods cleanse the earth with a flood of waters ... Your people remember only one deluge [that of Deukalion], though there were many earlier ...'
>
> *Timaeos*, 22C-23B

There is also a full descripton of the conflagrations and floods from Philo Judaeus,[13] which may derive from Theophrastos:

> Destructions of things on the earth, not of all of them together but of most of them, are attributed to two principal causes, indescribable onslaughts of fire and water; they say that each of these descends on the world in turn, after very long cycles of years. So, when a conflagration occurs, a stream of fire from heaven is poured out from above and scattered far and wide, spreading over great regions of the inhabited earth; when there is an inundation, every sort of water rushes down; rivers fed by their own springs, and winter torrents, not only flow in spate but exceed the usual level to which they rise and either break down their banks or leap over them, rising to the greatest height. Then they overflow and pour out over the adjacent plain and ... become a great expanse of sea as the many lakes are joined together. And by these conflicting forces those who dwell in opposite places are destroyed in turn. The fire destroys those who dwell on the mountains and hills and in places where water is scarce, since they do not have abundant water, which is the natural defence against fire.
>
> *De aeternitate mundi*, 146-8

When the time for *pralaya* to be performed duly arrives through passage of Time, the enneagram or 'circle of nine points' goes into reverse. The Earth at nine is subsumed by Water at eight as torrential rains cover the land and mountains. The Earth is reduced to small particles by the Great Waters and then Fire at seven, in the form of the heat of the Twelve Suns burns up the whole liquid substance. Then air at six enters into a Great Whirl and blows away the whole solar and other systems. The Ether, which stands at five in both the outward and returning thrusts of Creation, is withdrawn into the constituent parts of *ahaṅkāra*, which is itself withdrawn into the *avyakta prakṛiti*, which is the force itself. This in turn merges into the *Brahman* or Creator and the Creation is no more. All that remains is *AUM*, *aham*, *dhātu* and the natural alphabet, which are therefore all called *akshara*, being 'indestructible'. This is the number ten, where the Creator at one stands alone with the unmanifest Creation as zero.

Finally, just as *pralaya* involves the withdrawal of all the elements in succession, so the actual change from one *yuga* or 'age' to another is accomplished by the elements in turn. Thus, the story of Noah's Ark in the Old Testament records the floods that covered the earth with water as the *yuga* moved from the bronze age to the iron age. Vedic astronomy can even date this change to slightly more than 5,000 years ago, and traditionally the date accepted as the beginning of the current *kaliyuga* or 'iron age' is 18 February, 3102 B.C.;[14] this means that there are approximately 427,000 years to go before the end of the *kaliyuga* or iron age. Plato refers to these changes in the *yuga* and mentions 'the thousands and thousands of cities' that have 'come into being and perished'[15] and 'the many destructions of mankind that have been caused by deluges and pestilences, and in many other ways'.[16] He refers to the small numbers of survivors, who happen to be hill shepherds, for they kept to the high ground and avoided destruction.

10

The Seven *Ṛishi* of the *Veda* and of Delphi

In the vast timescale of the great cycles, which take in countless generations of mortal men, the *Ṛishi*, Prophet or Seer performs a special function within the human race, for he sows in the conscious imagination of the age the ideas that fashion spiritual and secular values, codes of conduct, laws, and institutions for subsequent generations. The *Ṛishi* is 'a singer of sacred hymns, an inspired poet or sage, any person who alone or with others invokes the deities in rhythmical speech or song of a sacred character, who were regarded by later generations as patriarchal sages or saints, occupying the same position in Indian history as the heroes and patriarchs of other countries. They are the inspired personages to whom the Vedic hymns were revealed, and such an expression as 'The *Ṛishi* says' is equivalent to 'So it stands in the sacred text ...'.[1] This has the same emotive force as an ancient Greek quoting Homer, as Sokrates often did in the midst of earnest dialogue, or a Christian swearing on the Bible to save his life.

Homer, the inspired poet of ancient Greece, probably composed his songs between the ninth and seventh centuries B.C.[2] They were then transmitted orally by the rhapsodes and bards till the beginning of the sixth century B.C., when the quadrennial Panathenaic festival at Athens required special legislation and probably some form of manuscript in order to stabilise the text for competition purposes. However, it was not until the second century B.C. that the vulgate text of the songs emerged in Alexandria, under the guidance of the scholiast Aristarchos of Samothrace.[3] In the *Vedāṅga*, or 'limb of the *Veda*', we find a similar process in the transmission from oral to literary form, together with a statement on the need for the creation of manuscript copy: 'The *Ṛishi* had direct experience of *dharma*. They, by oral instruction, imparted the *mantra* to later generations destitute of the direct experience, who, declining in power, recorded the *Veda* and its auxiliary treatises in writing in order to understand their meaning';[4] (see Appendix III). *Dharma* and *mantra* are two mighty concepts: *dharma* means 'law or virtue', and in a wider sense, 'all that supports life';[5] *mantra* means 'incantation of a sacred text or speech, such as a Vedic hymn'.[6]

The *Ṛishi*, Prophet or Seer acts at the level of civilisation, culture and nation, and the conscious impulse imparted through him takes a form appropriate to the age. Hence the Ten Commandments given by God through Moses at the birth of the Judaeo-Christian civilisation may be cited; or the Old Testament prophets, for example Jeremiah, to whom the word of the Lord came, saying: 'Before I formed thee in the belly I knew thee; and before thou camest forth out of the womb I sanctified thee, and I ordained thee a prophet unto the Nations'.[7]

For most Hellenists, the term *Ṛishi* will summon up the name of Homer, the 'Blind Seer'. The first *Ṛishi* of ancient Greece, however, appeared long before the Homeric tradition, at around the time of the founding of the temple of Apollo at Delphi. The above definition of *Ṛishi* continues as follows: 'seven *Ṛishis* are often mentioned in the *Brāhmaṇas* and later works as typical representatives of the character and spirit of the pre-historic or mythical period. They are also called *Prajāpatis* or patriarchs; in astronomy, the seven *Ṛishis* form the constellation of "the Great Bear"; metaphorically they may stand for the seven senses or the seven vital airs of the body; ... a symbolical expression for the number seven; the moon; an imaginary circle; a ray of light ...'.

Plato provides one of several lists of names of the seven 'wise men who met together and dedicated in the temple of Apollo at Delphi, as the first-fruits of their wisdom, the far-famed inscriptions, which are in all men's mouths – "Know thyself" and "Nothing in excess" '.[8] These utterings are noted by Plato as being 'short, memorable statements', which are sutraic in nature. Just as the seven *Ṛishi* who appeared at the beginning of each *manvantara* or 'great age'[9] are named in the ancient Vedic texts, that is *Gotama*, *Bharadvāja*, *Viśvāmitra*, *Jamadagni*, *Vasishṭha*, *Kaśyapa* and *Atri*, so Plato proposes a list of the names of the seven wise men of early Greece, namely Thales, Pittakos, Bias, Solon, Kleoboulos, Myson and Khilon. These are essentially historical figures, no doubt formulated long after the foundation of the oracle itself. Plutarch gives a delightful account of the great men of Greece who deigned to accept recognition as the wisest of such an august gathering:

> But what increased their reputation even more was the affair of the tripod, which circulated amongst them, passed through the hands of all seven and was declined by every one in turn, each striving to outdo the other in modesty and goodwill. The story goes that some men of Kos were hauling in a net and a number of strangers from Miletos purchased the catch before they had seen what was in it. It turned out to contain a golden tripod ... The Milesians began by quarrelling with the fishermen about the tripod, and then their respective cities took up the dispute and

finally went to war. At this point the Pythian priestess of Apollo declared to both parties that the tripod must be given to the wisest of men. So it was sent first of all to Thales of Miletos and the Koans willingly presented him personally with the object for which they had fought the whole population of Miletos. Thales, however, declared that Bias was a wiser man than himself, and the tripod was sent on to Bias, who again passed it on to another candidate wiser than himself. So it was declined and passed on by each sage in turn until it came to Thales for the second time. Finally, it was conveyed from Miletos to Thebes and dedicated to Apollo of the Ismenus, a nearby river. According to Theophrastos, however, the tripod was first sent to Bias at Priene, and after that to Thales at Miletos at Bias's request. In this fashion it went the round of all the wise men, until it returned once more to Bias and was eventually sent to Delphi.

Plutarch, *Life of Solon*, 4

Nothing certain is known of the origins of Delphi. According to one tradition, the oracle was originally the shrine of *Gē*, the earth goddess, and was protected by the serpent Python. Apollo established his oracle by taking on the appearance of a dolphin leaping aboard a Cretan ship and forcing the crew to help him slay the Python, and the name of the oracle was thereby changed from Pytho to Delphi, the Greek for dolphin being *delphis*; however, another tradition claims it is derived from *delphus*, meaning a womb. Apollo's forename was Phoebos, meaning 'bright' or 'pure', and he was the God of the Sun, in the sense that the oracles were transmitted from the Gods through the Pythian priestess, just as 'the moon's an arrant thief, and her pale fire she snatches from the sun', and for this reason the priestess received the word of Apollo facing the full moon; not surprisingly, the moon itself is one of the meanings of *Ṛishi*.

That the oracle at Delphi was most ancient and was held in great reverence by the ancient Greeks is well attested. Homer refers to the temple of Apollo at Pytho on several occasions, and in terms that suggest that the pre-eminence of Delphi was well established. Much later, at his trial in 399 B.C., Sokrates attempts to explain in serious terms the meaning of the oracle's statement, namely that he was the wisest man in all Greece.[10] Plato similarly refers to Delphi in reverent terms on several occasions; for example, he says of Apollo that 'he is the God who sits in the centre, on the navel of the earth, and he is the interpreter of religion to all mankind';[11] and in *Laws*, Plato proposed that Delphi would be the ultimate authority on all religious matters.

The Greeks believed, as Plato recorded, that Delphi was the centre of the earth and a round stone was placed in the temple to commemorate this, called the *omphalos*, or navel; for the myth held that Zeus had sent two eagles to the ends of the earth, considered to be a flat disc, in order to determine its centre, and the divine birds had met on their return journey at Delphi. There is a special significance attaching to the concept of the navel of the earth and these two verses from the *Ṛigveda* elucidate this:

Other fires, O *Agni*, are your branches,
In these all mortals are rejoicing;
Vaiśvānara! Thou art the navel of the people,
Upholding beings like a firm rooted pillar.

Head of heaven, navel of the earth is *Agni*;
He thus became the messenger twixt earth and heaven;
Vaiśvānara, the gods produced thee,
A god to be light unto the Aryans.

Ṛigveda, Ch.I, Canto 59, vv.1-2

Agni is the Vedic god of fire and of speech, and it is the element fire that provides the form of things, which are spoken into existence by the *Logos* or 'the Word'. There are certain similarities here to Apollo, who was the perfect image of athletic beauty, the ideal of vigorous, manly beauty in art, and the God of oracles. *Vaiśvānara* means 'relating or belonging to all men, omnipresent, universal, relating to the Gods collectively and relating or sacred to *Agni Vaiśvānara*'.[12]

The *Ṛigveda* continues:

This altar is the supreme limit of earth,
This sacrifice the navel of Creation;
This *Soma* the seed of the prolific horse;
This *Brahman* the highest heaven of speech.

Ṛigveda, Ch.I, Canto 164, v.35

The altar is the symbol of all actions performed in the spirit of sacrifice or surrender and represents the point where heaven meets earth, where life enters matter and where the all-pervading *Brahman* or 'Supreme Being' is ever present:

All creatures are the product of food,
food is the product of rain,
rain comes from sacrifice,
sacrifice is born of action.

Know that action comes from *Brahman*,
and that *Brahman* comes from the Imperishable.
Therefore, the all-pervading *Brahman*
is ever present in sacrifice.

Gītā, Ch.3, vv.14, 15

The references to the 'prolific horse' and *Soma* may need further explanation. The horse represents all vital energies, the finest of which is speech, the fundamental human attribute, of which the finest form is the utterances of the Gods, received on earth through the divine medium of the oracle. The horse is a favourite form for a God to take when mating with a Goddess or earthly female; for example, Poseidon and Medusa begat Pegasos,[13] the winged horse entrusted with the thunderbolt of Zeus, and Poseidon himself assumed the horse-form when he mated with Demeter. *Soma* is the nectar of the Gods and 'is identified with the moon ... and with the God of the moon',[14] and is the *rasa* or 'sweet taste of the Lord',[15] which entered the Creation at its beginning, and which is made available through the sacrifice, rising up as speech in the act of prophecy; for prophecy, the ancient Greeks relied implicitly on the oracle at Delphi, the first institution of ancient Greece, centred at the navel of the World.

11

The Epics as Spiritual Allegories

The epic cycle of ancient Greece, of which the two songs of Homer, the *Iliad* and the *Odyssey*, form the greater part, was composed at the dawn of Western Civilisation and was the most significant development following the establishment of Delphi. Indeed, epic poetry often emerges in the formative stages of a nation and almost invariably originates from an oral tradition, for even the purely literary creations, such as Virgil's *Aeneid* or Milton's *Paradise Lost*, are inspired by strands and texts that were themselves originally oral. In fact, many common elements can be found amongst the world's epics: Gods and Goddesses, wise men, blind seers, prophets, warriors and heroes, portrayed on the vast stage of Heaven, Earth and Underworld, over land and sea, on battlefields, in palaces and in humble crofters' cottages.

An epic is a song or poem which celebrates in a continuous narrative the achievements of the Heroes of history or tradition. Perhaps the world's greatest epic and incomparably the longest is the *Mahābhārata*, composed by *Vyāsa*; this and the *Rāmāyaṇa*, composed by *Vālmīki*, are the great epics of India and encapsulate the mighty spiritual teaching of that sub-continent. The fact that scholarship cannot even date the origin of these works to within a millennium not only testifies to their great age but also evokes the problem of ascribing authorship, singular or multiple, to an orally-based epic. However, the name *Vyāsa* means 'Compiler' and is acknowledged to be a generic name for all the bards who contributed to that ancient tradition during its formative process; so when the *Mahābhārata* roundly proclaims there is nothing in the universe that is not included in its text, it is not simply an arrogant claim of 'the author'. From the Near East came the Sumerian epic of Gilgamesh and the Babylonian Creation Hymn, and from Europe the Teutonic poems such as *Beowulf* and the *Nibelungenlied* in the first millennium A.D., followed by the Celtic, Russian, Norse, Finnish and Icelandic poems and sagas, and more recent epics such as *La Chanson de Roland*, right down to the traditions of modern Yugoslavia that survive into the twentieth century. There are many points of similarity among them and in the European tradition the almost mandatory visit by the Hero to the Underworld is a feature of well over one hundred epics. For the present, it will serve to indicate the possibilities of a comprehensive comparative study of this vast subject and the role that the *Dhātu-Pāṭha* might play to reveal significant meaning.

The concept of the Heroic Age recurs regularly, for just as the *Mahābhārata* had looked back to the heroes of the Vedic Age, so Homer's Heroic Age recalled the late Akhaean period that had ended *c.* 1100 B.C. During the total illiteracy that followed for nearly three centuries, the Homeric Songs were kept alive as an oral tradition. Homer's Gods and Heroes and their epic deeds took root in the national character at an early stage and were the inspiration that guided men at the birth of European civilisation. It is fitting that Homer followed the name of the continent called after the mythological princess Europa and now emerging from the darkness, when he applied the epithet *euruopa* to Zeus, Father of the Olympian Gods and of men, for he was also God of the sky, light and consciousness.

Now *euruopa* is an artful compound, for it could mean one of two things: *euru* is simple enough and means 'wide' or 'far', but *opa* could mean 'voice' or 'sound' when the '*o*' sound is short, or 'vision' or 'seeing' when the '*ō*' sound is long, but both are equally possible in terms of meaning and equally appropriate as epithets of Zeus; it depends on the requirement of the scansion, as to whether a long or short measure is required in each hexameter. The Word of God is most certainly far-sounding and the consciousness of God is certainly far-seeing. As the evangelist said: 'the Word was God ... all things were made through Him';[1] or as an ancient grammarian stated: 'that beginningless and endless One, the imperishable *Brahman* of which the essential nature is the Word, which manifests itself into objects and from which is the creation of the Universe';[2] and the consciousness of Zeus most certainly runs far, for whatever action any individual may perform in the world is automatically witnessed on account of the consciousness associated with that action; this is the meaning of Hesiod's reference to the 'thirty thousand eyes of Zeus' that everywhere witness the actions of men, so that due punishment and reward may be meted out.

There is a delightful story told concerning the composition of the *Mahābhārata* that runs as follows: *Vyāsa* conceived a great epic of 100,000 verses. Clearly the taking down of so many verses called for a scribe of considerable skill and stamina. *Vyāsa*, not knowing who could carry out such a task meditated on *Brahmā*, the Creator, who then revealed himself before him. *Vyāsa*, having made obeisance, put his problem to the Creator, who replied: 'O Sage, invoke *Gaṇapati* and beg him to be your amanuensis.' Whereupon the Creator vanished and

Vyāsa meditated on *Gaṇapati* or *Gaṇeśa* the God of Wisdom, who immediately appeared before him. (The reason why such a feat is possible is that the physical elements are themselves made of that consciousness which the *mantra* is also designed to hold; when the force of the *mantra* is withdrawn, the apparition also vanishes.) *Gaṇapati* was the remover of obstacles and ruler of the categories, so he is naturally the patron of letters and the scribe who writes down the scriptures. *Vyāsa* addressed him as follows: 'Lord *Gaṇapati*, I shall dictate the story of the *Mahābhārata* and I pray you graciously to be pleased to write it down'; *Gaṇapati* accepted but proposed a condition to *Vyāsa*, that his pen must not stop while he was writing. *Vyāsa* agreed, but in turn put his own condition, saying, 'Amen, but you must first grasp the meaning of what I dictate before you write it down'; consequently, whenever *Vyāsa* needed to gain a breathing space in which to consider the next step of his marathon epic, he would deliberately compose some very subtle or complex stanzas, which would require *Gaṇapati* to pause until he had considered them thoroughly. The point of the tale may be to remind the reader or listener that in the great epic there is a deeper significance running beneath the apparent surface of events. For example, there is a scene common to the *Mahābhārata*, the *Rāmāyaṇa* and Homer's *Odyssey*, in which the Heroes, Prince *Arjuna*, Prince *Rāma*, and lordly Odysseus, participate in a contest to string a great bow and hit a target, the prize being the hand of *Draupadī*, *Sītā* and Penelope respectively. The three scenes are very similar, particularly in the *Mahābhārata* and *Odyssey*.

Arjuna is disguised as a *Brāhmaṇa* or 'priest', and Odysseus is disguised as a beggar; as each stands up to string the bow, a wild clamour breaks out amongst the onlookers, for both contenders appear incapable of performing the great task. *Arjuna* meditated on *Nārāyaṇa*, the Supreme God, in contrast to Zeus who thundered mightily as a propitious omen for Odysseus; both contenders then strung the great bow with ease; *Arjuna* immediately shot five arrows in quick succession through a revolving wheel right into the target, knocking it over, while Odysseus fired his arrows through twelve axe-heads.[3] *Rāma*, in his quest to find *Sītā*, actually breaks the bow while stringing it, and this causes a sound like thunder or the sound of the thunderbolt as thrown by the God *Indra*.[4]

The three stories clearly have a common origin in the oral tradition; thus it is reasonable to assume there may be an allegorical significance attaching to the action of stringing the bow. To penetrate this latent significance, it is useful to consult further the Vedic tradition:

> Taking hold of the bow, that is the great weapon familiar in the Upanishads, one should fix on it an arrow, sharpened with meditation.

Drawing the string with a mind absorbed in Its thought, hit, O good-looking one, that very target that is the Immutable.

AUM is the bow; the Soul is the arrow; and *Brahman* is called its target.
It is to be hit by an unerring man.
One should become one with it just like an arrow.

Second *Muṇḍaka* Upanishad, *Kāṇḍa* II, *Ślokas* 3 and 4

A beautiful exposition of the significance of these two verses is given by *Śaṅkarācārya* in his commentary: 'On that bow, one should fix an arrow. What kind of arrow? A sharpened arrow, that is to say purified by constant meditation. And after fixing the arrow and having drawn the string, that is to say, having withdrawn the inner organ (of mind) together with the senses from their objects, and concentrating them on the target alone, with the mind "absorbed in the thought of that *Brahman*, hit, O good-looking one, that very target that is the Immutable", the inner consciousness within life. Just as the bow is the cause of the arrow's hitting the target, so *AUM* is the bow that brings about the Soul's entry into the Immutable. For the Soul when purified by the repetition of *AUM* gets fixed in *Brahman* with the help of *AUM* without any hindrance, just as an arrow shot from a bow gets transfixed in the target. Therefore *AUM* is a bow, being comparable to a bow. The Soul is surely the arrow, the Soul that is but the supreme Self in Its conditioned state, that has entered here into the body as the witness of the modes of the intellect, like the sun into water. That Soul, like an arrow, is shot at the Self Itself that is the Immutable. Therefore *Brahman* is said to be the target of the Soul. It is called the target since, just as in the case of a mark, it is aimed at with Self-absorption by those who want to concentrate their minds. That being so, the target that is *Brahman* should be shot at by one who is unerring, who is free from the error of desiring to enjoy external objects, who is detached from everything, who has control over his senses and has concentration of mind. After hitting the mark one should remain identified with *Brahman*, like an arrow. The idea is this: just as the success of the arrow consists in its becoming one with the target, similarly one should bring about the result, consisting in becoming one with the Immutable, by eliminating ideas of self-identification with the body ...'

There is another point of significance which should not be lost sight of: *Arjuna* fired five arrows through a revolving wheel. It is easy to imagine the virtual impossibility of firing an arrow through, say, a revolving bicycle wheel; yet all five arrows went through the wheel and knocked over the target. This is clearly symbolic: *Arjuna*, being centred in the Self, was living outside the normally experienced time-scale and could consequently place the arrows through the revolving wheel without difficulty. Similarly, in the *Odyssey*, Telemakhos, Odysseus' son, digs one long trench for the twelve axe-heads and draws them 'true to a chalk line'; now an arrow has a trajectory, but the fact that Odysseus could fire the arrow straight down a chalk line indicates that the arrow was not subject to gravity, or in other words, his arrow or *mantra* was not subject to the forces of nature. It was these deeper significances, not obviously apparent to the casual listener or reader, that *Vyāsa* required the scribe *Gaṇapati* to penetrate fully before committing them to writing, so that their transmission to literary form would be imbued at that precise moment with the light of understanding.

In the above stories of *Arjuna* and Odysseus, one of the key components was the arrow. The Sanskrit word for arrow is *ishu* and the Greek word is *ios* and they both derive from root *ish*, shown in the *Dhātu-Pāṭha* as *isha*; it is important to remember that *dhātu* are monosyllabic and the final *–a* is a grammatical code indicating how the root conjugates as a verb; hence the root is the single syllable *ish*. This root means to 'let fly, throw, send out or off, discharge, impel etc.'[5] and the *Dhātu-Pāṭha* gives two *dhātvartha*,[6] namely *gati*, meaning 'manner or power of going, arriving at, art, method, state, condition';[7] and *ābhīkshṇya*, meaning 'continued repetition',[8] as when an archer fires a quiverful of arrows, or when one who meditates repeats the *mantra*. Similarly, a Sanskrit word for desire is *ishṭa* and in Greek there is *iotēs* and they also derive from root *ish*, shown in the *Dhātu-Pāṭha* as *ishu*; it conjugates differently from *dhātu isha* and though phonetically they are both root *ish*, they are in fact to be treated as separate roots. (This phenomenon of two roots being phonetically the same and yet differentiated in their expansion or conjugation is a common phenomenon, as is the fact that certain roots develop into two or more streams of meaning, particularly in later languages.) The *dhātvartha* for *ishu* is *icchā*,[9] and its meaning is 'wish, desire, inclination'.[10] It may not be purely coincidental that William Blake's hymn *Jerusalem* refers not only to the bow, but also to the arrow of desire, for the hymn is even composed in the Vedic *anuṣṭubh* metre, consisting of four quarter-verses of eight syllables each: thus far does the oral tradition travel with consummate ease down through the centuries, as has the perennial image of Cupid's arrow, albeit somewhat vulgarised.

12

Iliad and *Mahābhārata*

Homer's two songs are the central part of an epic cycle of which only secondary and later fragments have come down to us other than the *Iliad* and the *Odyssey*. This cycle ran from an imagined beginning of the World down to the end of the Heroic age. There were six poems that deal with the Trojan war and consequently the *Iliad* is placed after the beginning of the war, which had its origins in the judgment of Paris. Paris was one of the many sons of Priam, the king of Troy and he was distinguished by his good looks and known for his fairmindedness. He was invited by three Goddesses, Hera, Athene and Aphrodite, symbolising power, wisdom and beauty respectively, to settle a dispute amongst them, for Eris, the Goddess of Strife, had thrown an apple to them with the words: 'to the fairest'. Aphrodite promised as a bribe that he would be loved by the woman considered to be the most lovely of all mortals and Paris fell for the bait. He judged Aphrodite the winner of the contest and set off in search of the most beautiful mortal woman, which resulted in his abduction of Helen, wife of Menelaos, King of Sparta. In casting aside his good judgment, Paris chose to give chase to that perennial illusion, mortal beauty, that was to bring calamity not only to his enemies, but also to his own people. Now when Menelaos, meaning 'leader of the people', had won the hand of Helen originally, there had been many other suitors, so that Tyndareus, Helen's putative father and husband of Leda, decided that all suitors had to swear to accept Helen's choice of husband and to come to his help if at any time she proved unfaithful to him. Consequently, when Paris abducted Helen, Menelaos invoked the oath sworn by all her former suitors, and led by his brother Agamemnon, meaning 'good at waiting' or 'good at standing his ground', the Greeks arranged a federal invasion force to besiege Troy and to recover this most beautiful of all women.

In early Greek mythology Helen was the daughter of Leda and Zeus, who in order to fulfil his desires had changed himself into a swan and begotten Helen. It was appropriate that, as the offspring of the father of the Gods, Helen was the most beautiful embodiment of the female form on earth and consequently as worthy a *casus belli* for men as the Truth Itself. The debate has been waged ever since as to Helen's true nature: was she merely the innocent instrument of Aphrodite, who used her to bribe Paris? Or did Helen represent feminine infidelity and was she the cause of all the subsequent evils suffered by the Greeks and Trojans? The *Iliad* commences in the tenth year of the siege of Troy and is essentially a tale of the wrath of Akhilles; the name Akhilles is derived from the Greek word *akhos*. The link between Akhilles and grief was a prophesy that he would have either a short and glorious life or a long and ignoble one; or possibly that he would grieve for Patroklos, or even the grief he would bring to others through his wrath. The initial cause of the wrath of Akhilles was Agamemnon's depriving him of a serving girl, Briseis, who had been given to him as booty. A priest of Apollo had come to the Greeks and requested the return of his daughter, who was being held captive by Agamemnon; but the latter refused the proffered ransom and so the priest prayed to his God for vengeance and Apollo inflicted a damaging plague in response. Akhilles advised Agamemnon to consult a seer to learn the cause of the God's wrath: the answer was the captivity of the priest's daughter. Agamemnon said he would only release the priest's daughter if Akhilles made up his loss by handing over Briseis in return: Akhilles was forced to do so and vowed to desist from fighting until Briseis was returned to him.

The fact that anger was capable of bringing about the downfall of the human Soul became part of the developing Greek tradition: 'It is hard to fight with anger; for what it wants it buys at the price of the Soul'.[1] In the *Mahābhārata* there stands the dialogue between the Prince *Arjuna* and the Lord *Śṛī Kṛishṇa* called the *Gītā*, which conversation takes place on the sacred battlefield of *Kurukshetra*, meaning 'field of action': this battle between the *Kauravas* and *Pandavas* was on a scale far greater than that of the Greeks' fight with the Trojans on the windy plains of Troy. The Lord *Śṛī Kṛishṇa* delivers the following warning:

> When a man dwells on the objects of sense, he creates an attraction for them; attraction develops into desire, and desire breeds anger.
>
> Anger induces delusion; delusion, loss of memory: through loss of memory, reason is shattered; and loss of reason leads to destruction.
>
> *Gītā*, Ch.2, vv.63-4

Śaṅkara's commentary on the first verse states that anger is aroused when desire is frustrated by some cause or other, and the cause of Akhilles' wrath is possession of a mere slave girl. These two verses from the *Gītā* exactly epitomise the story and fate of Akhilles. For he develops and dwells on his honour and this is the cause of his overwhelming desire to keep Briseis as his booty; this in turn causes the anger of Agamemnon; Akhilles then withdraws from the Greek cause and idly watches their disastrous rearguard action; he then witnesses the death of his squire, Patroklos, who foolhardily puts on Akhilles' own armour to wage battle against the Trojans; he charges for the fourth time but goes too far ahead of his own troops, cannot retreat in time, and is killed by Hektor.[2] Patroklos was not destined to be the *svatantraḥ karttā* for the death of Hektor, for he did not have 'the system within himself' for that action; he only wore the armour of the man who did, which was a grave miscalculation.

The death of Patroklos is similar to an incident in the *Mahābhārata*, when a *cakrivyūha*, or 'circular array of troops', was set up by the enemy *Kauravas*, in a particular pattern, in which seven gates are created by clever troop deployments, one within the other. This is a tactical trap, which only *Arjuna* can unlock, but he is absent putting down a revolt in a far distant place. So his son *Abhimanyu*, who was still only a teenager, was made general for the day; however, he knew only how to deal with the first six gates, but it was agreed that after he had penetrated these, that the entire army would pit its full force and intelligence against the seventh gate. *Abhimanyu* succeeded in breaking the first six gates, but became trapped within the seventh, and having advanced too far, just like Patroklos, was cut off and killed.[3] The meaning is that the six gates of nature can be crossed by knowing the relevant regulations, but the seventh gate is *prakṛiti* itself (see Appendix I), which can only be crossed by true knowledge and the understanding necessary for victory, which is freedom. *Arjuna* enjoyed the *svatantraḥ karttā* for cracking the seventh gate, but his son *Abhimanyu* miscalculated and paid for it with his life; he had not yet reached the necessary level of knowledge and maturity, unlike Odysseus' son Telemakhos.

Meanwhile Akhilles, in remorse at Patroklos' death, enters the fray; he has the necessary *svatantraḥ karttā* for he does kill Hektor, but is himself fated to die as a result. For the myth of Akhilles records that his mother dipped him into the Styx, so that the waters of the infernal river would make his body invulnerable, but unfortunatly she held him by the heel, so that he was still vulnerable at that point and an arrow from Paris, who himself was fated to die at the hand of Philoktetes, eventually brought death to Akhilles. This is not actually recorded in the *Iliad*, though Akhilles' horses speak and foretell his death.

The first word of the *Iliad* is *mēnin*, which is the accusative of *mēnis*, meaning 'wrath' or 'anger'. In terms of the Greek language, *mēnis* derives from root *mā*, which branches into three main meanings.[4] The first sense is 'eager desire, yearning, intensity of purpose', as in the Greek verb *maō*, meaning 'to wish eagerly, strive, yearn, desire, covet', and has the sense of impetuosity. The second main meaning is close to the first and has the sense of 'excitement of mind', as in Greek *mania*, which is akin to English 'mania'. And the third meaning is 'persistency', as in Greek *menō*, meaning 'I remain'. Consequently, some of the verbs expressing 'desire' and 'coveting' have the same root in Greek as the verbs expressing 'excitement of mind' and 'madness'.

The way these words derive in Greek from the single root *mā* is in fact a simplification of the more complex root system as expressed in the *Dhātu-Pāṭha*, for the Greek word *mēnis* derives from *dhātu mantha*,[5] whereas the Greek verb *maō* derives from *dhātu marga*;[6] *dhātu mantha*, from which *mēnis*, the 'wrath' or 'anger' of Akhilles is derived, has for its *dhātvartha viloḍane*, which means 'stirring up, churning, agitating, alarming'.[7] As in Greek, the words *mēnis* and *mania* are closely related through the root structure, so in Sanskrit there is the word *māna*, which means 'opinion, idea, wish, design, self-conceit, arrogance, pride, honour, the wounded sense of honour, anger or indignation excited by jealousy, caprice, sulking'.[8] The dictionary definition virtually follows the path to destruction taken by Akhilles in his violent reactions to the dispute over Briseis, which ultimately leads to his own destruction. Sokrates said in Plato's *Kratylos* that the Heroes are not begotten of the love of a God or Goddess for a mortal, but the semi-divine Akhilles was the son of the Goddess Thetis and the mortal man Peleus; there is more than a hint of the *Avatāra* concept implied in such generation, namely the descent of a divine being into an earthly form.[9] These Demi-Gods or Heroes appear at the onset of the iron age and they are all destroyed according to their fate: Patroklos is killed by Hektor, who in turn is killed by Akhilles, who as a result is himself fated to die at the hand of Paris, who himself is mortally wounded, while Agamemnon is murdered with his wife, Kassandra, by his former wife Klytemnestra, on his return home. In the *Iliad*, no less than three hundred and eighteen heroes meet violent deaths. Before their deaths, however, the Heroes prove to be mighty warriors, who tower over the ordinary rank and file, surpassing them in strength, courage and in their competitive spirit in search of *timē*, or 'honour', which is their main goal. Indeed, the cause of Akhilles' wrath was very simply that his honour was at stake over the issue of Briseis; and for the same reason, Peleus advised his son 'to be always best in battle and pre-eminent beyond all others'.[10] Now when Lord *Śṛī Kṛishṇa* addressed *Arjuna* as follows, it might well have been Agamemnon addressing Akhilles, when the latter was sulking and refusing to fight:

> If you refuse to fight in this righteous cause, then, having abandoned your duty and your fame, you shall incur only sin.

Men will recount forever your disgrace; and to the noble, dishonour is worse than death.

Gītā, Ch.2, vv.33, 34

The Lord *Ṡṛī Kṛishṇa* is asking *Arjuna* to fix his mind on him and fight, in the sense of surrendering the notion of the individuality of his mind; he was not asking *Arjuna* to fight with his mind split between the battle on the one hand and Lord *Ṡṛī Kṛishṇa* on the other, but to act from the Will of the Creator rather than from his own desires or aversions: *Arjuna* was ordered not to fight as '*Arjuna*' but to fight as the *Brahman*, thereby gaining release from the individual ego. The essential message of the *Gītā* is 'surrender yourself'; the *Iliad* depicts the disastrous consequences if you do not. By this surrender, the creative power of the *Brahman* is released from the *avyakta prakṛiti* or 'unmanifest nature' and becomes *vyakta* or 'manifest' and available. As long as a hold on to the limited ego is maintained, a man is bound by habit; this was exactly the predicament of Odysseus, one of the great warriors of the siege of Troy, when he was detained on Kalypso's island. Odysseus, however, having lead the Greeks to victory by the ruse of the wooden horse, did escape from the island and returned home after another ten years of wandering on the seas in search of his wife Penelope and his native Ithaka.

13

Odyssey and *Rāmāyaṇa*

The first word of the *Odyssey* is *andra*, the accusative of *andros*, meaning 'man', whose prime duty as set out in the *Gītā* is to 'surrender himself'. Odysseus and *Rāma* both endured long absences from their palaces, ostensibly for different reasons, but both had to learn 'to surrender' in their different ways before they could be reunited with their real creative power, represented by Penelope and *Sītā* respectively. In the case of Odysseus, during his great wanderings he is gradually deprived of everything and returns to Ithaka with nothing. When *Rāma* entered the forest in order to give up everything in the tradition of the ascetic, *Bhārata* was asked to rule the kingdom, but he refused to do so and went after *Rāma* to seek his advice. *Rāma*, however, compelled him to rule on his behalf during his fourteen years of exile and instructed him to maintain it in good order until his return. *Bhārata* understood what he meant and took *Rāma's* golden sandals back with him. He put them on his sovereign's throne and conducted the affairs of state as his regent. This story is an allegory of 'surrendering oneself', but the whole of the *Odyssey* can be viewed as a saga of a man who had to be stripped of everything in the process of 'surrendering himself'.

The qualities of a man demanded by such an ordeal are manifold, as are indicated by the epithets of Odysseus, such as goodly, lordly, and *polumētis*, meaning 'man of many wiles'. Once again, Homer loses no time in pointing out the subtle aspect of the name Odysseus, for he invites comparison between *Odusseus* and the verb *odusao*, which is the second person singular of the aorist middle tense of the verb *odussomai*, meaning 'I hate'.[1] In fact, it is said that even 'the Gods are jealous and do not wish that man obtains knowledge'.[2] Odysseus was hated in particular by Poseidon, and this for two reasons: first, Poseidon, together with Apollo, had built the walls of Troy for Laomedon, and Odysseus organised the stratagem of the Greeks at the time of the sacking of Troy; secondly, Odysseus blinded the Monster *Kuklops* or Cyclops, Polyphemos, meaning 'speaking with many voices', who was begotten of Poseidon. Poseidon relentlessly persecuted Odysseus on his return journey and exacted terrifying revenge on the Phaeakians, the magical people, who conveyed Odysseus in a deep sleep to his native Ithaka, turning the ship and crew into stone at the suggestion of Zeus, by striking their boat with the flat of his hand and blocking the entrance to the Phaeakian harbour in the process. And yet, it is necessary to look rather carefully at the part played by Poseidon in Odysseus' homecoming, for as has been already noted, the Gods often play an apparently obstructive role in order to create the necessary tests which the returning Hero must overcome. For as the Goddess Ino said to Odysseus when Poseidon had shipwrecked him: 'And yet he will not do away with you, for all his anger'.[3] Shortly afterwards Poseidon sees Odysseus swimming in the sea and says to him: 'There now, drift on the open sea, suffering much trouble. Only you come among certain people who are the Gods' fosterlings. Even so, I hope you will not complain that I stinted your hardship'.[4] Poseidon could either have been gloating with irony or have been genuinely pleased to have provided the obstructions that turned Odysseus from a distinguished warrior into a returning Hero.

The name Odysseus, however, warrants closer examination. Liddell & Scott suggest that the initial *O-* is an euphonic prefix and thus the root becomes *dus*,[5] and *dus* always signifies something bad or difficult, being the contrary prefix to *eu*, meaning something good or worthwhile. The *Dhātu-Pāṭha* gives roots *dvisha* and *dusha*.[6] The meaning of root *dvisha* is 'to hate, show hatred against, be hostile or unfriendly, to be a rival or a match for'.[7] Odysseus' aspirations to return home to his powers made him a rival and match for the Gods, being equal in particular to the obstructions caused by Poseidon; and the Gods are jealous of those who can rival their powers. The meaning of the root *dusha* is 'to become bad or corrupted, to be defiled or impure, to be ruined, perish; to sin, commit a fault, be wrong'.[8] Odysseus in a frank moment of self-examination freely admits the errors of his past.[9] It may well be significant that the root *dusha* appears in the *Dhātu-Pāṭha* in the fourth *gaṇa* or 'family of roots', which is the level of *ahaṅkāra* in the enneagram.

The *dhātvartha* for *dvisha* is *aprītau*, meaning 'dislike, aversion, enmity, pain';[10] and the *dhātvartha* for *dusha* is *vaikṛitye*, meaning 'modified, undergoing change, hatred, enmity, hostility'.[11] It is clear that Odysseus is undergoing change throughout his return journey, as indeed is his son, Telemakhos; for his infant son from the time the Greek force left for Troy has, during his father's twenty years' absence, been growing to manhood. In fact, the name Telemakhos means 'fight from afar': in order to assist his father's return and eventual destruction of the suitors, it has been necessary for Telemakhos to grow in strength, discrimination and intelligence, in fact in all those qualities that denote manhood, a growth that was parallel to his father's own development. It may be significant that the root *dvisha* appears in the second *gaṇa*, which is the level of *avyakta prakṛiti* or 'unmanifest Creation'.

The name of Odysseus' wife, Penelope or *Penēlopeia*, means 'weaving worker' from Greek *penē* meaning 'a bobbin or spool' and root *op*, with *opeia* implying a feminine *nomen agentis*;[12] for under pressure she agreed to marry one of the suitors when she had finished weaving the shroud for her husband's father, Laertes. She maintained her fidelity to Odysseus throughout the twenty years while Telemakhos was growing to manhood, and resisted the evil suitors by weaving through the day and unstitching her work at night after the suitors had retired; in this way the evil of the suitors was kept at bay by her extreme wakefulness and by the perfect action of unstitching the shroud, thereby ensuring no result or seed for further actions. For there was nothing that she could do, except undo the result of her doing, which was all that was necessary.

The chief suitor is Antinous, meaning 'opposite to intelligence'. The suitors are essentially evil and are wasting the substance of Odysseus in his absence and are not worthy of the hand of Penelope in marriage. Whereas it is necessary for Odysseus to be reunited with his powers, symbolised by Penelope and his throne, the corollary is that the very nature of the suitors precludes them from marriage with her. Indeed, in the marvellous description of the suitors spoken by Telemakhos, he refers to them, though still living, as 'ghosts',[13] and he draws no distinction between them as ghosts living in Odysseus' Palace and the ghosts that will shortly 'hasten down to Erebos beneath the darkness'.

The action of the *Iliad* is relatively straightforward and uses the siege of Troy as a backcloth to depict the destruction of the Heroes and the roles of Gods, Heroes and men in the great play of Creation, in which the paradox of the demi-divine Akhilles pitted against the forces of the world is dramatised in a great battle; but the *Odyssey* is a tale of a mortal man in the Iron Age struggling to regain his powers, set against an extremely complicated and often fanciful background; and it is necessary to penetrate this story, in the manner of *Gaṇapati* in the *Mahābhārata*, to see its deeper significance.

The *Odyssey* opens with a description of the divine scheme for Odysseus' homecoming and from Book 1 (Line 95 to the end of Book IV), there is the description of Telemakhos' vain search for his father. In Book V the divine council that decrees the time as appropriate for his homecoming is repeated and Hermes is sent to visit Odysseus, who is languishing on Kalypso's Island. Kalypso's name means 'I hide', from the verb *kaluptō*. The Goddess Kalypso had been carrying on a secret liaison with Odysseus and hence she hid him on her island; but she also hid the truth in the sense that his destiny was to return to Penelope. Odysseus obeys the instructions of the God and builds a raft and sails to Skheria, the mythical home of the Phaeakians, the magical people descended from the Gods, who give safe passage to men on their spiritual journeys across the restless seas. 'Restless seas' are themselves a symbol of the troubles of man in the iron age, and in one sense Odysseus' journey is to a life beyond the restless seas. Having arrived at Skheria, Odysseus proceeds to outline to his hosts the seven years of his great wanderings that have preceded his arrival on Kalypso's island. During these wanderings Odysseus has had to face twelve major obstacles, which are in fact spiritual tests of his developing powers. At the outset he is surrounded by many companions, but they are *nēpioi*, meaning 'foolish', and they are gradually lost or killed, until Odysseus alone returns to Ithaka.

The first test involves a battle for three nights with the Kykonians, followed by the second test of the incident of the Lotus-eaters, people who have lost the will to return home and merely enjoy passing pleasures.[14] The third test is the episode involving the *Kuklops* or Cyclops, Polyphemos, and Odysseus only escapes from his cave hidden beneath a sheep by declaring that his name is *outis*, meaning 'nobody'; Polyphemos shouts that no one is escaping, so nobody comes to his aid; but the name indicates in terms of the spiritual allegory that Odysseus' personality was being dissolved as part of his approach to 'surrendering himself'. The fourth test involves Aiolos and the bag of winds, which are unfortunately let loose by one of his foolish companions, when Odysseus has fallen asleep. Whenever the returning Hero falls asleep, he fails a particular test of consciousness and suffers a major reverse. The fifth test is the attack of the giant Laistrygones.

The sixth test is Odysseus' meeting with Kirke, whose name may be derived from an ancient Greek verb *kukeō*, meaning 'I mix a potion'; for Kirke changes men who come within her presence in a state of impurity into animals, and she actually turns Odysseus' companions into swine. A remarkable incident is now described by Homer: Odysseus is already on his way to visit Kirke when Hermes is sent by the Gods to give him protection; Hermes picks up a root that is lying nearby and gives it to Odysseus as an antidote to overcome Kirke's powers. Homer says that the Gods call this root 'Moly'.[15]

Sokrates stated that extreme caution must be used to discern the real meaning when Homer talks in these terms.[16] The notes to Stanford's edition of the *Odyssey* state that the root for Moly is *mūla*,[17] which *dhātu* has two *dhātvartha,* namely *rohaṇe* and *pratishṭhāyām*.[18] The *dhātvartha* of *rohaṇe* means 'a medicine'[19] and this adequately fits the description, for Hermes clearly gave Odysseus some form of medicinal root. It may well be significant that the root *mūla* appears in the *Dhātu-Pāṭha* in the tenth *gaṇa* or 'family of roots', which is the Creation and the unmanifest Creation at number ten in the enneagram. The *dhātvartha* of *pratishṭhāyām* is a compound and means 'that which stands at the very beginning'; now that which 'stands at the very beginning' is *prajñā* or 'consciousness'[20] which, says the Lord *Śṛī Kṛishṇa*, means the Self:

> I am the Self, O *Guḍākesha* [*Arjuna*], seated in
> the heart of all being;
> I am the beginning and the middle, and also the
> end, of all beings'.
>
> *Gītā*, Ch.10, v.20

This is also a most acceptable explanation: there are several examples of wise men who on account of the purity of their Souls are able to resist poison, by breaking its constituent elements down into its own original and pure elements. For example, St Paul is bitten by a snake on his arrival at Malta and this has no effect on him, so the natives call him a saint.[21] It is no doubt significant that root *mūla* here stands in the first *gaṇa* or family of roots, that is in the *bhvādigaṇaḥ*, or the '*gaṇa* beginning with *bhū*', or 'being', which is found in *sattā*, or 'purity'.

With the help given by Hermes, Odysseus is able to neutralise the powers of Kirke. There is another point that should be noted, for the Hero has now recounted to the Phaeakians the first six tests and the time is now approaching midnight.[22] The number twelve is significant and it is no coincidence that Homer chooses to point out that the Hero is halfway through his twelve tests at the same time as the middle of the night approaches, symbolising that the spiritual struggle was entering its darkest and most difficult hour. Kirke instructs Odysseus to visit the underworld to seek Persephone, who represents the archetypal tragic state of the human soul since the beginning of the iron age; Odysseus must meet her and experience this eternal feminine archetype before he returns to Penelope. Odysseus must also meet Herakles, who was the most recent Demi-God known to the Greeks, and he must also hear the prophecy of the blind Seer, Teiresias, who reveals the mysteries of birth and death by explaining the past and foretelling the future. In Hades, Odysseus first meets the spirits of the mothers, beginning with Antikleia, his own mother, who reveals the mysteries of birth and life before birth. Birth is commonly understood to imply birth of a new being, but in fact birth relates to the past, for it is past lives that determine all aspects of a new birth.[23] Then Odysseus meets the spirits of the fathers, beginning with the Trojan War Heroes, namely Agamemnon, Akhilles, Patroklos, Antilokhos and Ajax; then the fathers of the legendary past, namely Minos, Orion, Tityos, Tantalos, Sisyphos and finally Herakles.[24] Herakles relates the story of Kerberos, the Hell Hound, whose destruction was his last labour, accomplished with the help of Hermes and Pallas Athene. It is significant that Herakles relates to Odysseus his final labour, and it is of even greater significance that at this stage Odysseus has only met eleven fathers; for he himself will be the twelfth, destined to achieve the goal of the final journey.

On returning from the Underworld, Odysseus' next test is to resist the enticing song of the Sirens, who attracted sailors to their deaths by the magical sweetness of their song. Their name is commonly derived from *seira*, meaning 'a cord' or 'rope', for their song drew and bound their victims, whose dry bones lay round about them.[25] Having successfully resisted their temptations, Odysseus must now sail past two sea monsters guarding a narrow channel, namely Skylla and Kharybdis. Skylla is a revolting monster, who makes puppy-like squeals, and hence her name, for *skulax* means 'puppy'. Kharybdis is the more dangerous to seamen, for three times a day she sucks in the water and creates a whirlpool. Skylla and Kharybdis represent the twin dangers to the man on his return journey, namely revulsion and attraction respectively, which is exactly the condition of *Arjuna* on the battlefield of *Kurukshetra*. In the next episode, contrary to the strict instructions of Kirke, the cattle of Helios are eaten by the remaining companions, once again while Odysseus is sleeping. The eleventh test for Odysseus is his successful resisting of Kalypso's charms. Finally, having been shipwrecked, he rejects marriage to the beautiful Nausikaa. On the next day the Phaeakians take Odysseus to Ithaka and during this journey Odysseus experiences a sleep most like to death or 'surrender':

> The boat carried a man with a mind like the gods for
> counsel, one whose
> Spirit up to this time had endured much suffering and
> many pains: the wars of men, hard crossing of the big
> waters; but now he slept still, oblivious of all he
> had suffered'.
>
> Book XIII, ll.89-92

Throughout the great wanderings, which are recorded in Books IX to XII, Athene, the Goddess of Wisdom, has been absent from Odysseus, but now on his return to Ithaka she appears before him by the cave of the Naiad Nymphs, which have a special significance. Porphyry, the third-century A.D. commentator, repeats earlier authorities and states that the ancients consecrated caves and grottoes to the Cosmos as a whole; for caves are surrounded by the limitless mass of earth and the Cosmos is a natural reality and is by its very nature joined to matter, which is signified by stone and earth, as they are inert and resist form.

Caves were dedicated to the nymphs because of the waters that flow either from above or below and the Naiads are the powers that preside over these waters. Souls were also called Naiad Nymphs, for the ancients thought that Souls settled by water into genesis and that the waters were divinely inspired. Porphyry then quotes Herakleitos, who customarily dealt in paradoxes and apparent contradictions, and who wrote: 'It is a delight, not death, for Souls to become moist', and 'The dry Soul is wisest and best'.[26]

The inference is that the Soul comes into being from moisture, but whereas its true state is made of fire, so it is destroyed when it turns entirely into water. Porphyry states that the looms described by Homer as being in the cave are symbols of the Souls going to genesis, to the creation of a new body. The sea-purple garments are the flesh and bones and are as stone to the body. They are sea-purple for they are woven from blood, just as purple garments are woven from wool dyed in the blood of shell-fish, and the body is the garment of the soul, a wonderful sight. He states that the amphoras are filled with honey because of its cathartic and preservative powers: honey is a symbol of purification, of preservation against rotting and of pleasure in the descent to genesis, and is well suited to water nymphs to symbolise the uncorrupted nature of the waters which they preside over, their purifying powers and their co-operation in genesis. Porphyry explains the two entrances to Homer's cave as representing the winter and summer tropics, namely the most southern and most northern, in Capricorn and Cancer respectively, and that Souls due for rebirth go by the southern route, whereas those Souls that have become immortal leave the cave via the northern route, just as Plato later talked of two orifices, one through which Souls ascend to the heavens and the other through which they descend to the earth.[27] As Lord *Ṡṛī Kṛishṇa* said to *Arjuna*:

> Now I will tell thee, O chief of the *Bhāratas* [*Arjuna*]! of the times at which, if the mystics depart, they do not return.
>
> The sages who know the *Brahman* go forth with fire and light, in the daytime, in the bright fortnight, in the six months of the northern [summer] solstice, attain *Brahman*.
>
> The Yogi who departs in gloom, in the night-time, in the dark fortnight, in the six months of the southern [winter] solstice, then attains to the lunar light and is born again.
>
> These bright and dark paths out of the world are everlasting; by the first path a man goes and does not return, but he who goes by the latter path, returns.
>
> *Gītā*, Ch.8, vv.23-6

Porphyry also quotes from the sixth-century theogonist, Pherekudes of Syros, who 'talks of recesses and pits and caves and doors and gates, and through these speaks in riddles of the becomings and deceases of Souls'.[28] Homer states that there was an olive tree planted outside the cave and Porphyry says that this is a symbol of the cosmos, for it is the plant of Athene, and is therefore a symbol of the wisdom of God. The bright part of its leaves turn upward in summer and are reversed in winter; olive branches are held in front by men in prayer, auguring for themselves a transformation of their darkness into brightness.

Porphyry concludes: 'In this cave, says Homer, every external possession must be laid down; and one is required, having stripped oneself naked, just as a beggar, withered in body, having cast off all superfluity, and averse to sense perception, to take counsel with Athene, seated with her at the foot of the olive tree, as to how one might eliminate the treacherous passions of one's Soul. When the wisdom of antiquity, all the intelligence of Homer, and his perfection in every virtue are taken into account, one should not reject the possibility that in the form of a fairy tale the poet was intimating images of higher things'.[29] This is in fact the description of Odysseus' act of Self-Surrender.

The above interpretation clearly echoes the words spoken by Lord *Ṡṛī Kṛishṇa* to *Arjuna* on the subject of self-control:

> He whose Self is satisfied with knowledge and wisdom,
> who remains unshaken, who has conquered his senses,
> who looks upon a lump of earth, a stone and gold
> with an equal eye – he is said to be a saint.
>
> Let him try constantly to keep the mind steady,
> remaining in seclusion, alone, with mind
> and body controlled,
> free from desire, and without possessions.
>
> *Gītā*, Ch.6, vv.8,10

With the help of Athene and Telemakhos, Odysseus regains his palace, strings the bow, slaughters the suitors and is reunited with Penelope. But Odysseus has to inform his wife that there are still further troubles to come and that there is yet a further and final journey which he must fulfil.[30]

The ancient commentators, Aristarkhos and Aristophanes of Byzantium, said that line 296 of Book XXIII was the last line of Homer's *Odyssey*, which means that the re-telling of Teiresias' prophecy by Odysseus to Penelope represented the end of Homer's work; it is significant that the song ended with that prophecy.[31] For Teiresias' prophecy indicated that Odysseus' journeys over the 'restless seas' would one day be ended, and that Odysseus would know this when a wayfarer, seeing the oar that he carried, would think that it was a winnowing fan, the very symbol of the Vedic God of Wisdom in the form of *Gaṇeśa's* ears, which kept the words of untruth and of the unwise away from his Soul, for they guarded the porch of his ears by their winnowing. Significantly, Teiresias then ordered Odysseus to make sacrifice to the Lord Poseidon; and Teiresias concluded that death would come to Odysseus 'far from the sea, a death so gentle' that would come to him in old age and that his people would dwell in bliss around him; the nature of the death prophesied for Odysseus is reminiscent of Hesiod's description of death in the Golden Age, which 'overcame men with sleep',[32] as the ultimate surrender and return to the Creator. The bliss is known in the *Veda* as *saccidānanda*: *sat* is 'that which is'; *cit* is 'the consciousness of that which is'; and *ānanda* is 'the bliss of the consciousness of that which is', signifying Self-Realisation, and *saccidānanda* is the name of the number ten, when the process of *pralaya* leaves only the Creator and his unmanifest Creation.

The *Rāmāyaṇa* has many correspondences with the *Odyssey* and the *Iliad*. However, the sequence of events is somewhat reversed from the *Odyssey* in that the youthful *Rāma* is required at the outset to slay the *rakshasas* or 'demons' who, like the suitors' waste of the substance of Odysseus, are destroying the sacrifices of *Viśvāmitra*, one of the seven *Ṛishi*. Having killed the female monster *Taḍāka* and *various other demons, Rāma* is taken by *Viśvāmitra* to the palace of King *Janaka*, where in attempting to string the great bow, he breaks it, but wins the hand in marriage of the king's daughter, *Sītā*. *Rāma*, his new wife *Sītā* and his brother *Lakshmaṇa* are now required to enter the forest for fourteen years, while *Bhārata* reigns in *Ayodhyā* with *Rāma's* golden sandals on the throne,[33] whereas Odysseus' great wanderings preceded his being reunited with Penelope.

During their stay at *Pañcavati*, the female monster *Śūrpaṇakhā* announces her love for *Rāma* and her desire to marry him, but *Lakshmaṇa* attacks her for this insolence and cuts off her nose and ears. Two of her brothers retaliate and are killed, but the third brother, *Rāvaṇa*, plots with her and other demons to abduct *Sītā* and kidnap her away to the island of *Laṅkā*, just as Paris had abducted Helen to Troy. *Rāma* is enticed away by *Mārīca,* the offspring of the monster *Taḍāka*, who is disguised as a deer, as a preliminary to the plot to abduct *Sītā*. *Rāma* chased the deer and shot it with an arrow, but as the Soul left the body, *Mārīca* gave up the form of the deer and employed his power of illusion instead to imitate the cry of *Rāma* calling for help. *Sītā* became concerned for *Rāma's* safety and rebuked *Lakshmaṇa* for not following *Rāma*, saying: '*marama vacana jaba Sītā bolā*', meaning 'when *Sītā* uttered those hurtful words', implying that

Lakshmaṇa was letting his brother die. The verb *bolā* meaning 'he spoke' is masculine, though it should be the feminine form of *bolī* to agree with *Sītā*; the apparently wrong grammatical form emphasises the tension and terror that overtook *Sītā*: this is a pure stroke of linguistic genius on the part of the writer of this *Avadhi* dialect version, Saint *Tulasidasa*.[34] *Rāma* and *Lakshmaṇa*, with the help of *Sugrīva*, king of the monkeys, lead an army to recover *Sītā*, just as *Agamemnon* led the Greeks to Troy in the *Iliad*; and just as Athene, the Goddess of Wisdom, helped Odysseus on his return journey, so *Hanuman* helps *Rāma* in his struggle to overcome *Rāvaṇa*. *Hanuman* was a celebrated semi-divine, monkey-like being, whose name meant 'having large jaws'.[35] He was the son of *Maruta*, 'the Wind', could assume any form at will and possessed paranormal powers, for example to remove trees and mountains, mount the air and seize clouds. *Hanuman* represents discipline or system and his symbol of the club in his right hand represents reason; the meaning of the symbol is that only when reason is applied to dispel the egotism of *ahaṅkāra* (which enters at level four in the enneagram of Creation), does it run for its life and reveal the real *aham*.

The first problem for *Rāma's* army is that *Laṅkā* is one hundred kilometres south of the tip of India and it is not even known where *Sītā* is held. However, *Hanuman* climbs Mount *Māhendra*, whence he jumps the ocean in a single leap. *Māhendra* means the Great *Indra*,[36] or 'pure mind', with which he could survey everything and which could jump 'injurious distance' by the power of thought. Arriving in *Laṇkā*, *Hanuman* watches *Sītā* while hidden in a tree; *Rāvaṇa* approaches her and reminds her that only two months are left from the twelve months within which she is required to agree to marry him. *Sītā* raises a blade of grass, which is a Vedic symbol of the purity of the Self, between herself and *Rāvaṇa* and tells him to set aside false hopes, for she is as inaccessible to a *rakshasa* as salvation is to a sinner.[37] *Hanuman* meets *Sītā*, but is rendered unconscious by *Rāvaṇa*; for he knows that monkeys love their tails, so he orders that *Hanuman's* tail be tied with old rags and set on fire, to get rid of him. However Hanuman recovers consciousness, jumps on a building seven stories high and wreaks terrible damage on the city of *Aśokavanikā* with his fiery tail, before returning to *Rāma* to tell him that *Sītā* is alive.

The moral of the tale is this: *Rāma* is the *mantra* for the *Ātman* in the individual, *Hanuman* represents reason, *Rāvaṇa* is the *ahaṅkāra* and the demons or *rakshasas* are lust, greed, anger, attachment, avarice and the other qualities of lower nature as displayed, for example, by the suitors at Odysseus' palace. *Sītā* when abducted by *Rāvaṇa* represents the lost peace of the individual; in the search to restore this peace to the *Ātman*, *Hanuman* or reason has to play havoc to destroy the *rakshasas* and subdue the *ahaṅkāra*. This is why

Hanuman as reason had to establish the whereabouts of peace, as personified by *Sītā*, and then went on to challenge the *ahaṅkāra*, by setting fire to the city of *Rāvaṇa* with his blazing tail. *Rāma* is greatly saddened by his enforced separation from *Sītā*, but says she must be repeating his name only. The name *Rāma* means 'causing rest, and in most meanings is from root *ram*',[38] which is also a *mantra* extensively used in meditation. So *Sītā* maintained her purity by repeating the *mantra* of her husband's name and thus kept *Rāvaṇa* at bay, as Penelope kept the suitors at bay by stitching and unstitching the shroud of Laertes. The *dhātu ram* is given in the *Dhātu-Pāṭha* as *ramu*, which has *dhātvartha krīḍā*,[39] which is the first word of the long compound (on p. 24) to describe the root *divu* and the activities of the Gods, meaning 'sport, play, pastime, amusement, amorous sport'. *Gauḍapāda* stated, however, that whereas some say that God created the universe for his enjoyment and some say it was for his sport, it is 'God's very nature, for what desire can he have, whose desire is ever filled'.[40]

Rāma's army built a bridge in five days, crossed over to *Laṅkā* and with *Hanuman's* help destroyed *Rāvaṇa*, freed *Sītā* and returned in triumph to *Ayodhyā* for his coronation. *Rāma* had great difficulty in his fight with *Rāvaṇa* although he was using his best arrows. However, *Rāvaṇa's* brother, *Vibhīshaṇa*, explained that *Rāvaṇa* had a secret love for *Sītā* and kept remembering her in his heart: unless the memory of *Sītā* is expunged from his heart, he will continue to keep drawing nectar from her presence and will not be killed. The nectar is the very substance of *ānanda* or 'bliss' which is the true being of each individual. *Rāma* had to aim his arrows first at *Rāvaṇa's* head so that he would lose all memory of *Sītā* and then aim at his heart, and in this way *Rāma* overcame *Rāvaṇa*. The coronation marks the end of the original poem, but just as the *Odyssey* is clearly written by a lesser hand from the end of Teiresias' prophecy in Book XXIII, so the last Canto of the *Rāmāyaṇa*, namely the thirty chapters of *Uttara Kāṇḍa*, are a subsequent edition by a different poet or poets. Whereas Teiresias prophesied an additional journey for Odysseus which was not undertaken in that song, in the *Uttara Kāṇḍa*, *Sītā* actually leaves *Rāma* for the following rather feeble reason: she became pregnant soon after her return to *Ayodhyā*, but *Rāma* was upset by gossip about her lengthy stay with *Rāvaṇa* and, concerned with his role as king, decided to abandon her. *Sītā* went to *Vālmīki's* hermitage in the forest, gave birth to twin sons called *Kuśa* and *Lava*, who were trained by *Vālmīki* and soon proved mighty in battle. The four of them returned to *Rāma* and for a second time there was great rejoicing. There was a public ceremony, but *Sītā* looked down and prayed to Mother Earth, that if she had been faithful to *Rāma*, to open up before her; the ground opened and a throne shining like the sun appeared with Mother Earth seated upon it, who swiftly embraced *Sītā* as they both disappeared beneath the earth, leaving *Rāma* desolate with his two sons, whom *Vālmīki* had instructed to sing the *Rāmāyaṇa* in all quarters of the 'irresistible city'.

Penelope represented the powers of Odysseus, for being *strīliṅga* or 'feminine' she was the force of the forceful, with which he had to be reunited in order to make the final journey, but the *Uttara Kāṇḍa* is silent on the effect of *Sītā's* second absence from *Rāma*, when she gives birth to his sons before being reunited with him. Here again, the order is the reverse of that in the *Odyssey*, where Books II-IV, called the Telemakhy, trace the growth of Odysseus' son Telemakhos to manhood before Odysseus' great wanderings. A clue may lie, perhaps, in *Sītā's* name, which means 'a furrow; the track or line of a ploughshare',[41] for her father found her while ploughing ground in preparation for a sacrifice; and the names of her sons, *Kuśa* and *Lava*, mean 'the sacred grass, and a rope made of this grass used for connecting the yoke of a plough with the pole', and 'a little part, cut or shorn off' or lower end, respectively;[42] for when they were born, *Vālmīki* ordered that the elder be wiped with the heads of the *kuśa* grass and the younger with the lower ends. The plough in Vedic literature is a symbol of the sacred enquiry, which necessarily proceeds through unknowing, like the sharp point of a ploughshare cutting deeply through the dark earth; the furrow is the straight path trodden by the true disciple; the yoke is the teaching that provides the connection to the teacher, who guides the pole and who in the final journey of the *Rāmāyaṇa* is the sage *Vālmīki*, for he guides *Sītā* and her two sons back to *Rāma*. With her sons reared to manhood and having returned them to *Rāma*, her lifetime duties are complete and she is free to disappear beneath the earth whence she came.

These our actors,
As I foretold you, were all spirits, and
Are melted into air, into thin air;
And like the baseless fabric of this vision,
The cloud-capped towers, the gorgeous palaces,
The solemn temples, the great globe itself,
Yea, all which it inherit, shall dissolve;
And, like this insubstantial pageant faded,
Leave not a rack behind. We are such stuff
As dreams are made of, and our little life
Is rounded with a sleep.

Shakespeare, *The Tempest*, Act 4, Scene 1

PART III
The Philosophies

14

Teacher and Student

The first recognisable educational movement in Europe was Sophism, a generic title for those teachers who travelled throughout *Magna Graecia* from the middle of the fifth century B.C. onwards. Although they did not originate from a common school, they tended to profess common themes and teach similar subjects with similar aims. Sophism was a movement towards humanism and away from the natural philosophers. There was also another factor behind this shift towards humanism that arose from developments within society itself; in particular, practical politics began to dominate men's thinking as the City-State concept grew in importance and became the focal point and aim of men's ambitions and actions: Greek society was becoming steadily more geared to the Assembly. Hence it is hardly surprising that the most readily recognisable feature of Sophistic teaching was the development of the powers of oratory. This teaching was therefore highly practical, and its main aim was the inculcation of *aretē* or 'virtue'; thus the pupil should be seen to be able to defend himself in public and gain power in politics. The Sophists' other main distinguishing feature was a common scepticism about the possibility of absolute knowledge: the senses as sources of philosophic knowledge and faith in the unity and stability of the phenomenal world had both been severely shaken, if not actually destroyed, by the middle of the fifth century and the intellectual vacuum thereby created provided the opening for Sophism to flourish.

The most important lesson taught by the Sophists was the art of oratory: *aretē* to them was political *aretē*, oratorical ability in fact. The Sophists' concentration on oratory naturally led to extensive studies of grammar and dialectic, and these three studies, the trivium, became the basis of an educational tradition which, when allied to the quadrivium of arithmetic, geometry, music and astronomy, persisted throughout the ages as the seven liberal sciences. In the *Dissoi Logoi*, written by an unknown Sophist towards the end of the fifth century, there is an insight into their method, namely the ability to attack and defend the same thesis. For example, opposing concepts like Good and

Evil are selected, and then the interlocutor trained by the sophistic method asks an imaginary supporter of the opposing thesis questions which make him contradict himself. 'Are you good to your parents?' 'Yes.' 'Then since you say Good and Bad are not distinct, you are bad to them', but it is hardly surprising that the person contradicts himself as he is already committed to saying good and bad are not distinct. Protagoras was the most influential of the Sophists and two tenets of his demonstrate clearly enough the philosophical basis of his teaching:

> Man is the measure of all things, of the reality of those which are, and the unreality of those which are not.
>
> As to the Gods, I cannot know whether they exist or not; too many obstacles are in the way, the obscurity of the subject and the shortness of life.

Plato interpreted the first statement as meaning that the way things appear to one man is the truth for him, and the way they appear to another is the truth for the other, while the implications of the second statement are obvious. The degree of scepticism held by the Sophists is further highlighted by the standpoint of Gorgias, the most famous orator of the movement, who parodied the general title chosen by natural philosophers, namely 'on Nature (*phusis*) or the Existent', by naming his book 'On Nature, or the Non-existent', in which he set out to prove three points: first, that nothing exists, in fact nihilism; secondly, that if anything did exist, men could not know it; and thirdly, if men could know anything, they could not communicate it to their neighbour.

This irreverent scepticism of the Sophists was a direct challenge to the previously unchallenged sanction of law, which was based on a belief in its divine origin. Lykurgos, the legendary lawgiver of Sparta, was believed to have been inspired by Apollo, whereas Protagoras, when drawing up the constitution for the new colony of Thurii in 443 B.C., resorted to a form of law that was basically a social contract between men: he said in effect that men at an early stage had been obliged to band themselves together into communities for their own protection and mutual advancement, and the convention had naturally arisen whereby the stronger pledge themselves not to attack and rob the weak, simply because they are the stronger. The premise in fact is that laws and moral codes were not divine in origin, but man-made and imperfect. The Sophists, in removing the basis of law from the divine sphere, had unwittingly left the way open for the more radical pupils of Sophism, such as Kallikles in the Platonic dialogue *Gorgias*, to maintain the natural right of the stronger to have his own way and to run society for his own ends, holding the weaker in subjection or even enslavement; the strong man had a natural right to employ his superior powers in gratification of his own ends.

Indeed, fifth-century thinking was dominated by the antithesis of *nomos* or 'convention' on one hand and *phusis* or 'nature' on the other: 'discussion of religion turned for example on whether Gods existed by *phusis*, in reality, or only by *nomos*; of political organisation, on whether states arose by divine ordinance or by natural necessity; of cosmopolitanism, on whether divisions within the human race are natural or only a matter of convention; of equality, on whether the rule of one man over another (slavery) or one nation over another (empire) is natural and inevitable, or only by convention; and so on'.[1] The logical conclusion of Protagorean and Gorgian subjectivism is moral and political anarchy; there is no all-embracing 'good for man', but the pragmatic standard of 'better or worse' depends on the actual conditions that any particular state is subject to, and it is the duty of the Sophist, with his power of persuasive oratory, to diagnose the particular situation and prescribe the best course.

It is at this point that the clash with Sokrates, and with Plato and Aristotle, really occurs, for Sokrates insisted that there was one universal Good, Knowledge of which would give the key to right action for everybody everywhere. Sokrates thereby questioned whether the Sophists could teach or impart *aretē* or 'virtue' and implied that knowledge that could be shared in this way was non-existent. Sokrates reasoned that the *aretē* of any human activity, be it philosophy or shoe-making, depended upon the final object or end and how to achieve it being clearly known and capable of definition: the Sophists were professing to teach a practical efficiency in living for any man and so there must be an end or function which all human beings have to perform: if a man is to acquire this universal human nature, he must discover what the function of man is, but the first stage in Sokrates' approach to knowledge is to convince the would-be aspirant that he knows nothing. This departure point was actually the main cause of Sokrates' criticism of the Sophists for taking fees, for they thereby forfeited their licence to teach their pupils this very point, that knowledge begins with not-knowing. For as the Vedic tradition declares:

> *Brahman* is known to him to whom it is unknown;
> he does not know to whom It is known.
> It is unknown to those who know It well,
> and known to those who do not know.
>
> *Kena* Upanishad, Ch.II, v.3

This acknowledgment of not-knowing precludes an easy definition of the aim of man; instead, Sokrates reasoned that if men could be brought to see the truth of the statement that 'virtue is knowledge', then they would then realise the truth of his second main formulation that 'no one does wrong willingly', for if they understood the first statement they would automatically choose the right. The corollary follows naturally that evil is only due to ignorance of the truth.

The path to truth now becomes a search in companionship with the man who has come to appreciate that he too does not know, by means of the procedures defined by Aristotle, namely 'inductive argument' and 'general definition'. For example, to define piety requires a collection of pious acts in which the common quality exists by which they are all named as pious. This common quality is the essence of piety; 'inductive' implies a leading on of the mind from individual instances to the understanding of the general definition. Euthyphro says 'piety is what I am doing now', but he has first failed *logon dounai* or 'to give a general definition'. The point of Sokrates' scrupulously analytical approach is this: if a man has no clear definition of Goodness or Justice, for example, how can he become a 'good or just man'; and this is precisely what is lacking in the Sophistic approach, for their teaching was not related to a truly rational foundation.

Sokrates reasoned that if order was to be restored to human conduct, the first necessity was to decide what justice, goodness and the other virtues really are. Sokrates' philosophy required an observant and sustained effort, so that the third main tenet of his teaching, that man should constantly attend to the care of the *psukhē* or 'Soul' might be realised. In the dialogue *Alkibiadēs I*, (which may or may not have been written by Plato), Sokrates takes Alkibiades, who desires to be a leader of men, both in politics and in war, through the following steps: first, he ought to have some understanding of such concepts as right and wrong; but Alkibiades contradicts himself over their definition. Secondly, ignorance is not important, but ignorance that you are ignorant is; for there is no harm in knowing nothing of the art of seamanship if one is content to be a passenger and leave the steering to the skilled helmsman. Next Alkibiades agrees that to be successful you have got to take care of yourself, and Sokrates shows you cannot tend and improve a thing unless you know its nature: 'knowing how' must be preceded by 'knowing what', for the Delphic command 'Know Thyself' must be taken seriously. The *psukhē* or 'Soul' controls the body and the Delphic command is directed to the Soul as the ruling element. Sokrates is the lover of Alkibiades because he loves his *psukhē*, or Alkibiades Himself, as opposed to his body, which is to the Soul as a belonging only. Finally, the *aretē* or 'virtue' of the *psukhē* is wisdom, and its function is to rule, govern and control.

This genuine search for the truth in a partnership of not-knowing is compared by Plato in *Gorgias* with the relationship between Sophist and fee-paying pupil as potentially being one of *kolakeia*, which is defined as a relationship of 'flattering and fawning'.[2] Its significance, however, goes beyond pandering for position and favours and implies a whole system of spurious knowledge, a counterfeit world of false relationships and untruth that nevertheless has the appearance of being reasonable, but it aims at another's pleasure and not at his good.[3] It is the teaching of deception that substitutes *tekhnai* or 'skills' that only have an empirical basis and do not have a logical or moral basis, for ones that have. Sokrates names the various subdivisions of *kolakeia*, where sophistry replaces legislation, rhetoric displaces corrective justice, cosmetics supplant gymnastics and cookery usurps medicine, whereas Gorgias had stated that the ability to speak well had the same beneficial effect in bringing order to the Soul as medicines had on the body.[4]

The Sophistic approach has nevertheless influenced western education right down to the present day and there is no doubt that much of its teaching, for example in language, was permanently useful. The clash with Sokrates, however, shows up the paucity of such an approach in the all-important virtue of tending the Soul, in expounding the way, the truth and the life. The idea (which flourishes to this day in the West) that education is to equip a man for life or a career, for example as an accomplished orator at the Assembly, was to Sokrates a denial of the true purpose of man, which was to realise his divinity. Plato calls such an aspirant 'a lover'; a characteristic of 'the lover' is a tendency to have a rich artistic or literary sense either to appreciate or to create. Plato recounts the journey of 'the lover' and his teacher into the realm of the unknown in this memorable passage:

> Whenever a man, ascending on the return journey from these mortal things, by a right feeling of love for youths, begins to catch sight of that beauty, he is not far from his goal. This is the correct way of approaching or being led by another to the realm of love, beginning with beautiful things in this world and using them as steps, returning ever on and upwards for the sake of that absolute beauty, from one to two and from two to all beautiful embodiments, then from beautiful embodiments to beautiful practices, and from practices to the beauty of knowledge of many things, and from these branches of knowledge one comes finally to the absolute knowledge, which is none other than knowledge of that absolute beauty and rests finally in the realisation of what the absolute beauty is.
>
> *Symposium*, 211A-211C

The lover surpasses the nihilism of Gorgias and the limitations of Protagoras; for he that 'loves the beautiful is called a lover because he partakes of it'.[5] In Sanskrit there is no *karttā* or 'subject' of love, for although the inner and outer realms of this Creation are caused by love, yet all the different forms in Creation are expressions of love and are all related to and through the love. The depiction of Sokrates accompanying the disciple into the unknown or 'realm of love' is in essence very similar to the *Guru*-disciple relationship expounded in the Vedic tradition. The obvious advantage, however, was that the ancient Aryans enjoyed the benefit of the *Vedas* themselves (see Appendix III) as a traditional touchstone of spiritual teaching and as a firm-footed guide.

The Upanishads describe the *Guru*-disciple relationship in many different ways, but one of the most complete descriptions is the conversation between the boy *Naciketā* and *Yama*, the God of Death. *Naciketā* states that he is 'full of faith',[6] both in the existence of the *Ātman* and also in the *ācārya* or 'teacher', for the latter is the link between the aspirant and the teaching, 'with discourse joining them',[7] just as in a Sokratic dialogue. This faith arises from *citta*, the source of right actions, and is guided by belief in that which is true, which is based on *buddhi* or 'discrimination'; when these two grow in strength together, the faith turns to love which trancends them both. In the Vedic tradition, there is no restriction or set pattern for the discourse between aspirant and teacher; rather, the teacher uses his own knowledge of the Self or of his *sadhana* or 'spiritual wealth' as an efficient cause[8] to lead the aspirant to knowledge in a manner particular to the nature of the aspirant. In the case of the dialogue between the Lord *Ṡṛī Kṛishṇa* and the Prince *Arjuna* depicted in the *Mahābhārata* on the battlefield of *Kurukshetra*, called the *Gītā*, the entire dialogue is even set in the context of the forthcoming battle. *Arjuna*, seeing that the enemy are his own cousins and relatives and that his own commander is his teacher, is overtaken by *moha* or 'delusion'[9] and the *Gītā* was spoken to dispel this ignorance or loss of memory. At the end of the discourse, *Arjuna* says to the Lord *Ṡṛī Kṛishṇa*:

> My Lord! O Immutable One! My *moha* has fled.
> By Thy Grace, O Changeless One, the light has dawned.
> My doubts are gone, and I stand before thee ready to do Thy Will'.
>
> *Gītā*, Ch.18, v.73

There can clearly be no set rules for such an intimate relationship, intimate that is between the indwelling *Ātman* of the teacher and the indwelling *Ātman* of the aspirant, which Sokrates called 'the right feeling of love for youths'.

Setting out in a state of faith and firm conviction, which is the natural state of *citta*, the aspirant must submit to discipline: 'By *tapas*, by *jñāna*, by continence and by truth is the Self to be attained'.[10] A key requirement of the *Veda* and of Sokrates was for the aspirant to be *satyam* or 'truthful' as a *sine qua non* to realisation, for 'the very nature of *Brahman* is truth'.[11] By following the scriptures and the words of the *Guru*, the disciple's life is given to truth in a state of faith and steadfastness. 'O Beloved *Naciketā*', says *Yama*, 'truly thou art faithful and steadfast; would that I always had such a disciple'.[12] This steadfast devotion to the teacher is beautifully portrayed by the master teacher of the *Veda*, *Śṛī Ādi Śaṅkarācārya*, in a hymn called *Gurvashṭakam*:

Eight Verses in Praise of the *Guru*

1. śaṛīran surūpan sadā rogamuktam
   yaśaścāru citran dhanam merutulyam.
   manaścenna lagnaṅ guroraṅghripadme;
   tataḥ kin tataḥ kin tataḥ kin tataḥ kim.

   Though your body be perfect, ever free from illness,
   Your honour unsullied, wealth high as Mount *Meru**;
   If your mind does not dwell on the Lotus Feet of the *Guru*,
   What use is all this? What good will it bring you?

2. kalatran dhanan putra pautrādisarvam
   gṛiham bāndhavāḥ sarvametadhi jātam.
   manaścenna lagnaṅ guroraṅghripadme;
   tataḥ kin tataḥ kin tataḥ kin tataḥ kim.

   A dear wife, sons and grandsons, beloved relations,
   Household and friends, all these you may have in abundance,
   If your mind does not dwell on the Lotus Feet of the *Guru*,
   What good are they all? What joy will they bring you?

3. shaḍaṅgādivedo mukhe śāstravidyā
   kavitvādi gadyaṅ supadyaṅ karoti.
   manaścenna lagnaṅ guroraṅghripadme;
   tataḥ kin tataḥ kin tataḥ kin tataḥ kim.

   The whole *Veda* and Holy Tradition lives on your lips,
   And foremost amongst seers you write inspired verse and prose;
   If your mind does not dwell on the Lotus Feet of the *Guru*,
   What use will it be? What good will it serve you?

4. videśeshu mānyaḥ svadeśeshu dhanyaḥ
   sadācārarvṛitteshu matto na cānyaḥ.
   manaścenna lagnaṅ guroraṅghripadme;
   tataḥ kin tataḥ kin tataḥ kin tataḥ kim.

* Meru is the mountain at the centre of the Earth; it represents the spinal column in man.

Though you be honoured at home and famous abroad
Thinking no one excels you in the practice of virtue,
If your mind does not dwell on the Lotus Feet of the *Guru*,
What will it lead to? What good will follow?

5. kśamāmaṇḍale bhūpabhūpālavṛindaiḥ
sadāsevitan yasya pādāravindam.
manaścenna lagnaṅ guroraṅghripadme;
tataḥ kin tataḥ kin tataḥ kin tataḥ kim.

Though your own Lotus Feet by Emperors be worshipped
And by hosts of the rulers of this earthly globe,
If your mind does not dwell on the Lotus Feet of the *Guru*,
So what? What good will come of all this adulation?

6. yaśaśced gatan dikśu dānaprātapāt
jagadvastu sarvaṅ kare yatprasādāt.
manaścenna lagnaṅ guroraṅghripadme;
tataḥ kin tataḥ kin tataḥ kin tataḥ kim.

Though your might and gift-giving be renowned in all quarters,
If your mind does not dwell on the Lotus Feet of the *Guru*,
From whose grace all wordly objects are in your grasp,
What good will it do you? What good will follow?

7. na bhoge na yoge na va vājimedhe
na kāntāmukhe naiva vitteshu cittam.
manaścenna lagnaṅ guroraṅghripadme;
tataḥ kin tataḥ kin tataḥ kin tataḥ kim.

Though it delights neither in riches nor the pleasures of beauty,
Nor in strength, nor intelligence, powers of yoga or enjoyment,
If your mind does not dwell on the Lotus Feet of the *Guru*,
What good will come from all this asceticism?

8. araṇye na vā svajya gehe na kārye
na dehe mano vartate me tvanarghye.
manaścenna lagnaṅ guroraṅghripadme;
tataḥ kin tataḥ kin tataḥ kin tataḥ kim.

Though my mind turns not to the forest, nor to my own household,
Nor to actions, nor to the body, nor to that which is priceless;
If my mind does not dwell on the Lotus Feet of the *Guru*,
What good will come from all this detachment?

9. gurorashṭakan yaḥ paṭhatpuṇyadehi
yatir-bhūpatir-brahmacārī ca gehī.
labhedvāñ-chitārtham padam brahmasañjñām
guroruktavākye mano yasya lagnam.

That virtuous one who recites this eightfold praise of the *Guru*,
Be he an ascetic, a king, a student or householder,
He will attain the desired state which is known as *Brahman*,
Whose mind always dwells on the words of the *Guru*.

Śaṅkarācārya Bhagavatpāda

The hymn refers to various types of *upādhi* or 'limitation and qualification' with which the individual is wont to identify. *Upādhi* means 'that which is put in the place of another thing, a substitute; anything which may be taken for or has the mere name or appearance of another thing, a phantom or the disguise of certain forms or properties considered as disguises of the Spirit'.[13] The hymn lists certain *upādhayaḥ*, beginning with the body and family relations, then learning, fame, power, wealth and finally intelligence. The roles a man may play, whether he be an astronaut or a doctor of philosophy or a lifeguard, become an *upādhi* for the individual when the role is believed to be real by that individual, for it disguises the true spirit in Self-qualification, as 'I am an astronaut, a doctor of philosophy, a lifeguard', for the nature of *upādhi* is *rūpa* or 'outer form' which is a type of illusion, which does exist but does not exist. *Upādhayaḥ* are legion and in society people play with *upādhi* – play with the role of lawyer, politician, expert or worker at this and that – but there is no lasting satisfaction from this limited play while the *upādhayaḥ* are taken as real. The main thrust of Sophism was to train a man to play just such leading roles in society, but these roles may become mere limitations and qualifications that add nothing to the substance; it is only the true teacher, declares the hymn, that can lead a man away from the phantom of *upādhi* and back to the Self.

A final question is posed by this profound hymn: *Śaṅkara*, the wisest commentator and teacher of the *Veda*, writes a hymn to 'his *Guru*', but who is his *Guru* and what is his name? The Vedic texts state that everyone's *Guru* is the indwelling *Ātman* or Self; thus the physically manifest *Guru* or teacher stands by means of the power of *Māyā* as a representative of the indwelling *Ātman*, and he stands as the *svatantraḥ karttā* in relation to the Self, for 'he has the system within himself as the agent of the *Ātman* for the action', which is the realisation that the indwelling *Ātman* is the *Brahman*, that the *jīva* or 'individual Soul'[14] is the *Brahman*.

15

Knowledge and Nescience

Sokrates questions Meno's slave and supplies the correct construction of a square that is double the size of an existing square,achieved by placing the second square on the diagonal of the first. The slave recognises that the seemingly obvious but wrong approach does not work, but then recognises that the correct construction is correct. Sokrates then concludes as follows:

> Either then he has at some time acquired the knowledge which he now has, or he has always possessed it. If he always possessed it, he must always have known; if on the other hand he acquired it at some previous time, it cannot have been in this life, unless somebody has taught him geometry. He will behave in the same way with all geometrical knowledge, and every other subject. Has anyone taught him all these?
>
> *Meno*, 85E

The answer to the question is a resounding 'No', for he is a slave. This geometrical experiment therefore reveals that there are three stages to arrive at knowledge: first, knowledge is unconscious; then opinion or belief is awakened from the unconscious by questions and dialectic; finally, opinion is converted into knowledge by giving an account of the relationship between the object of knowledge and the eternal 'Form' from which it is somehow derived. However, without someone present who already knows the answer, it will doubtless take longer to find out; perhaps Pythagoras was the first to reveal the solution, and if discrimination between right and wrong answers was not possible, there would be no hope of achieving the certainty demanded by the precise art and science, for example, of geometry.

It is at this final stage that the distinction between knowledge and opinion is really apparent, for knowledge is stable and unchanging, whereas the changing world of experience can only give rise to opinion or belief. Sokrates puts this in the following way:

> True opinions are a fine thing and do all sorts of good so long as they stay in their place, but they will not stay long. They run away from a man's mind, so they are not worth much until you tether them by working out the reason. That process, my dear Meno, is anamnesis, as we agreed earlier. Once they are tied down, they become knowledge, and are stable. That is why knowledge is something more valuable than right opinion.
>
> *Meno*, 98A

This relationship between knowledge and opinion is expanded in the extended Simile of the Line in *Republic*.[1] The Line represents the hierarchy of human knowledge or possibility of knowledge, a scale which is not in fact calibrated, but divided into four sections in an ascending ratio, to indicate the level of knowledge; hence level one or the first section represents Knowledge Absolute, and the lower three sections, the descending levels of knowledge (see Appendix V).

Starting at level three, the world of the senses, all forms may partake of The Good and The Beautiful, just as they can all be reflected in pools of water and polished surfaces at level four, and in the same way the universal form in level two may be found in the forms of level three. For the purpose of clarification, Plato keeps to the metaphor of geometry, so the square, circle and angles that the mathematician works with at level two are reflected in the physical objects of level three as the round stool, the square table and the rest. The Square Itself and The Circle Itself are universal, and what is true of one square is true of all squares. If the metaphor had been a moral one, such as piety, the result would be the same: the pious action at level three would be a result of knowledge of piety at level two. But the philosopher works at level one by the agency of pure perception, so that he may know that the universal forms with which he works can only be known in their dependence on the Universal Forms at this level, which can only be known in their dependence on The Good Itself. The Square Itself and Piety Itself are eternal and unchanging Forms held at level one, which can only be known in their dependence on The Good. The mathematicians and analogues of mathematicians, such as moralists perhaps, work at level two by means of the intellect, but at this level the forms are not known in their dependence on The Good Itself.

What is The Good? Sokrates declines to give an account, but offers an explanation of the child of The Good, and concludes as follows:

> This, then, which gives to the objects of knowledge their truth and to him who knows them his power of knowing, is the Form or essential nature of Goodness. It is the cause of knowledge and truth; and so, while you may think of it as an object of knowledge, you will do well to regard it as something beyond truth and knowledge, and precious as these both are, of still higher worth. And, just as in our analogy light and vision were to

> be thought of as like the sun, but not identical with it, so both 'knowledge and truth are to be regarded as like The Good, but to identify either with The Good is wrong. The Good must hold a yet higher place of honour.
>
> *Republic* VI, 508E-509A

Book VII of *Republic* opens with the parable of the cave which serves as an extended simile to depict the state of human knowledge and its relationship to the hierarchy of the Line, thereby illustrating the progress of the mind from the lowest state of unenlightenment to knowledge of The Good. The parable gives a warning about plunging untrained Souls into the discussion of moral problems, and then Plato sets out his ten-year course of pure mathematics, so as to habituate the intellect to abstract reasoning before moral ideas are called in question. The course in mathematics trains the intellect in the science of Dialectic, so that a man 'can dispense with sight and the other senses and follow truth into the region of pure reality'.[2]

In summary, Plato's metaphysical doctrine of Ideas or Forms grew directly out of Sokrates' search for general definitions and out of the moral vacuum created by the Sophists. In the early dialogues, the Ideas are not seen as existing transcendentally but as being immanent in the particulars themselves, which continues in *Meno*: 'All the virtues have an identical Form',[3] and in *Kratylos*, the Idea is embodied in the particular form of the shuttle; but in *Symposium*, Diotima speaks of 'the ever present Unity of Beauty Itself, in Itself with Itself',[4] which must clearly be taken as a transcendent unity.

In *Phaido*, both the doctrine of anamnesis and the Forms related to it are used in proofs of the Soul's survival after death, which also clearly implies the separate existence of Ideas. Just as snow participates in the Idea Coldness and retreats at the approach of heat, so the Soul participates in the Idea Life and retreats at the approach of death. The interesting question 'Is there an Idea of Death, or an Idea of a non-thing', is not put to Sokrates, which is clearly a serious omission. However, the example of snow has brought out the concept of properties and accidents: the property of snow is coldness, whereas its accident, that which is never present, except during the process of melting, is clearly heat.

In *Republic* the Idea of The Good acts on the world of Ideas in the same way as the sun acts in relation to sensible things, in that it is causal and the source of nourishment and the agency through which they are known and it gives the power of knowing to the knower. Plato also begins to hint at the fact that the inter-relationship of Forms with particulars and with other Forms will have to be examined, for 'each Form seems to be many because it everywhere appears in association with actions and bodies and with the other Forms'.[5] *Phaidros* takes the whole matter further in this direction, into the process of division of each genus so as to know that a single generic Form embraces a number of specific Forms and to know what the articulations within it are.

In *Parmenidēs* Plato's first real defence of the criticisms that could be levelled at the 'Theory of Ideas' is set out. The dialogue falls into two distinctive halves: first, Sokrates states his belief in Forms of Relationship, such as Likeness, Unity and Plurality; in ethical Ideas such as The Good and The Beautiful and in Ideas of manifest particulars such as Man. Parmenides asks Sokrates if he really believes there are Ideas for Man, Fire and Water, and then for Hair and Mud; Sokrates hesitates. Parmenides argues next that if the whole of an Idea is present in a separate manifest particular, it has become separate from Itself, and he proceeds by an argument of *reductio ad absurdum* to show that if a small particular has only a part of smallness, the Small Itself will be larger than that part, and that if a small thing acquires that part of smallness which at first it lacked, it will become smaller instead of larger by the addition. There are two reasonable answers to Parmenides' objections that Plato does not care to put forward. To the 'Mud' objection, doubtless Sokrates regarded such particulars as a by-product of a natural process or as a biological species; in fact, in the expansion of Creation there is a cut-off point for the principal Forms, though there is still a Form for everything of which a common name can be predicated; and to the second objection it could be said that the Form is an attribute, not a thing, and that Parmenides' spatial metaphor is inappropriate, although Plato has Parmenides use the spatial metaphor of the Sail in replying to that of the Day, which is not so obviously open to the same objection.

Parmenides' third objection is this: if the many large things participate in the Large Itself, there must be a further Form of Large common to the large things and the Large Itself, and yet another Form of Large common to all of these, and so on *ad infinitum*. Sokrates replies that each of the Forms may be a thought, which cannot exist properly anywhere but in a mind, so that each Form may be one; but Parmenides says that it must be a thought of something as opposed to nothing, and of something too that actually exists. Plato is thus claiming that the Forms have a substantial existence of their own, quite apart from a thought in the mind of a man or of God. Parmenides then proceeds to show up Plato's use of the verbs describing the nature of the participation of the Ideas in the particulars, namely *metekhein* and *metalambanein*, and this whole aspect of the theory is placed under a question mark; and yet the very arguments used by Parmenides infer that the nature of this relationship must be subtle, in the sense that it is an immaterial relationship which cannot be negated by materialistic objections. Again Plato does not say as much, but there is nowhere else for the argument to go: the simple, tautological, assertion made in *Phaido* that 'beautiful things are beautiful by participating in Beauty Itself' assumed too much to be acceptable any more.

The longer second half of *Parmenidēs* is capable of varying interpretations; however, the important point is that Plato is examining the logic of Parmenides, which he shows to be incorrect. Parmenides takes five pairs of opposite Forms – Unity/Plurality, Likeness/Unlikeness, Rest/Motion, Being/Non-being, Coming-to-be/Perishing and in respect of each pair argues from two premises: 'It is One' and 'It is not One', both in respect of One, the Form Itself, as the subject and in respect of things other than it, and *vice versa*. So in each case there are four arguments, with a pair of contradictory arguments in each case, thus giving eight consequences. To take the negative side of the fifth hypothesis as an example: if the Form of the One does not exist, it thereby admits existence of each member of many pairs of opposite predicates, implying the possibility of the existence of recurring duality.

In *Theaetētos*, Plato re-examines Protagoras' claim that the senses yield knowledge, which is tantamount to hopeless scepticism. Plato dismisses the idea that knowledge is true opinion and then digresses on false opinion and compares the mind to a waxen tablet and to an aviary: the process in the mind that leads to a false judgment, when the mind gets hold of the wrong piece of knowledge and interchanges it for the right one, is likened to the birds in an aviary, which have all been caught by the possessor, but this does not prevent him laying hands on a ringdove when he is hunting among his fluttering prisoners for a wood-pigeon. Finally, Plato proposes a third avenue to knowledge, which is 'true opinion with a *logos*' or rational base, which is clearly reminiscent of *Meno*. The discussion then moves in the world of appearances and proves that if a man tries to leave out of account the world of True Being, he cannot extract knowledge from sensible experience, from the world of transient becoming, for Being is grasped by 'the Soul Herself by Herself' without any aid from the senses.

In *Sophist*, Plato determines to put the Forms on a more secure logical basis and he examines intercommunication of the Forms amongst themselves. To begin with, there are three Forms that can be predicated for all other Forms, namely Being, Sameness/Likeness, and especially Difference/Unlikeness. Next it is reasoned that if all the other Forms could mix with one another, then everything could be everything, in that any predicate could be applied to any subject, and there would be no objective laws in the universe. So it is stated that some Forms can be found in close relationship while there are other pairs of Forms of which neither can be predicated of the other.[6] For example, Motion has Being and Likeness to Itself and Unlikeness to

Rest, but does not participate at all in Rest. It is stated that 'Every one of the Forms contains a certain amount of Being and an infinite amount of Non-Being'.[7] Whereas Being, Sameness and Difference are all-pervading, Motion and Rest divide all between them. The business of the philosopher is to employ the science of dialectic to collect and divide the Forms into their true hierarchy so as to rise up to the all-pervading level of Reality of these first three Forms; no doubt the final unity is the Form of The Good as set out in *Republic*, but the relationship between them is somewhat problematic and is not discussed here.

In *Philēbos* three problems are posed: Do the Forms exist? Do they continue to exist as units not subject to birth and decay? And how can they be present in many particulars and yet remain one? This last question is the single most important question: what is the relationship between the Forms and their manifest particulars? A general formula is put forward, concerning the Limit, the Unlimited, the Mixture and the Cause of the Mixture, which cover every instance of participation of the manifest many in the One. The One equates with the Limit, and Plurality with the Unlimited or Indefinite, often referred to as the More-and-Less. For example, Hotter-Colder is a continuum capable of infinite extension, but every actual object has a definite temperature, where Limit or Definiteness has been impressed upon the More-and-Less. Everything that exists has so much of each of its qualities. In *Sophist*, there is the concept of a number of infinitely extendable potentialities, one for every quality of man, and there is the Form Man, itself a focus of other Forms which combine to form Man. Each combining Form may be considered separately from a logical standpoint, and in each case the operation consists of the impress of Limit upon the Indefinite More-and-Less. Plato's solution, however, seems to explain the relation between generic and specific types of things rather than the relationship between universals and individual instances.

The importance of the function of Limit is to provide Measure, producing 'generation into Reality'.[8] The introduction of Measure is the fulcrum between the Forms and the question of pleasures and the good life, and the relationship between the Forms and Knowledge was discussed in *Timaeos*, which may have preceded *Philēbos*:

> If reason and opinion are different things, then Forms imperceptible by us, objects of thought alone, must exist by themselves; but if true opinion differs in no wise from reason, the things we perceive by means of the body must be deemed to be the most secure realities. Now we must say that reason and opinion are two things, since they differ both in origin and in nature. The one is produced by teaching, the other by persuasion; we can justify the one by true reasoning, the other is unreasoned; the one cannot be moved by persuasion, the other can; only God and a few men

possess the one, all men possess the other. We must therefore agree that there are Forms distinct from the copies of them.

Timaeos, 51ff.

Finally, mention must be made of the 'unwritten doctrines' recorded by Aristotle, in particular in relation to Ideas and numbers. For the Greeks, number connoted plurality, so that one is not a number, but the first principle of number, that from which number starts. For Plato, the 'great and the small' are the material element, the One is the essential or formal element in the Forms, the numbers (identified by Aristotle with the Forms) are produced by the participation of the great and the small (*i.e.* indefinite plurality) in the One. The Idea of the line was derived from two and the long and the short (*i.e.* indefinite length). The idea of the plane was derived from three, and the broad and narrow (i.e. indefinite width). The idea of solid was derived from the number four and the deep and shallow (*i.e.* indefinite depth). These numbers were also assigned to mental faculties. Reason was correlated with One because it is the direct apprehension of a Single Idea; science was correlated to two because it goes from a single datum to a single conclusion (according to Aristotle); opinion was correlated to three, because it moved indifferently from a single datum either to a true or false conclusion; and sensation is correlated to four, for four is assigned to solids and the objects in the sensible world are solids. These geometric figures were not accepted by Plato, but they served to remind the ancient Greeks that the eternal verities of the *Bonum*, *Ens*, *Verum* and *Unum* were transcendental.

Plato's Theory of Ideas set out to rediscover the beginning and cause of manifest Creation, of both concrete things and moral values, and in *Timaeos* the Forms are referred to as *paradeigma* or 'models' which were a *telos* or 'fulfilment' for an individual. Plato spoke in symbolic terms of that which is real and does exist, but Aristotle, his pupil of twenty years, was determined to discover the pathway that leads there. Aristotle's pragmatism sought to explain phenomena by seeking out their final cause: different members of the same species are different individual expressions of the same original Form but have developed differently; to understand a particular phenomenon is to lay bare the characteristics which distinguish it from other things. Aristotle, in seeking the purpose and explanation of Creation, had to reconcile a world of unstable phenomena which were perpetually changing and coming into existence and passing away again and never the same for two instants with that total stability which is the essence of the unmoving cause that he had no desire to question. Aristotle found the answer in two related concepts, the concept of 'immanent form' and the concept of *dunamis* or 'potentiality'.

First, behind the constant flux of the physical world are certain *arkhai* – 'basic principles' or 'causal factors' – which do not change and therefore provide the objects of true philosophy, such as the Unmoved Mover(s). *Arkhai* present in material forms, however, are not a set of substances existing apart from the sensible world, like Plato's Ideas, in which the transient in some obscure way participates. Aristotle's Forms do exist, and always manifest in some embodiment, as in 'this man', 'this horse'; in short, for Aristotle, this world was the expression of reality. Creatures of nature change through the presence of *arkhai* in them. An object consists at any given moment of a *hupokeimenon* or 'substratum', also called its *hulē* or 'matter', informed by or possessed of a certain *eidos* or form or 'quality'. The early thinking about the constant flux of Creation was that such movement took place between two opposites or contraries, from black to white, hot to cold and so on, which violated the law of contradiction, as Parmenides perceived. So Aristotle postulated the substratum, in which the heat left the substratum and the cold entered, but the substratum was without qualities and unchanging.

Secondly, as regards potentiality, the teleology of Plato and Aristotle demanded the actual existence of the *telos* or 'end', that is of a perfection under whose influence the activity of the natural world takes place. As Aristotle said: 'where there is a better there must be a best', which is a grammatical tautology, for comparisons are meaningless unless there is an absolute standard to which they may be referred. The ultimate *telos* of Aristotle's world is its God, who is the only pure Form, other than the heavenly spheres, existing apart from *hulē* or matter and therefore apart from body. He is not the Form of anything in the physical world, but *Ho Theos* or 'God' is the pure Form of *ousia* or 'Being'. For Aristotle, Plato's Ideas seemed like useless replicas of perceptible things: for God, having no matter and no substratum, has no possibility of change, and this concept is also expressed in the Upanishads in the following terms:

> One should meditate on that *Brahman* as the support;
> thereby one becomes supported.
>
> *Taittirīya* Upanishad, Ch.III, Canto X, v.3

At this point it should be pointed out that Aristotle's physical investigations into nature provided an empirical base for this metaphysical teleology. Even for the non-biologist, the concept of nature evolving towards an appropriate end for the particular form in question, whether it be man, an animal, a fish or a plant is clear, comprehensible and borne out by the evidence of the senses. The fact that a certain creature needing a certain kind of protection should be provided with an appropriate form of protection is eminently acceptable: the hedgehog has spikes, the skunk a smell and so on. In nature, the child looks to its adult, the parent in perfect form, the *telos* towards which it is developing; likewise the world looks to an absolute perfection for its continued maintenance. By realising as adequately as it can its own specific form, every creature may be said to be imitating, in its own limited way, the eternal perfection of God. The inward urge to do this is what is meant by the *phusis* or 'nature' of a natural object.

Aristotle felt the need to express motion and resolved this by formulating his notion of 'being', that each particular in relation to 'being' was either actual or potential. For example, water has the potential to become hotter, but can only become hotter by the agency of something that is actually hotter. *Dunamis* or 'potentiality' implies that that which is undergoing a genesis or act of change cannot already be in possession of the form which it is intending to acquire, and also the agent of the change must already be in possession of that form. Taken together, the two statements mean that nothing can move itself for to do so it would have to be both actual and potential in relation to the same act of change at the same time, which is a *reductio ad absurdum*.

The universe as a whole requires an external mover, 'external' in the sense of being distinct from what it moves, and as the universe is everlasting the cause must be eternal. This Being, which is eternal and perfect, contains no element of unrealised potentiality, so the concept of God as the Unmoved Mover is demonstrated. As God is incorporeal, so he is unmoved and unalterable, and as God is free from motion then he must be pure *energeia* or 'actuality'; God is all activity, though exempt from *kinēsis* or 'motion' and from being moved by anything else, and is eternally active within an activity which brings no fatigue, but is forever blissful. For '*hē gar nou energeia zōē*' means 'life is the activity of *nous*': God's pure mind can contemplate in a single instant, and does so eternally, the whole realm of true being. Aristotle could not accept Plato's initial postulate that God is Soul and Soul is Self-mover; for him, it had to be the final step in this chain of reasoning.

Plato had struggled long and unsuccessfully to define precisely how the phenomenal world participated in the Forms while Aristotle had still to explain the relationship between God and the world. Aristotle postulated four aspects of natural causation: first, the 'material' as in the wood for a table or the acorn from which the oak grew; secondly, the 'formal' meaning the shape of a table or the tendency of the acorn to grow into an oak tree as opposed to anything else; next, the 'efficient', or the carpenter or parent oak tree, and lastly, the 'final cause' which is the purpose to be fulfilled by the carpenter of a table or the fully grown oak tree to which the acorn grows. The fact that in nature there is no apparently premeditated purpose as there is in human activities does not vitiate the doctrine of *telos*, for the world as a whole, especially the heavens and perhaps human beings, 'moves towards God as the supreme object of desire';[9] whereas other creatures aim at their own well-being and the perpetuation in kind through their progeny. Aristotle decried the Homeric deference that 'a mortal man must confine himself to mortal thoughts', but advocated instead that 'man's highest nature is identical with God's; cultivate it and emulate the immortal'.

There is a marked contrast between Greek systems of knowledge and the *Veda*. The former deals with objects of knowledge, but the latter deals with objectless knowledge, namely knowledge of the Self. The *Vedas* maintain that the seer cannot be the seen for the seen is an object, but the seer can never be an object, for the seen refers to the seeing. In the Vedic tradition, knowledge is called *vidyā* and nescience *avidyā*. This Creation is the manifestation of *Brahman* through countless forms and *vidyā* is the knowledge that this is so; when the differentiated *prakṛiti* or 'nature' comprising *ahaṅkāra*, *citta*, *buddhi*, *manas*, the elements and the senses is taken to be true, and *manas* and so on to be the Self and involved in the movements of *prakṛiti* or 'nature', then this state of nescience is *avidyā*. In *vidyā*, *Ātman* only observes, and in this observation, in the seeing, hearing, touching, tasting and smelling, the being lives in accordance with its true nature of truth, consciousness and bliss. In a sense, *vidyā* and *avidyā* are inseparable, but they seem separate in Creation; however, a real knower does not claim to have attained *vidyā* and banished *avidyā*, for it is not in the nature of the indwelling *Ātman* either to claim or to disclaim anything, for such distinctions are absent in the pure state of just observing:

> He who knows these two, *vidyā* and *avidyā*, together attains immortality through *vidyā*, by crossing over death through *avidyā*.
>
> *Īśā* Upanishad, *śloka* 11

Vidyā is identified as arising from two quite different sources, and the *Vedas* themselves are similarly divided. Thus *śruti* refers at the first level to that 'which is heard or perceived with the ear' (it should be noted that the dictionary does not say 'by the hearer'); at the second level *śruti* is 'that which has been heard or communicated from the beginning, sacred knowledge orally transmitted by the *Brahmans* from generation to generation'; in fact, *śruti* means 'the *Veda*, that is the sacred eternal sounds or words as eternally heard by the *Ṛishis*'.[10] In the Vedic tradition, *śruti* only applied to the *Mantra Brāhmaṇa* portion of the *Veda*, but it was later extended to the Upanishads and *Darśanas*. *Śruti* is from *dhātu śru* meaning 'to hear';[11] it has *dhātvartha śravane*,[12] meaning; 'streaming, flowing, flowing off',[13] implying that it is a gift of Creation, not something that can be asked for or worked for, nor something that can be produced by human thought, for it can only be received as a revelation. The second source of *vidyā* is *smṛiti*, which refers to 'remembrance, reminiscence, calling to mind', and it refers to 'the whole body of sacred tradition or what is remembered by sacred tradition, including the six *Vedāṅgas* (see Appendix III), the Laws of *Manu*, and the epics';[14] thus the laws of grammar and *Dhātu-Pāṭha*, for example, are *smṛiti*. *Smṛiti* is from *dhātu smṛi* which has several *dhātvartha*, for example *cintā*,[15] meaning 'thought , care, serious thought about, consideration'.[16] This *dhātvartha* demonstrates how *smṛiti* and *śruti* are two very different streams of knowledge; in the former there is a clear parallel with the Sokratic doctrine of anamnesis, and the same root carries the same essential meaning of memory in Greek, Latin and English;[17] whereas in *śruti*, there is the definite sense of divine revelation that is of a different order. Plato caught the sense of those two terms when he distinguished between 'the knowledge which has a Soul, of which the written word is no more than an image'.[18]

Vidyā and *Veda* are from *dhātu vid*, as is the Greek *oida* meaning 'I know' and *eidos* or 'form' and the Latin *video* meaning 'I see'. The root *vid* appears five times in *Dhātu-Pāṭha* and an analysis of the *dhātvartha* is revealing.[19] First, *dhātu vid* is found in *jñāna*, or 'knowledge', which is found in *sattāyām*, so 'knowledge of the Self' is implied. This knowledge depends on *vicāraṇe* or 'discrimination' of what relates to the Self and what relates to the not-Self. This discrimination leads to the activities expressed in the *dhātvartha* compound of *cetana-ākhyāna-nivāsa*, where *cetana* is the 'conscious being', *ākhyāna* is 'the making known' of the conscious being and *nivāsa* is the state where the Self 'dwells deep within', which leads to *lābhe*, found 'in attainment' of knowledge of the Self.

In order to appreciate the related concepts of *vidyā* and *avidyā* more fully, it is necessary to examine the organs of the *antaḥkaraṇa*, namely *citta*, *buddhi*, *manas* and *ahaṅkāra*. Now *antaḥkaraṇa* means that which is 'concealed, hidden or internal to the action itself', namely the inner organs of heart and mind, and also 'the seat of thought and feeling, thinking faculty and conscience'.[20] For as the Upanishads declare, *satyam jñānamanantam Brahmā*: 'The Self is Truth, Knowledge, Infinite'.[21] True knowledge is of the Self alone, which is called *adhyātma-vidyā* or the 'science of Self-Knowledge'; thus the sacred texts expound the means whereby such knowledge is realised, and therefore on the workings of *antaḥkaraṇa*, and in particular of *citta*, which is at the heart of the matter.

Aham is the cause of *citta* and *citta* is the heart where the light of the *Ātman* is reflected, thereby illuminating the *antaḥkaraṇa* or organs of mind, the five senses and the physical body. The paramount quality of *citta* is goodness, hence human feelings are naturally good, but the impediments and impurities acquired by the individual form a husk around *citta* and reduce the amount of light available; the light of *citta* is not reduced, but it shines in darkness and the basic structure closely remembles the Judaeo-Christian concept of the light according to the Gospel of St John. *Citta* is both individual and universal and is designed to reflect all activities in the universe. In fact, actions in the world are a projection of the state of *samashṭi citta*, and pure *vyashṭi citta* reacts naturally to every situation while maintaining purity; but when *vyashṭi citta* is governed by *ahaṅkāra*, then the individual feels 'this is my existence' and the attachments and identifications to actions develop into individual personality. The wise man subsumes his traits of personality into the steady state of *citta*, which is undisturbed by pains, does not seek pleasures, and is free from actions, fear and anger:

> Undisturbed by the unpleasant, freed from attachments,
> fear and anger, is the steady state of *citta*.
>
> It is all encompassing and embraces everything,
> having no attachment, no sorrow, pure and peaceful.
>
> This is the steady state, O *Pārtha*;
> attaining this, one is no longer confused.
> Remaining in it even at the final hour,
> One finds absorption into *Brahman*.
>
> *Gītā*, Ch.II, vv.56-7,72

The wise man knows that *citta* is not the conscious being nor the Self, for it is the instrument of the experiencer, of the seer who sees an object; but when through attention the object refers to the seeing, it is experienced by the attention in *citta*. This is the glory of the indwelling *Ātman* and is held in *citta* until by grace the heart opens up and joy pours forth, which is the manifestation of the bliss of the knowledge of the Self, stored in *citta*. The light of the *Ātman* is reflected in *citta*, and when reflected from *citta* in whatever strength, it enlightens *buddhi*, the mental organ of discrimination, and if sufficiently strong it thereby enables *buddhi* to differentiate between what is true and what is not true, what is right action and what is wrong action. When the reflected light from *citta* illuminates *manas*, then *manas* makes sense of the senses as it fulfils its role of discursive mind.

Citta is from *dhātu cit*, which has four *dhātvartha*, carrying the meaning of 'consciousness, pure perception, in service of another [organ of *antaḥkaraṇa*], memory and being fully conscious'.[22] *Buddhi* is from *dhātu budha*, which has *dhātvartha avagamane*.[23] *Avagamane* means 'making known' and 'understanding, perception, knowledge';[24] the Greek verb *punthanomai* meaning 'I know' is from the same root.[25] Finally, *manas* is from *dhātu mana*, which has *dhātvartha jñāne*,[26] meaning 'knowing', in that *manas* is the link with the senses as their interpreter. A pure state of *citta* strengthens and purifies *buddhi*, so that as the seeker comes to the knowledge that the indwelling *Ātman* is the *Brahman*, that the seeker is the sought, then he can dispense with the functions of *antaḥkaraṇa*, such as reminding himself of any idea that the absolute nature is the Self, for then *Ātman* lives as *Ātman* and knowledge of the most profound aspect of *Veda* is attained.

This brief investigation into systems of knowledge propounded by various philosophic camps highlights the different viewpoints of the function of individual mind and universal Mind. Plato's *dianoia* or 'mind' worked at level two of the Line to study the universal Forms, which could be known at this level through the study of mathematics; they could only be contemplated by the *noēsis* or Mind which is capable of pure perception at level one, where the universal Forms can only be known in their dependence on The Highest Good. Neoplatonists, such as Plotinos, said there was no reality, except the ineffable One, that was outside the universal Mind. The Vedantist, in particular the Advaitist, would not accept the proposition that there can be a thinking subject and a thought object, for there is only the Self and a universal activity of thinking; and as far as Mind is concerned, Aristotle and Neoplatonists would agree with the Advaitist, but Aristotle would also insist that our embodied selves are as real as Mind, and the Neoplatonist would probably find himself nearer to Aristotle on this point than to the Advaitist. In fact, Aristotle could rightly be interpreted as emphasising non-duality by this view, in that 'as below' really is 'as above', for how could the Mind that knows on this earth be different from any other Mind? Aristotle would say to the Advaitist, 'you cannot maintain that "the indwelling *Ātman* is the *Brahman*" in your terminology, implying that the Creation is the manifestation of *Brahman* through countless forms, and at the same time deny the validity of what I mean when I say "this man, this horse", because allowing for language, time and place, we may even be saying something not so dissimilar. For what does your teaching mean otherwise, when it says: "This Self [*Ātman*] is also of the individual Soul [*purusha*]"?'[27] Aristotle could probably count on the Neoplatonist for support in promoting such a discussion, as the latter would give the individual Soul more of reality than the Hindu, for he is accustomed to the Platonic tradition of the images and imitations in the physical world rather than the Indian idea that it is an illusion.

16

Birth and Death

In terms of a single life, birth necessarily precedes death; but if the transmigration of the Soul from one body to another is an accepted premise, then death necessarily precedes birth, and an investigation into death will yield knowledge of its inevitable contrary of birth. Belief in survival of the *psukhē* or 'Soul' after death in some form or other runs throughout Greek civilisation; even the Mycenaeans believed that the dead lived on in the tomb with their human needs, much as they were when living, and consequently requiring household objects to be buried with them, as evidenced by the alleged tomb of Agamemnon. Homer depicted the dead dwelling together in a common subterranean abode, the realm of the God Hades and the Goddess Persephone, dark and gloomy like the grave. Homer's *psukhē* was a kind of breath or vapour which animated the body but in turn was dependent on the body for its efficiency. At death, the body perished and the *psukhē* slipped away, gibbering and squeaking into a pale and shadowy existence without mind or strength. On Odysseus' visit to the underworld, 'the strengthless heads of the dead' had to imbibe blood to recover their wits in order to speak to him. This twilight world so appalled Akhilles that his ghost told Odysseus: 'I would rather follow the plough as thrall to another man, one with no land allotted him and not much to live on, than be a king over all the perished dead'.[1] Homer and Hesiod held out the possibility that certain favoured heroes, exempt from death, are taken by the Gods to the Isles of the Blest, or Elysium situated at the ends of the earth. For example, Menelaos, by the very fact of his marriage to Helen, will go to Elysium.[2]

According to the Homeric Hymn to Demeter, the Eleusinian Mysteries promised their initiates a happier lot in the after-life; there, as in this world, they will continue to celebrate the Mysteries. Similarly, Pindar (born 518 B.C.) ascribed to men a prolongation of existence, which did not equal immortality; also, Glory, which lasts into the future, passes the bounds of mortality by making itself known to the dead. Pindar was still really quite close to Homer, as indeed were Sappho[3] and Theognis,[4] as he envisaged a judgment of the dead in which certain spirits are rewarded and others punished. The judge is an unspecified *Tis* or 'Someone', who rewards the good and punishes the evil. Pindar was undecided, however, as to the exact home of the favoured few, as to whether it was 'beyond the ocean' in the Isles of the Blest, where they displayed their bliss by weaving garlands,[5] or below the earth, where they pursued earthly sports and pastimes.[6] Pindar was also in two minds over reincarnation, a concept for which he is the first Greek literary source. His first notion was that a few heroes who have passed three lives 'in either world' pass at death by the highway of Zeus to the Tower of Kronos on the Isles of the Blest,[7] a teaching taken up by Plato; then, at a different place, the wise and strong are born as a result of their merit in previous lives:[8] these two concepts can clearly be combined.

Pythagoras in the sixth century and Empedokles in the fifth century both had fully developed teachings on the transmigration of the Soul.[9] Although the former left no extant writings, for his was an oral tradition, there are references; for example, Porphyry states that Pythagoras maintained 'that the Soul is immortal; next that it changes into other kinds of living things, also that events recur in certain cycles, and that nothing is ever absolutely new; and finally that all living things should be regarded as akin'. 'Pythagoras', he says, 'seems to have been the first to bring these beliefs into Greece', and Herodotos had earlier stated quite clearly that such beliefs were maintained by the Egyptians. The consequence of Pythagoras' views was that the Soul had to undergo a process of purifying itself through successive embodiments until finally 'there can be little doubt that the ultimate aim was the annihilation of Self in reunion with the divine'.[10] The Pythagorean views were also shared by other mystical sects, particularly those who taught in the name of the mythical Orpheus.

There is considerable correspondence with the view of the Soul's life or journey between Empedokles' poem 'Purifications' and Pythagorean teaching. The Cycle of the Soul for Empedokles consisted of four stages: starting at Unity or Peace, it falls into Disorder or Strife, recovers, and so begins again. Through a process of metempsychosis, the human Soul slowly recovers from its fall over thirty thousand *hōras* or 'seasons' during which it walks with Discord, and then ascends the scale of lives back to human form and thence to immortality: 'For already have I once been a boy and a girl, a bush and a bird and a dumb sea fish'[11] and 'I go about among you an immortal God, no mortal now'.[12] It is an open matter, on the extant fragments, to determine whether Empedokles believed in individual survival, as the question turns on the degree of figurative and material use of language. The interpretation of Hippolytos, writing much later, assumed that Empedokles professed reabsorption into the 'Sacred Mind'.

The fifth century ended with the death of Sokrates in 399 B.C., and in the *Apology* no definite view of the after-life is promulgated. Sokrates was convinced, however, that no harm can come to a good man, and said that either death was a dreamless sleep, a deep sleep in which the Soul experiences total peace and contentment, or the Soul survived and would join the company of the Gods and the deathless heroes. It remained to Plato to pick up the strands of teaching from Sokrates, Pythagoras, the Orphists and earlier philosophers and to supply a philosophic basis to eschatology. The Sokrates of the *Meno* who develops the theory of anamnesis, that all knowledge lies dormant within the Soul which has seen the truth in its disembodied state and in former lives, and of *Phaido*'s doctrine of immortality are generally recognised to be Platonic extensions. Similarly the ethical considerations as set out in the Myth of Er in *Republic* and the Theory of Ideas involve an after-life and a metempsychosis. Plato's teaching on reincarnation involves ethical and moral considerations as well, as he invariably introduces his eschatology as an adjunct to a dialectical discussion on morals or knowledge, often in the form of a myth. In *Phaido*, Sokrates sets out to prove the immortality of the Soul on the actual day of his execution; it is significant that the real subject of the dialogue is the art of correct living rather than the fate of the Soul after death, and Sokrates seems generally more interested in this aspect of Soul. However, those who do not practise the separation of Soul from the body while living end up with Souls that become heavy and body-like, and after death they wander as shadowy ghosts on the outskirts of the physical world until they are once more attracted into the bonds of the body, or indeed descend into animal life.[13] The fate of those who are ruled by ambition rather than love of possessions is not so bad, and politicians perhaps become bees or ants. But high above them all the Soul of the philosopher, freed from the pleasures and pains which nail body and Soul together, freed that is from the body, contemplates 'the truth and the divine ... and when It dies It goes to that which is like unto Itself and is freed from the evils of human life'.[14] There is more than a definite suggestion here that the final aim of the Soul is its reunification in its appropriate eternal, absolute Form.

Sokrates' statement in *Phaido* that the Soul is indestructible throughout the whole of time has implications for each individual and his actions. In particular, the unjust man can no longer assume that he will escape any penalty for any wicked act he might perform; for even if he evades his prosecutors on this earth, as death is not the end of the Soul's life, he will surely not escape the divine assize and the punishments of Hades. In an age which knew many tyrants and witnessed many outrageous acts, this was not only a solemn warning to the evil-doers, but was also a source of comfort and support to the oppressed, who might easily assume that those in power were beyond any authority that could be imposed in this world; indeed, it answered the common man's complaint that there was no justice amongst men. Secondly, Plato emphasised that men should choose philosophy as their way of life, as no other way provided truth and goodness for the Soul, that required great care throughout its successive lives if it were to regain its original pure state. The only way to ensure the Soul's best interests in this life and its successive embodiments was to cease neglecting it and to provide the proper education and nurture. Sokrates states that 'if anyone is going to neglect it, now the risk would seem fearful'.[15]

Sokrates in *Phaido* commences his proof of the immortality of the Soul by stating a principle that opposites come from opposites, and that there are cyclical processes between every pair of opposites. Just as the weaker are the opposite of the stronger, so life is the opposite of death, and they are generated out of each other, for the weaker can only become weaker from the stronger; there is a fallacy in this argument, for it simply is not true that every weak thing that comes to be was previously strong. Plato argues, however, that the process of generation cannot just be linear; if it was just a passage from living to dying, then everything would end in death and everyone would end up like Endymion, fast asleep. Then Sokrates proceeds to the doctrine of anamnesis, that the process of learning is but a recollection of what the Soul knew in a former state. Sokrates gives examples of what he means; the mind appreciates the notion of absolute equality and is reminded of this on seeing two equal sticks or stones, but the equality of the objects is imperfect whereas the concept of absolute equality is perfect, unchanging and eternal, and not being evident as such in the physical world, the Soul must have acquired the knowledge of these absolute qualities either before birth or at birth: but not everyone has this knowledge; so it is not innate, and indeed it is only known through reminiscence. If it was not given at birth, it must have existed before birth, and so the Soul must have existed in a former state and had intelligence. The objection to the 'equality' argument is that a man may surely form the concept of equality by extrapolation from the more or less imperfect that he has seen; the claim that when one thing suggests another, that there must have been previous experience of the second one is clearly false.

Simmias and Kebes, the interlocutors, here object that this only proves the pre-existence of the Soul, but Sokrates asks them to join this argument to the cyclical notion of the living coming from the dead and the two arguments together prove the immortality of the Soul. Sokrates gives a dissertation on the nature of the Soul, comparing it to the nature of the body; the Soul is relatively immutable and partakes of the eternal attributes of the Forms; she rules and directs the body, being the image of divinity whereas the body is mortal and human and capable of being weighed down by its own desires. Simmias is still not convinced, and poses the probability that the Soul is a *harmonia* or 'harmony', or rather 'an attunement', that exists in the body, which will vanish when the instrument is broken. Sokrates points out that an attunement is an effect whereas Soul is causal, and quite unlike an attunement, for she does not admit of varying degrees, in the sense that what can be more or less attuned is clearly not itself an attunement. The whole practice of a philosopher in attaining to purity, the principle process on the way to immortality, consists in his Soul resisting the affections of the body, and he refers to Odysseus whom Homer describes as 'rebuking his heart'; for by definition an attunement cannot oppose itself.

Sokrates finally resorts to the Theory of Ideas, which states that there is an unmanifest, single, determinate and immutable concept that is the causal form of every significant, manifest form, whether manifest physically as a body or in the mind as an idea, that can be appreciated only by *hē noēsis* or 'pure perception', and by 'perception' the senses are in no way implied. A beautiful thing thus *metekhei* or 'participates' *auto to kalon* 'in Beauty Itself'. As for the proof of immortality, Sokrates argues that all phenomena have an essential character that partakes of a particular Form, and that such things never partake of or admit an essentially opposite or incompatible Form; Sokrates is small and has the attribute of smallness and cannot therefore become tall, for the smallness in him drives out tallness. This doctrine of mutual exclusion is not only true of the opposites themselves, but also of other characteristics, which are inseparable from them. For example, the number three excludes the number four because three is odd and four is even, and the odd is opposed to the even. Similarly, it is an essential characteristic of a Soul to be alive, to partake of the Form of Life: it refuses to partake of the form death, just as life also excludes death. Furthermore, if the odd principle were imperishable, then the number three would not perish but would remove itself at the approach of the even principle; but the immortal is imperishable, and so the Soul on the approach of death does not perish, but removes.

Phaido is the first real attempt in western literature to apply logic to the proof of immortality. The crucial argument is that the immortal is imperishable, for if this is not proven, the argument only shows that there can be so such thing as a Soul that is dead, that dead Souls do not exist, which is a long way from proving the immortality of the Soul. The arguments in *Phaido* for immortality are not in themselves independent and individually complete, but rather complementary and placed in a sequence that is designed to present a total case for the Soul's survival. The principal objection by critics to the cyclical argument is that it assumes the existence of the Soul in an unembodied state, which is the very point that has to be proved, for there is no reason why a 'new' life of a 'new' Soul might not be embodied at any birth; the Endymion corollary assumes no potential for 'new life'. Critics are also quick to point out the various ambiguities of the verb *gignomai* meaning 'become', 'be born', 'arise' and so on, and that it obviously suited Plato to use this word to describe the rather vague process of 'opposites' being generated from 'opposites'. Also, the argument makes no attempt to prove the immortality of each Soul, or personal immortality. These criticisms cannot really be answered, but the real purpose of placing the cyclical argument first is probably to set before the audience a working model of the Soul's journey; before the proof can begin, the proposition must be stated, and that is all that is really accomplished in the logically argued passages of the dialogue.

Critics have also argued that the example chosen by Plato of equality relies initially on the sense perception of sight, whereas at many other instances, even in *Phaido*, he has warned of the danger of relying on sense perceptions. However, such criticisms overlook that the true mode of pure perception of the true equal, as with all the other Forms, resides in the *nous* or Soul; the senses merely perceive the physical equal, and the *nous* connects with the true equal which the physical equal can never equal, but Plato never stated that the senses should be made redundant; rather, they are for information only, as the agent for the stimulation, by association in this case with that which only the *nous* or Soul appreciates, the eternal and unchanging Forms. Plato does not attempt to describe the method whereby the Soul attains to the vision of true Forms in *Phaido* for the doctrine of anamnesis is not really analysed fully, but merely uses the existence of the Forms to posit the evidence of the existence of the Soul in a disembodied state. It is often stated, as Simmias indeed does state, that the recollection argument only proves the pre-existence of the Soul and in no way proves its existence after death. Sokrates' invitation to unite the cyclical and recollection arguments is logically fair, but of course imports the real weakness of the former argument, that it has not been proved that there is no other source for the living other than from the dead, and Plato did not raise the all-important theme of a finite number of Souls until *Republic*.

Plato's description of Sokrates' manner in meeting his death is a living example of the supposed validity of the logical arguments. To the man who meets death with a sense of loss, lamentation and weeping, in fact just as the assembled company behave at Sokrates' imminent death, it is clear that his Soul has not developed sufficiently, in this embodiment at any rate, along the true philosophical path. To such a man the Theory of Ideas has remained a theory; it is the experience of the actual pure perception of their true Forms that takes a man beyond the theoretical, beyond that which is supported by logic to true knowledge.

In *Republic*, Plato distinguishes three parts of the Soul: *to logistikon* or the 'reasoning' part; *to epithumētikon* or the 'appetitive' part; and *to thumoeidēs* or the 'feeling' part.[16] This threefold aspect of Soul immediately poses problems for the idea of immortality propounded in *Phaido*, where the Soul was considered as a single entity which survived death. In *Timaeos* it is the reasoning part alone that is immortal, as it is the most divine part of the Soul, being akin to the Gods and created by God HimSelf, whereas the other two functions of the Soul were created by lesser Gods at the time of embodiment, but the work of God himself must be everlasting. Those aspects of Soul that carry physical desire and ambition do not survive, so human personality is mortal. The nature of the immortality of the reasoning part is not precisely described, but there is a passage in *Republic* that claims the direction of this immortal part is eventually to lose its individual identity by 'becoming incorporate with very Being', or Reality.[17] Both Sokrates and Plato, however, put the emphasis rather on the care of the Soul while embodied, in the firm conviction that to the good man nothing but good can come.

Aristotle likewise denied the power of survival to all but the intellectual part of man's Soul. This part survives as it 'comes in from outside' and also exists after the body's death.[18] As with Plato, Aristotle omits to say whether the part of the Soul that survives death does so in an individual form or is merged in some wider spiritual unity. This active reason in the Soul goes beyond the individual, and it would appear to be identical in all individuals: 'when it has been separated it is that only which it is essentially, and this alone is immortal and eternal; and without this nothing knows'. Aristotle also says: 'Intuitive thought and contemplation, then, die away through the destruction of something else within [the body], but are themselves impassible. But reasoning and loving or hating, are affections not of reason but of its possessor, in so far as he possesses it. Hence when he perishes there is neither memory nor love; for these belonged not to reason but to the composite being which has perished; reason is doubtless something more divine and is impassible.'[19] Hence Aristotle depicts the immortal reason as being devoid of sensibility after death. The Homeric hero surviving after death in Elysium, with his personality intact as in life, has been refined into that part of the Soul that is the source of knowledge in each man and in each particular instance survives, but shorn of the individual personality manifested in life.

In the Vedic accounts of death, the process of modification of mind and matter is called *gati*, a very widely used Sanskrit word denoting 'movement' in all its various forms, including the whole process of metempsychosis.[20] At the time of death, the process of *gati* starts with the absorption of speech into *manas*, and then all the other functions of the organs, such as seeing, hearing and touching, (but not the organs themselves), also merge into *manas*. Then the process of *gati* removes *manas* into the *prana* or 'vital breath', just as one who sleeps is seen to breathe through his senses when the mind is not functioning. Then the *prana* merges with the *jīva* or 'individual Self', which is encumbered with the *karmic* effect of the residues from previous actions; quite simply, *vāsanā*[21] or 'what has been meditated, valued and dwelt upon in life and has entered into the individual's nature' will come into the memory at this stage and what has not entered memory will not be at hand. The breathing stops and death of the body occurs. The five gross elements forming the physical body return at death to earth, water, fire, air and ether; *manas* and *buddhi* also return to their universal forms, for there is no loss at the universal level of *samashṭi*.

The process next moves the *jīva* into the *tanmātrās* or five subtle (as opposed to physical) elements; they form a *sukshmaśarīra* or 'subtle body' that encloses the encumbered *jīva*, just as the gross body did while living, and it resides in consciousness in *citta* or 'the heart'. As the external organs have stopped functioning, the consciousness is governed at this point entirely by past actions, which in turn govern the *vāsanā* which will determine the direction taken by the subtle body as it leaves the heart. The emphasis put by Sokrates, for example, in *Phaido*, on the care of the Soul while living takes on a new significance in the context of *vāsanā*. Finally, the *sukshmaśarīra* and *jīva* leave the heart by one of the many arteries or veins and the *citta* that has lived in the steady state departs in peaceful majesty from the dead gross body.[22] The subtle body then journeys either by the northern path, the way of the Gods, to the sun or by the southern path, the way of the fathers, to the moon, as was depicted in Homer's allegory of the Cave of the Nymphs. In the Vedic tradition, there is also a third path, taken by those who have neither knowledge nor the benefits of adherence to ritual obligations, which leads to *Yama*, the God of the dead, who passes judgment on their Souls.

The immortality of the Soul or Self pervades the Vedic tradition and is clearly stated on many occasions:

> The Self is neither born nor does it die.
>
> *Kaṭha* Upanishad, Ch.1, Canto 11, v.18
> & Ch.2, Canto 18, v.17

The traditional Indian view is that birth and death are witnessed by onlookers in the physical world and they falsely assume that someone is born and someone has died. No one can remember his birth and no one can remember a time of not-being; this is because there is no birth of the Self and there is no not-being of the Self; therefore there can be no death of the Self, for there was never a time when it was not; for as *Śaṅkara* of *Puri* was wont to say: 'No man has ever said "I am dead".' The body, however, changes and by the constant association with the body and attachment to it and caring for its needs, which was Sokrates' complaint in *Phaido*, the individual thinks that he himself is going through the modifications, but the indwelling *Ātman* does not go through any change. It is for this reason that the father of the new-born child chants this hymn during the Vedic post-natal ceremony:

> I create and sustain earth for you.
> I create and sustain atmosphere for you.
> I create and sustain heaven for you.
> I create and sustain the whole earth,
> atmosphere and sky for you.
>
> *Bṛihadāraṇyaka* Upanishad, Ch.6, Canto 4, v.25

In essence, the hymn declares that the *Ātman* indwelling in the father and the *Ātman* indwelling in the child are one and the same and that the Creation and all that it provides are but projections of this *Ātman*; it appears to change with the many forms it inhabits but it experiences no change, for it remains ever the same.

17

Law and Justice

The Greek and Vedic words for law or justice, *dikē* and *dharma* respectively, have a very wide gamut of meanings, and include the whole notion of conduct, righteous behaviour, mode of living, the final judgment and all aspects of the laws of Gods and men besides. As there are numerous levels in Creation, there are necessarily many levels and spheres of law, both natural and man-made, operating in the divine, causal, subtle and physical worlds. Greek *dikē* is from *dhātu diśa*, which has *dhātvartha atisarjane*,[1] meaning 'the act of giving away, granting liberality, killing, sending out of this world' and 'consigning to the flames, separation'.[2] Indeed the prime purpose of justice is to maintain liberality by curbing excess and abuses, and the purpose of justice is to purge sins and faults and the ultimate sanction is execution. The *dhātu* of *atisarjana* itself is *sṛja* which has *dhātvartha* of *visarga*[3] meaning 'letting go, liberation and final emancipation',[4] for freedom is protected by justice and gained by obedience to the laws of Creation.

Homer meant either one of two things by the concept of *dikē*: it was the mark or characteristic of acceptable or traditional behaviour, with some sense of 'proper behaviour' being implied: 'the Blessed Gods love not rash deeds, but honour *dikē* and the moderate deeds of men'.[5] The second meaning Homer ascribed to *dikē* is evidenced in the settling of disputes, as depicted on Akhilles' shield[6] and in the dispute over who won the chariot race.[7] Disputes such as these could be settled by *biē*, 'by force', or by *dikē*, 'peaceful settlement'; now *dikē* comes to mean settlement of a dispute or a ruling given in a dispute. In this system a third party called a *dikaspolon* proposes a *dikē* or settlement in order to resolve the *dikai*, the 'opposing claims'. The verb for this act of proposing a settlement is *dikazein*, and in the absence of a *dikaspolon*, one of the parties to the dispute must *dikazesthai* (middle mood), 'propose his own settlement'.

Hesiod's use of *dikē* is only for Homer's principal meaning, that is the ruling or settlement applied to a dispute. Hesiod's full meaning of *dikē* is given in *Works and Days* and can be divided into three distinct parts:

first, an appeal is made to his brother Perses to listen to *dikē* and avoid *hubris*;[8] under the influence of the former the land flourishes and under the latter Zeus sends disaster. Then an appeal is made to kings, as the agents of Zeus and *dikē*, to ensure the maintenance of straight justice, to punish crooked *dikai* and so keep the paths of *dikē* straight.[9] A final summation is made to Perses: listen to *dikē*, avoid *biē*; further *dikē* and prosper; impede *dikē* and Zeus will bring you low.[10]

The second part is of particular importance: *dikē* is opposed to *biē* and *hubris* and is connected with oaths and with kings who dispense *dikē*, and with Zeus who administers *dikē* and who with the help of his thirty thousand agents observes violations of *dikē* and sends appropriate punishments, thereby enforcing *dikē*. The passage as a whole is a strong plea for justice. Hesiod does not mean divine justice either but rather an effective legal process of 'law' and 'due legal process'. Hesiod made a radical extension to the meaning of *dikē*, towards a litigation process and system, in fact to the rule of law. This is not surprising when the purpose of *Works and Days* as a whole is taken into account, for the poem is about material prosperity and how to obtain it; this depends not just on willingness to work hard and basic practical knowledge, but also on a peaceful society, so that men may feel secure in the possession of the fruits of their labour.

Hesiod's working man does not engage in the ambitious rivalry for chivalrous purposes of the aristocracy, but in the quiet strong rivalry of work. In the sweat of his brow shall he eat bread but that is not a curse, it is a blessing. Only the sweat of his brow can win him *aretē*, for Gods and men hate him who lives without work. 'His nature is like the drones, who sit idle and eat the labour of the bees ... work is no shame, but idleness is a shame.'[11] Hesiod created a culture of *aretē* for a social class who were debarred from joining Homer's aristocratic virtues; Hesiod's achievement and influence in fact spread further than just the peasant class, for he also had great influence in the subsequent development of thought and philosophy.

The Theogony was not just the first and most important of the early Greek cosmogonical myths, which influenced Pherekudes and others; it was also the first attempt to produce a regulated order in Creation, to perceive a common foundation of all things and a system of stable relationships in the affairs of men. The quest to define *dikē* began at the outset of Greek civilisation, but it was in the classical period that the debate reached its zenith, particularly in the Platonic dialogues, principally *Gorgias*, *Republic* and *Laws*. The dialogue *Gorgias* sets out to define rhetoric, but its true purpose is to define the just life.

Polus, 'a young colt', asks Sokrates in *Gorgias* for his definition of rhetoric: 'an empirical knack in producing a particular gratification or pleasure' and such a definition applies equally to cookery, replies Sokrates, and he proceeds to his analysis of the four branches of

Kolakeia or 'spurious knowledge', as they apply to Body and Soul. Polus' amazement is complete when Sokrates proceeds to state that politicians do not exercise more power than anyone else, as oratory gives them no scientific understanding of *to beltiston* or 'the best', and consequently he cannot know what is best for himself nor know what he really desires and so his actions can only be based on what 'seems' good to him. Sokrates continues to make further propositions and gives their verbal proof: first, he points out that transitive and intransitive actions both aim at 'the good'; the agent always seeks 'The Good', and any action that results in harm to him does not reflect his will. Then, in response to Polus' question whether Sokrates would not like to have absolute power to kill and rob whom he pleased, Sokrates replies that power would be unenviable if it was used justly, and pitiable if used unjustly; 'it is better to suffer injustice than to commit it'. Thirdly, the wicked man is necessarily unhappy, but is unhappy if he goes unpunished. Thus Polus is forced to admit, fatally, that doing wrong is more *aiskhion* or 'more disgraceful' than suffering wrong, while maintaining that suffering wrong is *kakion* or 'more evil'. Sokrates continues the proposition that anything *kalon* or 'beautiful' is either *hēdu* or 'pleasant' or *ōphelimon* or 'happy-making' or both, and that if doing wrong is less *kalon* than suffering wrong, then it is either less *hēdu* or less *ōphelimon* or both; but it is not less *hēdu*, so it is less *ōphelimon* and therefore worse. Sokrates states again[12] that it is a greater evil for the wrong-doer to escape punishment than to be punished. Polus admits that what is just is *kalon* and *kalon* here is *ōphelimon*, which Polus claimed[13] was *agathon* or 'good' and so it is good for the wrong-doer to be punished. Finally, Sokrates concludes with a comic inversion stating that an enlightened rhetorician would get himself or family or friends punished, when necessary, or save enemies from punishment when wanting to harm them: needless to say, Polus finds these conclusions 'strange'.

The definition of *kalon*, however, is suspect as it fails to differentiate between *kalon* as it affects the object and the observer; secondly, Polus agreed unconsciously with Sokrates' substitution of *agathon* for *ōphelimon*: thirdly, Polus (like Gorgias before him) retires through *aiskhunē*, after his acceptance that doing wrong is [more] *aiskhion* than suffering wrong; no full-blooded hedonist would ever accept that point. And this is precisely the point that Kallikles, the main interlocutor, refuses to be browbeaten on. He brings to the proceedings precisely what is needed to blow away all the verbal victories Sokrates has won, namely, the view that the full-blooded Machiavellian doctrine that Might alone is Right, that power is the *telos* or 'goal' or chief good. He upbraids Sokrates for having falsely taken advantage of Polus' admission that committing wrong was [more] *aiskhion* than suffering it; what Polus meant was that it was [more] *aiskhion* by *nomos* or 'convention', not at all by *phusis* or 'nature'; *phusis* says that it is far more disgraceful to suffer wrong, that *hoi nomoi* or 'the laws' were invented by the weak to protect themselves from the strong, seeking thereby to impose a slave morality on all. The strong man breaks out of the bounds of conventions, becomes master, satisfies his desires and does whatever he will for his own pleasure, and therefore for his own good.

Sokrates proves that committing wrong is worse or uglier than suffering it *kata phusin* or 'according to nature' as well. The masses are stronger and therefore better than the individual *kata phusin*, and their law is *to ison ekhein* or 'to hold the mean', and violation of this is contrary to nature. Kallikles did not mean mere physical strength, otherwise slaves would have all the power; he meant the man who is *kreitton* or is *beltion* or 'better' and is *phronimōteros* or 'wiser'; and *beltion* is further extended to include the qualities of courage, which together with his intelligence enable a man to gratify all his pleasures; *akolasia* or 'laziness' is condemned only by those lacking these very qualities, which deny them the possibility to satisfy their every desire. Without any doubt, Kallikles' well-thought portrayal of the great immoralist has clearly brought the issues into focus between the philospher and the fifth-century Athenian politician. The principal issues are whether or not there is a true ethical base for actions, and whether true happiness depends on those actions, and consequently whether the man living according 'to law' or 'to nature' is on the right path to achieve his goal. Sokrates senses victory and at this point reminds Kallikles that he must not change his ground out of shame. Sokrates then enters upon his vulgar analogy; 'can a man who itches and wants to scratch and whose opportunities of scratching are unbounded be said to lead a happy life continually scratching? ... But suppose the itch were not confined to his head? Must I take the analogy further?'

Sokrates now proves that the ignorant feel as much pleasure as the wise, the coward as the brave, for both derive pleasure from seeing the enemy retreat. Kallikles in order to maintain his position cannot now relinquish his concept that pleasure and good are synonymous, but he is compelled to agree that some pleasures are better and others worse.[14] Sokrates takes this to mean that some pleasures are therefore good, and some harmful, and he extracts from Kallikles his agreement to the principle that since all actions ought to aim at The Good, pleasures are to be sought for the sake of what is good, and not what is good for the sake of pleasure, a matter which requires considerable discrimination. Thus Sokrates arrives at his fundamental view that knowledge is the aim of the just life and philosophy is vindicated; The Good for man depends on Self-control. Excellence, whether in a fool, an organism or the mind depends on the principle of order and that principle in the human mind is *sōphrosunē* or 'Self-control'. So human excellence, and consequently the Good of Man, depends on Self-control which produces *eudaimonia* or 'happiness'; Kallikles, however, is not persuaded. *Gorgias* is clearly not just about rhetoric; it concerns the moral basis of all actions as well as human happiness, and it contains the seed of the debate on true justice. The principal matter under dispute, which Sokrates reminds his co-dialecticians of at several points, is how a man should conduct his life. It starkly contrasts The Good and the pleasant, in the context of which one a man should follow, and shows that the solution of this depends upon knowledge and discrimination. It was Kallikles' refusal to accept that The Good was the pleasant that led to his downfall.

In *Republic* Book I, Sokrates attempts to define justice but reaches no firm conclusion, though the discussion enables him to deliver a subsequent description of the just man:

> In reality justice was such as we were describing, being concerned, however, not with the outward man, but with the inward, which is the true Self and concernment of man: for the just man does not permit the several elements within him to interfere with one another, or any of them to do the work of others; he sets in order his own inner life, and is his own master and his own law, and at peace with himself; which may be compared to the higher, lower, and middle notes of the scale, and the intermediate intervals when he has bound all these together, and is no longer many, but has become one entirely temperate and perfectly adjusted nature, then he proceeds to act, if he has to act, whether in a matter of property, or in the treatment of the body, or in some affair of politics or private business; always thinking and calling that which preserves and co-operates with this harmonious condition, just and good action, and the knowledge which presides over it, wisdom, and that which at any time impairs this condition, he will call unjust action, and the opinion which presides over it ignorance.
>
> *Republic*, Book IV, 443C-444A

In *Laws*, Plato gives proof that the Gods exist, that they are concerned with the fate of mankind and that they cannot be bribed by sacrifices. Plato planned a legal foundation for religion by incorporation of these three propositions into an unalterable legal code, imposing legal penalties on disbelievers. Plato's plans for counter-reformation were, however, not as influential as he had hoped.

The Sanskrit word for law is *dharma* and it has an extremely wide gamut of meanings, including: 'that which is established or firm, statute, ordinance, law; practice, customary observance or prescribed conduct, duty; right, justice; virtue, morality, religion; justly according to the nature of anything'.[15] *Dharma* means 'natural law' or the laws that sustain everything in Creation at all levels and in all spheres.

Consequently, the Indian tradition defines *dharma* as 'the command of the Lord'.[16] This is also referred to as the *Sanātana Dharma* or 'Eternal Way', by which realisation of the ultimate is achieved. For those who do not aspire to follow this higher *dharma*, the Upanishads decree imprecatingly: *jāyasva mriyasva*, meaning 'be born and die',[17] which is also a manifestation of *dharma*. *Sanātana Dharma* goes far beyond any concept of right and wrong, which are considered in the Vedic tradition as being only relative to each other, that is for the enlightened man who has realised the bliss of *Brahman*:

> Him indeed this remorse does not afflict:
> 'why did I not perform good deeds,
> and why did I perform bad deeds?'
> He who is thus enlightened [knowing *Brahman*
> as non-dual] knows both good and bad as
> identified with the Supreme Self.
>
> *Taittirīya* Upanishad, Ch.2. Canto 9, v.1

King *Parikshit*, the King of *Ayodhyā*, observed that human life is such that no one can escape from doing something 'wrong' in life, but the Vedic tradition embraces the purgatory powers of confession and resolution that can provide immediate release from the sinful deed, provided it is surrendered to the universe. In fact, it is impossible to describe *dharma* adequately without describing first the law of *karma* or 'action', for *dharma* is cause and universal effect and is closely related to *karma* which is action in the individual. *Karma* is from *dhātu kṛiñ* or [*ḍu*] *kṛiñ*, which has two *dhātvartha*, namely *hinsāyām* and *karaṇe*:[18] *hinsa* means 'injury or harm' and 'destruction'[19] and *karaṇa* means 'activity', which itself has *dhātu* [*ḍu*]*kṛiñ*.[20]

In *dharma*, the cause, the activity and the result are all united. An action may be prompted by a whim, by a gratifactory desire or by a firm resolution based on underlying knowledge, which knowledge is itself the product of *dharma*, and whatever the cause of the action, a result must follow. In the law of *karma*, actions are either *sakarmaka*, where the action and the fruit or residue of the activity are separated, or *akarmaka*, where the action and fruit of the activity are one. In *sakarmaka* activity, the subject or action desires an object or result, thus producing a separate *karma*, which itself has a complete cycle of activity which is capable of repetition; it is the same as *ahaṅkāra*, which in the cycle of space, time and the *guṇāḥ* keeps on repeating. *Aham*, however, is beyond time, space and the *guṇāḥ*, although the immanent presence of the Self is experienced within these measured concepts in an *akarmaka* state; there is no *sakarmaka* activity as such in *Aham*, for the knower of all knowledge cannot be known, as it can only be experienced in the *akarmaka* state.

In approaching the law of *karma*, it is necessary to begin with the meaning of *saṁskāra*, comprising the prefix *sam-* meaning 'harmonious unity' and *kāra* meaning a 'doer or actor',[21] also from *dhātu* [*ḍu*]*kṛiñ*. *Saṁskāra* therefore holds out the idea of a complete law governing all individuals' actions in their totality. The residue of each individual's past actions, including from previous lives, are held in the heart of the individual, in *citta*, as substances which form a husk or cloud around the heart, which obstructs the pure light of the *Ātman* which shines there. This is very similar to the Greek concept of *miasma* or pollution, or 'stain, taint of guilt or defilement', which was the actual or supposed presence of any substance, of whatever kind, which was believed to hamper a man's relation with the supernatural; for example, the greatest pollution was caused by homicide.[22] These substances constitute the secondary nature of the individual and form the subtle or unconscious mind of the *jīva* or 'being', which is carried over from one embodiment to another. These residues of past actions are called *sancitta karma* and a certain portion of this capital is advanced, so to speak, at birth and this advance is called the *prārabdha karma*, comprising those residues that are ripe for use. *Prārabdha* means 'what is begun, an undertaking' and also 'fate and destiny'.[23] Armed with this capital, the individual goes forth to meet his destiny, which is called *kriyāmāṇa*, the third aspect of *karma*, meaning 'an act of performance or execution'.[24] In short, the way in which the individual plays his role in the face of destiny and all that it presents him with is determining the nature of his future *sancitta*, in terms of purity and impurity, which will be potentially available for the next embodiment.

Sancitta is a precious substance, which is only available to those born into the human race; hence man is responsible for *sancit*. All the other 8,400,000 species of creature are only governed by *prārabdha karma* and they cannot create any *kriyāmāṇa* because they are not designed to be consciously responsible beings; hence the *Vedas* maintain that the animal and plant kingdoms are not responsible for their actions, for they simply suffer the misdeeds of past lives. Man alone is provided with the tools of consciousness, and he stands at the crucial point, where right use of consciousness leads to liberation from the cycle of birth and death and to realisation of truth, consciousness and bliss. The key to right action for man is to respond positively to conscious activities and to reduce all other activities, for every action has an equal and opposite reaction; in this way actions are either *puṇya* or 'meritorious', or *pāpa* meaning 'sinful', or partaking of both; that is they are either good, bad or indifferent.

There is a delightful story in *Rāmāyaṇa* about *puṇya*.[25] The *ṛishi Vasishṭha* went to *Viśvāmitra* and out of respect for him the latter gave *Vasishṭha* one half of the *puṇya* or 'virtue' which he had acquired during a long life of *tapas* or individual 'discipline'. *Vasishṭha* repaid the compliment and offered *Viśvāmitra* the *puṇya* from one *satsaṅga* or one 'conversation in good compamy'.[26] *Viśvāmitra* was upset and felt humiliated, but *Vasishṭha* claimed that his offer was greater. They went together to *Śesha*, the thousand-headed serpent beneath the earth, to adjudicate; the serpent said that as he carried the burden of the whole universe on his head, his mind was not light enough and that the burden would have to be lifted before he could give a true judgment. *Viśvāmitra* proposed to balance the burden against the remaining half of his *puṇya*, but the burden on *Śesha's* head could not be lifted. *Vasishṭha* therefore proposed that only one half of the *puṇya* from one *satsaṅga* be used to balance the burden, and this proved adequate and *Śesha* was temporarily released from his duty. *Viśvāmitra* asked for the judgment, but *Śesha* said that it had already been made, for the personal *puṇya* did not measure up to the *puṇya* of *satsaṅga*, the company of the good, which has the power to lift subtle burdens off those present. When *Śesha* had originally agreed to undertake his great task, *Brahmā* had said: 'O *Śesha*! O best of snakes! Thou art the God *Dharma*, because alone, with thy huge body, thou supportest the earth with everything on her, even as I Myself, or *Indra* can.'[27] For *dharma* or 'law' supports everything; it is from *dhātu dhā*, which is shown in the *Dhātu-Pāṭha* as [*ḍu*]*dhāñ*, which has the compound *dhātvartha* of *dhāraṇaposhaṇayoḥ*,[28] meaning 'preserving, protecting, maintaining' and 'nourishing and supporting'.[29]

This chapter naturally concludes with a comparison of the Vedic and Greek eschatological myths of the Day of Judgment. *Yama* is depicted in *Ṛigveda* and *Mahābhārata* as the Vedic God of death, the sovereign of the infernal regions; sinister and fearful, he judges the dead whom his messengers drag before his throne. He is the embodiment of *dharma* or 'righteousness' and the *dharma-rāja* or 'king-of-justice'. In the *Veda*, *Yama* is the First Ancestor and the king-of-Ancestors. He rules over the kingdom of the dead where the Ancestors dwell. He is *preta-rāja* or 'king of ghosts'. He has the full rank of a God, for *soma* is pressed for him.

The word *yama* means 'binder, restrainer'. *Yama* is from *dhātu yama* or *yam* after removal of the grammatical suffix. It has *dhātvartha uparama*,[30] meaning 'cessation, stopping, giving up and death'[31] and *pariveshaṇa*,[32] meaning 'waiting, surrounding and enclosing'.[33] It is *Yama* who keeps mankind in check: he binds, he decides what are the actions of the living beings that bear or do not bear fruit and he who controls all beings without distinction is *Yama*, the binder; as the *yamana* or 'restrainer' of men he is called *Yama*. *Yama* also means 'twin', for he is the God of death and of *daṇḍa* or 'punishment', the Eternal Law on which the universe rests, for 'the whole world rests on the law'. He is the judge, restrainer, and punisher of the dead. (The Greek word *zēmia* meaning 'penalty or punishment' is also from *dhātu yama*.) *Yama* is himself called *Mṛityu* or 'death' and *Antaka* 'the End'. He is *Kāla* or Time, *Kṛitānta* the 'Finisher', *Ṡamana* the 'Settler' and *Daṇḍadhara* the 'Rod-bearer'; as *Bhima-śāsana*, his decrees are dreaded. He is the noose carrier and Lord of Ancestors and Lord of Memorial Rites; as the ruler of the southern direction, *Yama* is also called Lord of the South.

Yama is of fearful and grim appearance, for his body is ugly and ill-shaped. He is of dark green complexion with glowing red eyes and dresses in blood red garments. His hair is tied on the top of his head and he wears a glittering crown. He holds a noose and a staff, and also carries an axe, a sword and a dagger. He rides a black buffalo and sometimes appears himself in the form of a buffalo. When identified with *Kāla* or 'Time', he is shown as an old man with a sword and a shield. In many stories he is, however, described as a handsome man: 'for a moment he saw a man clad in yellow, his tuft of hair bound. He was splendid like the Sun, of faultless blackness, beautiful, with red eyes. A noose in his hand, he inspired fear.'

The virtuous and the sinners see *Yama* in different forms. To the virtuous, he appears to be like *Vishṇu*: 'he has four arms, a dark complexion. His eyes resemble open lotuses; he holds a conch, a discus, a mace and a lotus. He rides on *Garuḍa* or the "Wings-of-Speech"; his sacred string is of gold; his face is charming and smiling; he wears a crown, earrings, and a garland of wild flowers. To the sinner, however, his limbs appear three hundred leagues long; his eyes are deep wells; his lips are thin, the colour of smoke and fierce; he roars like the ocean of destruction; his hairs are gigantic reeds, his crown a burning flame; the breath from his wide nostrils blows off the forest fires; he has long teeth and his nails are like winnowing baskets; stick in hand, clad in skins, he has a frowning brow.'

Yama's city is the *Samyaminī* or 'City-of-Bondage'. *Citra-gupta* or 'Manifold-Secret' is his scribe. His ministers are *Caṇḍa* or 'Wrath' and *Mahācanda* or 'Terror'. *Dhumorṇa* or 'Shroud-of-Smoke' and *Vijayā* or 'Victory' are his beloved ones. The place of judgment is below the earth. The messengers of death are his attendants who, dressed in black, have red eyes and bristling hair. Their legs, eyes and noses are like those of crows. *Yama*'s charioteer is *Roga* or 'Sickness'; he is surrounded with demons who are the different diseases, but there are also many sages and kings who assemble in his court to pay him homage, and musicians and heavenly dancers charm his visitors. At the door of the judgment hall is a guard called *Vaidhyata* or 'legality'.

When the Soul leaves the body, the messengers of *Yama* lead the tired being through a barren district without shade or water till he reaches the city of *Yama*. There the dead ones go alone without friends or family, but their deeds accompany them. After the record-keeper

Citra-gupta has read an account of the dead man's actions, kept in a book called *Agra-samdhānī* or 'Main Records', the Soul is brought to receive its sentence before the throne of *Yama* who appears gracious to the just, but fearful to the evildoers. The sinners, entering from the southern gate, have to pass a gate of red-hot iron and cross *Vaitaraṇī*, which is a fetid and boiling river called 'Abandonment', filled with blood, hair and bones and peopled with fearful monsters.

The righteous accumulate *puṇya* or 'merit from good deeds' and enjoy the fruits of heaven after death; they can stay there as long as the *puṇya* lasts and then the law of transmigration brings them back to embodiment on earth. Those who have not learned the goodness of righteous deeds accumulate *pāpa* or 'sin from unrighteous deeds' which can only be repaid after their death; they can only return to an embodiment on earth after going through the torments apportioned to them in hell. The cycle of transmigration continues until liberation is achieved by the wise men who have merged their being with the *Paramātman*, the Supreme *Ātman*, by the accumulation of *puṇya* that swamps the inevitable *pāpa* of human life. 'Confess yourself to heaven' advised the Bard; 'repent what's past, avoid what is to come, and do not spread the compost o'er the weeds to make them ranker. Forgive me this my virtue, for in the fatness of these pursy times, virtue itself of vice must pardon beg.'

The description of *Yama* at the final judgment is very closely paralleled in the Myth of Er by Plato,[34] a tale which is reminiscent of the Vedic concept of *saṁskāra*. Er was a warrior who fell in battle and his Soul was taken to the Kingdom of Tartaros, where the three judges of the dead presided, namely Minos, Rhadamanthus and Aiakos;[35] at his funeral, however, Er was detected still to be alive and so he was able to recount what he had seen, for he was not required to drink of the waters of the River of Lethe or 'forgetfulness'. Er said that there were two openings in the earth and two in the sky and the judges sat between them, and the just ascended by the heavenly way on the right hand and the unjust descended on the left hand. The just Souls were describing the heavenly delights of Elysium, while the unjust were weeping and sorrowful as they told of their journey beneath the earth, a journey which lasted for a thousand years, for they suffered tenfold for every wrong they had committed.

Seated around the Spindle of Necessity are found the three Fates, the daughters of Necessity, namely Lakhesis, Klotho and Atropos. Then an interpreter took from the knees of Lakhesis lots and samples of lives and mounting a high pulpit, said '... Mortal Souls, behold a new cycle of birth and death. Your genius will not be allotted to you, but you will choose your genius ... Virtue is free, and as a man honours or dishonours her he will have more or less of her; the responsibility is with the chooser. God is blameless'.[36] The spectacle of the Souls choosing alternatively the life of a tyrant and other evil lives was 'sad and laughable and strange; for the choice of the Souls was in most cases based on their experience of a previous life';[37] and the Souls that lacked philosophical training made unwise choices. The wisest choice was that of Odysseus, who searched for 'the life of a private man who had no cares'; he found it eventually, for it had been neglected by the other Souls, and he said he was delighted and would have chosen it anyway even if he had had the first choice.

After making their choice, the Souls went to Lakhesis, who ratified their choice; next Klotho turned the spindle and confirmed their destiny; and then Atropos spun the thread and made that destiny irreversible. Without turning round they passed beneath the throne of Necessity and proceeded across a dry plain in order to drink from the River of Lethe or 'forgetfulness' before their rebirth. Lakhesis is from the Greek verb *Lankhanō* meaning 'I obtain by lot or by fate' and *Atropos* is the negative prefix *a-* and *tropos* meaning 'a turn', so compounded they mean 'no turning back'. Klotho is from the verb *klōthō* which means 'I spin' and they are both from *dhātu grantha* which has *dhātvartha sandarbhe* and *bandhane*.[38] (It is worth noting once again how often the phonetic changes, here from *ga* to *ka*, are within the same *gaṇa* or 'category' of the Sanskrit alphabet, in this case the guttural category.) *Sandarbha* means 'weaving, collecting and mixing'[39] and *bandhana* means 'binding, fasting, holding fast; a bond, rope, tether; capturing, confining and mundane bondage'.[40] These are very apt *dhātvartha* for Klotho, for she binds into the Soul the effect of past actions according to the choice of life, and it is not suprising that this *dhātu* is also the *dhātu* for Sanskrit *granthi* which means 'the knots of the heart', the cumulative result of past actions which can only be dissolved by the due process of natural and divine law, clearing the way to freedom.

18

Eudaimonia and *Saccidānanda*

Herakleitos and Anaximenes were the first men in the western world to introduce the concept of Soul into philosophy. 'I searched Myself' was Herakleitos' own description of his method. Herakleitos' formulation of the relationship between the Soul and the universe is so complete and original it seems unlikely that he was following either Anaximenes or Pythagoras. Whereas the Milesian 'scientists' had been content to examine the natural world, Herakleitos was utterly dismissive of such an approach; he replaced their divine primary substance by a universal *Logos*; he was the first man to turn this key word to philosophic account and imbue it with a far deeper significance and meaning.

One of his departure points to explain the universal *Logos* was Anaximander's conception of the universe as an essential conflict of opposites, but there the similarity ends; it was precisely in these warring opposites that Herakleitos saw the key to the universal unity of *Logos*: 'Other men do not apprehend how being brought apart it is brought together with Itself; there is a *palintropos harmoniē* or "backstretched connection" as in the bow and the lyre'. The *Logos* spans the Creation but could not exist without this cosmic tension. In the physical universe, change is the law of all being: 'you cannot step twice into the same river'. This continually changing state is the law of all being, together with the perpetual conflict, and *Logos* must be found in this very condition. This represents the very antithesis of the Pythagorean search for the eternal and unchanging, for the two members of each pair in the opposites such as hot-cold, light-dark, male-female were equally natural and necessary for Herakleitos, whereas for the Pythagoreans only one of each pair was philosophically 'alive' or creative.

The Soul can understand Creation only by perceiving that behind these opposites there is the immanent *Logos* that orders all Creation, but it is hidden and not seen by ordinary men, as they fail to understand the relationship between *Logos* and their own Soul, which is essentially a relationship with unity. The universal *Logos* holds sway over the warring opposites and keeps them in balance: 'this world is the same for all beings; neither Gods nor men have created it; it always has been, it is and it always will be a living fire burning in the same proportion as it dies.' *Herakleitos* has taken another step in equating the universal ordering principle to an everliving fire, which is the common element throughout Creation: 'All things are changed into fire and fire into everything, just as merchandise is exchanged for gold and gold for merchandise.' The meaning of *Logos* now embraces not just reason or principle, but also proportion and measure as well; and in a particularly cryptic statement, the *Logos* is described as 'the thunderbolt' and 'the thunderbolt steers all things'; and the thunderbolt was the Self in the Vedic tradition. *Logos* rules the universe by its ability to give proportion and measure to the unceasing flow of the opposing forces in nature. It is the medium of exchange of all things into each other and this cyclic, ever-returning process is 'the way up and the way down'.

The relationship between the Soul and universal *Logos* and Fire is direct, for the Soul is composed of the ever-living fire. Consequently, 'a dry Soul is wisest and best'. The moist Soul is likened to a man who is drunk and 'for Soul it is death to become water, for water it is death to become earth; from earth water comes to be, and from water Soul'. Waking, sleeping and death are related to the degree of fieriness in the Soul; in sleep the Soul is partly cut off from the world-fire, and so decreases in activity. The important point is that virtuous Souls, partaking of fire rather than water, do not become water on the death of the body, but survive eventually to join the cosmic fire; hence Herakleitos states that 'Souls slain in war are purer than those [that perish] in diseases', for in war the spirit is roused to a fiery state. This is the first indication in Greek philosophy that the Soul has an ultimate aim to be reunited with that which is eternal. In this process, Herakleitos identified Self-knowledge and moderation as essential activities, a theme that was to be developed much more fully in the fifth century.

Herakleitos also propounded a cosmology in which the heavenly bodies are bowls of fire, which are nourished by exhalations from the sea, and the life of the cosmos is also regulated by *Logos*. This cosmology does not feature as an essential part of Herakleitian philosophy, which seeks rather to establish the Soul in the pattern of the physical universe and deduce knowledge of the best conduct of life from that relationship; the cosmological teachings are elementary and could not be classified as original, as compared say with his formulation of the opposition of contraries and the law of becoming that governs them.

Herakleitos stated that the 'real constitution of things is accustomed to hide itself' and 'human disposition does not have true judgment, but divine disposition does'. Herakleitos was dismissive of polymathic systems that employed extended prose and evolved his own style of short, concise, cryptic statements, that make use of etymologies, puns, antitheses and portmanteau words. His sayings, like Vedic sutras, were deliberately engineered to reflect the hidden reality of what they treated; they were meant to be reflected upon over a period of time, rather than read as prose, so that they might reveal that which is hidden. His sentences were formulae for exhibiting the reality of the intelligible principle of the universe not only in an external order like the Milesians, but primarily in the depths which the philosophic Soul discovers within Itself and cannot easily fathom because It Itself deepens them: 'You would not find out the boundaries of Soul, even by travelling along every path, so deep a measure does it have'. Herakleitos dived far deeper into these depths than any of his predecessors and he set the scene for Sokrates' and Plato's fuller analysis of Soul.

Eudaimonia and *Saccidānanda* in the Greek and Vedic traditions both refer to their respective perceptions of the perfect and natural state that subsists in the Soul, whether individual or universal. Plato's Myth of the Soul in *Phaidros* is one of the most inspired writings of all the dialogues and the grace of the Muses must surely have touched his brow when he wrote:

> Of the nature of the Soul, though her true form be ever a theme of large and more than mortal discourse, let me speak briefly, and in a figure. And let the figure be composite, a pair of winged horses and a charioteer. Now the winged horses and the charioteers of the Gods are all of them noble and of noble descent, but those of other races are mixed; the human charioteer drives his in a pair; and one of them is noble and of noble breed, and the other is ignoble and of ignoble breed; and the driving of them of necessity gives a great deal of trouble to him. I will endeavour to explain to you in what way the mortal differs from the immortal creature. The Soul in her globality has the care of inanimate being everywhere, and traverses the whole heaven in divers forms appearing: when perfect and fully winged she soars upward, and orders the whole world; whereas the imperfect Soul, losing her wings and drooping in her flight at last settles on the solid ground and there, finding a home, she receives an earthly frame which appears to be self-moved, but is really moved by her power; and this composition of Soul and body is called a living creature.
>
> *Phaidros*, 246A-B

The winged horses and the charioteer recall Plato's tripartite division of the Soul; the feeling and appetitive parts are the noble and ignoble steeds and the charioteer is the reasoning part. The wing is the nearest part of this 'mortal creature' to the divine, for it is the limb for the flight to the Gods. The wing is nourished by the divine beauty, wisdom and goodness and soars aloft, but if it is fed upon evil, it wastes and falls away. Plato then depicts Zeus holding the reins of the winged chariot of Soul and body as he leads the way, followed by the Gods and Demi-Gods. The chariot of the Gods glide rapidly, but the others suffer from the vicious steed who drags the Soul back to earth. This vision and symbolism is expressed in the *Veda* in similar terms:

> Know the Self [*Ātman*] as master of the chariot, and
> the body as the chariot.
> Know the intellect [*buddhi*] as the charioteer and mind
> [*manas*] as the bridle.
>
> They call the senses [*indriyāṇi*] the horses ...
> But the senses of that intellect become unskilful
> whenever associated with an uncontrolled mind,
> like the vicious horses of the charioteer.
>
> But of that intellect that becomes discriminating,
> being ever endowed with a controlled mind,
> The senses are controllable like the good horses
> of the charioteer.
>
> *Kaṭha* Upanishad, Ch.1, Canto 111, vv.3-6

Plato completes the myth of the revolution of the worlds in which the Soul beholds the Truth, for as he declares, he must dare to speak the Truth when Truth is his theme:

> There abides the very being with which true knowledge is concerned; the colourless, formless, intangible essence, visible only to pure perception, the pilot of the Soul. The divine intelligence, being nurtured upon mind and pure knowledge, and the intelligence of every Soul which is capable of receiving the food proper to it, rejoices at beholding reality, and once more gazing upon truth, is replenished and made glad, until the revolution of the worlds brings her round again to the same place. In the revolution she beholds justice, and temperance, and knowledge absolute, not in the form of generation or relation, which men call existence, but knowledge absolute in existence absolute; and beholding the other true existences in like manner, and feasting upon them, she passes down into the interior of the heavens and returns home; and there the charioteer putting up his horses at the stalls, gives them ambrosia to eat and nectar to drink.
>
> *Phaidros*, 247D-E

Plato's ambrosia and nectar is the supreme goal, which in the Vedic tradition is the all-pervading *Brahman*:

The man who has a discriminating intellect as his
charioteer, who controls the reins of the mind,
Attains the supreme goal, the highest place of *Vishṇu*.

Kaṭha Upanishad, Ch.I, Canto III, v.9

Eudaimonia or 'happiness' is a central theme in Aristotle's concept of how human life should be lived; *eudaimonia* means a 'good state of the Soul' and there was for Aristotle no exclusion of *hēdonē* or 'pleasant feelings' arising from external stimuli, provided they were not excessive. Aristotle regarded ethics and politics as parts of a single inquiry differing from science or first philosophy in that ethics has a practical aim, that is human 'happiness'. The object of the State, therefore, is to secure the good of the community as a whole. The best constitution is that in which every man, whoever he is, can act best and live 'happily',[1] although the number of people who can reach full virtue or happiness may be very restricted. The fact that ethics was essentially a practical affair was a marked development away from Plato, whose Theory of Ideas attempted to make the study of ethics and moral philosophy a scientific affair, in which knowledge would partake of something akin to mathematical accuracy. Plato's Ideas are stable and unchanging, but Aristotle sought to make men and their actions better, and so *ex hupothēsi* the material of ethical study is that which can be changed. Hence Aristotle frequently pointed out that ethics was not a branch of first philosophy, of *theōrētikē epistēmē* or 'contemplative epistemology' as opposed to *praktikē* or *poiētikē* epistemologies, but was really *praksis* or an 'empirical skill': 'the present inquiry does not aim at knowledge like our others. Its object is not that we may know what virtue is, but that we may become virtuous.'

The final goal of human life and the ultimate aim of all activity is 'happiness', the realisation of the '*aretē*' of man, which is the proper state of right condition for a mature man, namely *to anthrōpinon agathon* or 'the human good'; it is an activity, the *energeia* of man as such, commensurate with the function or *ergon* of man, and the early Greek idea that a man can only be happy when dead was totally alien to Aristotle's concept. Aristotle defines The Good for man as 'activity of Soul according to *aretē* or complete virtue'. Now man is partly emotional and sensitive and partly a rational being, and Aristotle distinguishes between two kinds of virtue of the intellect, *sophia* or 'theoretical wisdom', which is acquired by teaching, and *phronēsis* or 'wisdom', which comes from habituation,[2] and they are perfected by training and habit. *Aretē* or virtue is acquired by practising virtuous acts: *sophia* is a component of happiness and *phronēsis* is a productive agent that requires skill in intuitive application in given situations.

Few men, no doubt, will attain the higher intellect or virtue of *sophia*, but every man requires *phronēsis*. Virtue is what makes us aim at the right mark, practical intelligence is what makes us take the right steps to achieve the right end.[3] Aristotle does not lose sight of man's material predicament and states that a moderate supply of wordly goods is necessary, but he refuses to regard them as belonging to the essence of happiness.

A fuller definition of Aristotle's concept of *aretē* can be formulated: moral virtue is a state of character concerned with choice, lying in a mean relative to ourselves (*i.e.* not a rigid arithmetical middle), determined by a rational principle and in the way by which the man of practical wisdom would determine it. This doctrine of the mean was traditional in Greek popular morality, deriving from the Delphic injunction 'Nothing in Excess'. The general rule is that virtues and vices relate to affection and actions in which there is a scale of excess, intermediate and defect, with virtue lying in the intermediate between the two extremes.[4] Thus courage is a mean between cowardice and foolhardiness, temperance a mean between abstinence and self-indulgence, generosity between meanness and extravagance and so on; the important proviso is that the mean is always 'a mean relative to ourselves', varying according to the individual's temperament and general situation but always fixed for members of the same society in similar situations. Man is potentially good, with the *dunamis* of virtue inherent which may be developed into the *energeia* forming right habits. However, anything that is only potential is capable of developing in the opposite direction, as its matter or substrate may receive either the *eidos* or its contrary: man being potentially good is also potentially bad, so he must exercise his power of *proairesis* or 'choice'.

Aristotle has now arrived at the important matters of choice and responsibility and he maintains that each man is at least partly responsible for the settled state of character which he ultimately acquires, whether it be good or bad.[5] Greek thought generally did not treat with the notion of will, and Aristotle's analysis proceeds from a man's natural inclinations to virtue of character that does not arise by nature, but only after a careful process of habituation, from which process men emerge differently. Aristotle diagnoses three classes of action: first, *to hekousion* or 'voluntary', *to ouk hekousion* or 'non-voluntary'; then, *to akousion* or 'unwilling action', which may be either *to biaion*, meaning 'compulsory action', or actions taken in ignorance of particular facts. Man is largely governed by habit and after a certain time he no longer has the power to transform his disposition by any act of choice; but that disposition is none the less his and represents the prevailing trend of his past deliberate actions, a view which is very akin to the Vedic concept of *saṁskāra*. This view does not mean that Aristotle is defending Free Will, but it is some way from the Sokratic tenet that no one errs willingly.

Aristotle proceeds to analyse various types: the man of *phronēsis* or practical wisdom in whom habitual rightness of desire is combined with habitual validity of judgment is contrasted with the man who for various reasons fails to attain to steady pursuit of The Good; the logical opposite is the man in whom wrong desire is constantly allied to false judgment, and ends up pursuing *akolasia* or 'selfish pleasure, incurable self-indulgence'. Between these two poles there may be a man who retains true perception of The Good, but does not wish for it with such force that he does the right thing; his rebellious impulses are likened to an epileptic fit. Aristotle often said 'moral virtue makes us pursue the true end, practical wisdom enables us to take the right means'. For Aristotle pleasures are good, bad or indifferent according to the quality of the activities in which they are found. But in judging both the activities and the pleasures, reference must be made to the good man as the standard and measure of what is truly Good or truly pleasant. The conclusion of Book I of the *Nicomachean Ethics* was that 'happiness' is activity of the Soul according to virtue and in Book X it is activity according to the highest virtue, corresponding to the highest activity of the Soul or *nous*.[6] The activity of *nous* is *theōria* or 'contemplation', and 'the highest life and true end for man is divine in comparison with man, then life according to reason is divine in comparison with human life … we must, so far as we are able, make ourselves immortal, and do everything we can to live in accordance with the best thing in us',[7] namely the Soul.

The *Vedas* propound that the absolute substratum of being is *saccidānanda* (a compound of *sat* – *cit* – *ānanda* before *sandhi* or crasis), the threefold nature of being, where *sat* is the purity of being, *cit* is the consciousness of being and *ānanda* is the bliss of being, and the being is eternal. The Vedic substratum is very different from the Aristotelian, where the substratum, in the sense of matter, is ontologically inferior. The journey of the Vedic Soul through birth, existence and death remains forever in the fullness of *saccidānanda*, for it is stored in the causal body and awaits reactivation by memory, by the teaching or the teacher, just as the Sokratic doctrine of anamnesis was demonstrated by the example of *Meno*'s slave who recalled the construction of a square that is double the size of an existing square.

Saccidānanda can also be expressed in terms of pure consciousness, for it is the very substance of consciousness: *sat* is 'that which is'; *cit* is the 'consciousness of that which is'; and it is *ānanda* or 'the bliss' of which it is conscious. The knowledge of all three states is simultaneous and they never cease to exist. Now the *citta* is the light of the *Ātman* and has no force of its own, so the individual's failure to experience this state of consciousness called *saccidānanda* is caused by the stains or blemishes wrought by the individual's attachments, desires and habits, which have clouded the *citta* and reduced its power to reflect the pure light of the *Ātman*, so that we indeed see 'through a glass darkly'.[8] It is not the light of the *Ātman* which has lost power, but the knots of the heart which have diffused, filtered and deflected it, which is compounded by the claim of the individual to the reflected light that is still available, mistakenly taking this residue as his own actual source of the light, and unwittingly adding to his inner darkness by increasing the diffusion and deflection by this identification. The wise man, however, being free of desire and attachments, knows Himself as the source of the light and that *citta* is the reflector and so more knowledge and memory is available to him. This is akin to the state of Plato's winged Soul drawn by the noble steed, which soars effortlessly upwards.

The *sat* of *saccidānanda* is from *dhātu asa*, which has *dhātvartha bhūvi*, where *bhū* meaning 'being' is itself the first *dhātu* of all, with its *dhātvartha* of *sattā* meaning 'pure existence and reality'. *Cit* is from *dhātu cita* which is expressed in the *Dhātu-Pāṭha* with its grammatical suffixes as *ciṭa* and *citī*; they have four *dhātvartha*:[9] *sañjñāne* meaning 'consciousness and pure perception'; *parapreshye* meaning 'in service of another', for the *citta* serves the *antaḥkaraṇa* or 'the inner organs of action'; *smṛityām* meaning 'memory'; and *sañcetane* meaning 'to be fully conscious'.[10] *Ānanda* is from *dhātu nand*, which on account of grammatical rule changes is shown as [*ṭu*]*nadi* in the *Dhātu-Pāṭha*, having *dhātvartha samṛiddhau*,[11] meaning 'great prosperity, welfare and perfection'.[12] The Greek word *eudaimonia* comprises the prefix *eu-* meaning 'good' and *daimonia*, which has the same root and stem as in Sokrates' consultations with his 'inner *daimon*'. This word is from *dhātu daksha*, which has two *dhātvartha* compounds:[13] first, *vṛiddhau śīghrārthe ca*, where *vṛiddhi* means 'growth, prosperity and happiness',[14] (*ca* is the conjunct 'and') and *śīghra* means 'speedy or quick',[15] for the Soul is faster than the mind, or as the Upanishads declare 'the Self outruns pursuit'.[16] Secondly, *dhātu daksha* has the *dhātvartha* compound *gatihinsanayoḥ*, where *gati* may mean in this context 'origin, place of issue, motion manner or power of going, procession and condition';[17] *hinsana*, however, means 'killing',[18] which is harder to interpret as a state of the Soul, but the possibility cannot be left out of account that it may refer to the Soul's final procession or condition (*i.e. gati*) of reabsorption into the universal mind, for *hinsana* often carries the sense of dissolution into original substances.

19

'Madness in Great Ones'

Sokrates states that there are four types of madness, which are the greatest boon to men, provided they are given by the Gods. The first divine madness is prophetic frenzy, whose patron God is Apollo; then telestic or ritual madness, whose patron God is Dionysos; thirdly, there is poetic madness, inspired by the Muses; and lastly erotic frenzy inspired by Eros and Aphrodite.

> I told a lie when I said that the beloved ought to accept the non-lover when he might have the lover, because the one is sane and the other mad. It might be so if madness were simply an evil; but there is also a madness which is a divine gift and the source of the chiefest blessings granted to men. For prophecy is a madness, and the prophetess at Delphi and the priestesses at Dodona when out of their senses have conferred great benefits on Hellas, both in public and private life, but when in their senses few or none.
>
> *Phaidros*, 244A

Sokrates continues by stating that language links prophecy with madness, and therefore madness could not be a dishonour but rather there was an inspired madness, 'for the two words, *mantikē* and *manikē* are really the same and the letter *-t-* is only a modern and tasteless insertion'.[1] In fact, Greek *mantikē* or the 'faculty of prophecy', *mantis* a 'prophet', *mainomai* meaning 'I am mad' and *mania* or 'frenzy or madness' are all from root *mana*,[2] which has for its *dhātvartha* the important word *jñāna*,[3] meaning 'knowledge, especially the Higher Knowledge derived from meditation on the one Universal Spirit'.[4] The Upanishads declare that '*Brahman* is Truth, Knowledge and Infinity',[5] and this may be taken as the Knowledge of level one of Plato's Line, where pure perception reigns (see Appendix V). The *dhātu* for *jñāna* is *jñā*, which appears three times in the *Dhātu-Pāṭha* and which has *dhātvartha* which describe fully the *adhyātmavidyā* or 'science of Self-knowledge', which leads to an inner union arising from the natural application of knowledge.[6] Sokrates declares that this madness is superior to *sōphrosunē* or 'a sane mind', for the one is only of human, but the other of divine origin:

> Again, where plagues and mightiest woes have bred in certain families, owing to some ancient blood-guiltiness, there madness has entered with holy prayers and rites, and by inspired utterances found a way of deliverance for those who are in need; and he who has part of this gift, and is truly possessed and duly out of his mind, is by the use of purifications and mysteries made whole and exempt from evil, future as well as present, and has a release from the calamity which was afflicting him.
>
> *Phaidros*, 244D

Sokrates declares that the third kind of madness is possession by the Muses, which takes hold of a 'delicate and virgin soul, and there inspiring frenzy, awakens lyrical and all other numbers, with these adorning the myriad actions of ancient heroes for the instruction of posterity'.[7] But the poet who is not touched by the Muses' madness in his Soul comes to the door and thinks that he will get into the temple by the help of his art, but he and his poetry are not admitted. Sokrates states that the sane man disappears and is nowhere when he enters into rivalry with the madman:

> I might tell of many other noble deeds which have sprung from inspired madness. And therefore, let no one frighten or flatter us by saying that the temperate friend is to be chosen rather than the inspired, but let him further show that love is not sent by the Gods for any good to lover or beloved; if he can do so, we will allow him to carry off the palm. And we, on our part, will prove in answer to him that the madness of love is the greatest of heaven's blessings, and the proof shall be one which the wise will receive, and the witless disbelieve.
>
> *Phaidros*, 245B

The Platonic concept of *katokōkhē* or 'possession by the Muses' is indispensible to the creation of the highest forms of poetry, for the finest utterances are alone within the gift of the Muses. Demokritos even spoke of the power of poetic ecstasy, when the finest utterances were created *met' enthousiasmou* or 'with enthusiasm' and with *hierou pneumatos* or 'a holy breath';[8] now 'enthusiasm' here is *entheos* or 'the God within', as when the Pythia was *plena deo*, when the God entered into her body, mind and Soul and possessed her entirely, so that her utterances really were divine; in this state she was *ekstasis*, or 'standing outside' her body and ordinary intellect, in the sense that she witnessed as a detached observer from the activity that her whole being was an agent for the divine presence experienced within. This form of trance or ecstasy takes place in stillness and is quite different from the interpretation of ecstasy usually applied to Dionysiac rituals, where dance mania and collective hysteria generate a carefree and effusive condition, similar in some respects to the erotic frenzy inspired by Aphrodite, but these states do not approach *katokōkhē*. The word itself is derived from *katekhō* meaning 'I hold back, gain possession of or am master of',[9] where the prepositional prefix *kata* denotes 'motion from above'[10] and the verb *ekhō* means 'have or hold' when transitive, 'hold oneself' when intransitive and 'keep oneself back' in the middle mood.[11] The key to *katokōkhē*, it seems, is in 'holding oneself back', as in a state of absence of self, so that possession from above may fill the being.

There are only five states in which a man normally lives according to the Vedic tradition: the waking, dreaming, sleeping and unconscious states, and *samādhi*. In *samādhi*, consciousness only observes and no action takes place. *Samādhi* comprises the preposition *sam* – meaning 'altogether as one', always implying 'harmonious unity'; *-ā-* meaning 'fully' and *dhi* meaning 'here present'; *dhi* is from *dhātu dhyai*, which has *dhātvartha cintāyām*,[12] where *cintā* means 'direction of thought',[13] probably here in the sense of 'direction of attention'. So *samādhi* is the state of 'being fully present in the unity revealed by the consciousness which is the very expression and substance of the unity'. There is, however, one more state which is only experienced by the fully realised man, called *turīya*. This is a state of total stillness and of complete balance of the *Guṇāḥ*, when consciousness has no desire and in which no activity occurs:

> When the five senses of knowledge come to rest
> together with *manas* [discursive mind]
> And the *buddhi* [intellect] is not active either,
> That state is called *paramām gatim* [the highest state].
>
> *Kaṭha* Upanishad, 2,3,9

It is as though all Plato's triangles have come to rest in the form of the equilateral triangle, from which no movement can be derived. The *dhātu* for *turīya* is *tuḍi*, which has the most extraordinary *dhātvartha* of *toḍane*,[14] meaning 'splitting and dividing'.[15] Such a *dhātvartha* can cause a hiatus in the mind of the user and doubts may assail him as to the validity of the whole exercise! Familiarity with the *Dhātu-Pāṭha*, however, confirms it as a faithful guide and a good friend and so a closer examination is called for. In fact, the *dhātu tuḍi* really is the root of *turīya* and the *dhātvartha toḍane* is entirely appropriate, once it is realised that this condition is a dissolution of Creation where everything is dissolved back into the primordial substance, namely the *Brahman*.

Similarly, the Vedic tradition of the *Soma* juice which was drunk at ceremonies to celebrate the Gods does not imply that the *Ṛishis* were engaging in some drunken party or bacchanal. That there was a libation called *Soma* is not in doubt, for the ninth *Mandala* of *Ṛigveda*, which comprises one hundred and fourteen verses, is a song of praise to *Soma*. The juice was obtained by pressing 'one of the milk weeds or *asclepias acida*, probably *sarcostema viminalis*, which grows on mountains; the quality that grew on the Mujavat mountains being specially renowned'.[16] This drink probably imparted a temporary frenzy or ecstasy:

> O Thou, all-seeing, the illuminating rays of Thee,
> Who art the Lord, encompass all the dwellings;
> *Soma*, with Thy natural powers,
> Thou pervadest [the all] and flowerest,
> Thou art the King and Lord of Creation.
>
> *Ṛigveda*, Ch.IX, Canto 86, v.5

Whereas there clearly was a *Soma* juice, it is also clear that the *Ṛishis* inferred a revelation of the divine essence of which the drinking of *Soma* was a ceremonial symbol of the 'Self-surrender' or sacrifice to the Gods. The *Vedas* are in fact referring to the *rasa* or 'divine essence' or 'sweet taste of the *Brahman*'[17] that pervades the Creation but is known only by the connoisseur for it is always hidden behind the apparent form of everything. The God that presides over the *rasa* of life is *Soma* the Lord of Delight, which is the *ānanda* or 'bliss' of the *purusha* or 'Soul'.

> He tastes not that delight who is unripe
> and whose body has not suffered the heat of the fire;
> They alone are able to bear that and enjoy it
> who have been prepared by the flame.
>
> *Ṛigveda*, Ch. IX, Canto 83, v.1

The 'fire' and the 'flame' are the *tapas* or 'discipline' undergone by the worshipper as he follows the sacred instructions and gives up what he is not, namely the attachments to pleasure and identifications with the not-Self. Thus the *rasa* or sweet essence of the divine fills the being of the worshipper and is kept ready for the delectation of *Indra*, the Lord of the Mind who rejoices at the gift.

> We have drunk the *Soma*, we have become the immortals;
> We have attained the Light, we have discovered the Gods.
>
> *Ṛigveda*, Ch.IX, Canto 113, v.9

The conclusion must be that *rasa* is much more than just an intoxicating liquor; true, *Soma* is a wine, but it is the Wine of Immortal Delight which flows throughout Creation and in every living being, where it is kept alive and nourishes the *ānanda* or 'blissful essence' for which the very Gods are avid. This conclusion enables the symbolism of *Soma* to be explained more precisely. *Soma* was said to come from the mountains, which may be considered as standing for 'Creation and existence'; the peak of the mountains is higher consciousness, where the ecstasy of divine frenzy may be experienced by those who have reached the heights in their inner evolution of unity. The streams of *Soma* are the currents of *ānanda* which flow freely from the peaks, where there are no obstructions.

> This *Soma's* stream has come down from the loftiest heights, and discovered the rays of illumination in the wide spaces, hidden somewhere within the mountain [of being].
>
> This stream of *Soma* courses clear for thee, *Indra*, like lightning from heaven, thundering with the clouds.
>
> *Ṛigveda*, Ch.IX, Canto 87, v.8

The God *Indra* discovers the *Soma*, which is 'hidden somewhere', like the nest of a bird is concealed in a crevice in the rock, as the *rasa* can only be discerned by the connoisseur, by he who has undergone the fire of *tapas*, which awakens the God *Agni* within the being of the seeker; he clears the obstructions with his purgatory power of the thunderbolt and thereby enables *Indra* to enjoy the *Soma*. The *dhātu* of *rasa* is *rasa*, which has *dhātvartha śabde* and the compound *āsvādanasnehanayoḥ*;[18] *śabda* means 'pure sound'; *āsvādana* means 'the act of eating, tasting and enjoying' and *snehana* means 'unction' or 'anointment'.[19]

The *Soma* is held in the bowl called *śaryaṇāvat*, and this is the symbol of the inner sanctum of the heart, where the light of *citta* shines, that is the *citta* purified by *tapas*. The *Ṛigveda* states that the *Soma* flows in 'three extended strainers and once cleansed, is gathered into one'.[20] The 'three strainers' are *Agni* the God of Fire, *Vāyu* the God of Winds and *Sūrya* the Sun-God. *Vāyu*, as God of the vital airs, has brought *Agni* into the body and *Sūrya* has brought *Agni* into the mind of the *ṛishi*, and into still more conscious regions; thus *Soma* is filtered into the created being at all levels. The advent of these divine forces joins the consciousness of the purified mind to the vital airs of the original life-force and the way is open for the seeker to experience the spreading dawn of truth.

20

'That Thou Art' and 'Know Thyself'

The great message of Vedic and Greek philosophy is that the God of Creation is within the individual and that each individual is that God. This is the great truth, which is everyone's secret. There is no need for the individual to look for God outside himself or herself, or to look to heaven, or least of all to the Gods of others. The Vedic statement to affirm this great truth is '*Tattvamasi*', meaning 'That thou art', meaning 'Thou art that *Brahman*'; *tat* refers to 'the Supreme Self', *tvam* refers to 'the embodied Soul' and *asi* means 'thou art'. The corresponding Greek tenet is the imperative command '*Gnōthi seauton*', or 'Know Thyself', which in Vedic terms might be expressed as 'Know Thyself as the God within'. These two mighty sentences belong to a series of sutraic statements. In the Vedic tradition, the *Advaita* system of Non-duality is expounded from the five seats of *Śaṅkara* in India, one at each point of the compass and one at the centre, with the northern seat having been founded by the first *Śaṅkarācārya*. There are four great sentences from the *Veda* which are carved on each of the five thrones of *Śaṅkara*, and they are the great *ex cathedra* statements of the truth:

Tattvamasi	'Thou art that [*Brahman*]'
Prajñānam Brahmā	'The consciousness is *Brahman*'
Ayam Ātmā Brahmā	'This [indwelling] *Ātman* is the *Brahman*'
Aham Brahmāsmi	'I am the *Brahman*'

These sentences are for recitation and reflection, for they express the *Veda* in the pure language of Sanskrit and contain the power to assist the enquirer on the path to realisation of the Self, which is the *Brahman*. These *mahāvritti* or 'great sayings' are axiomatic sutras that require no proof in the Vedic tradition, where they are treated as *upadeśa* or 'received wisdom' or 'given truths'. They come from the Upanishads related to the *Sāmaveda*, *Ṛigveda*, *Atharvaveda* and *Yajurveda*, respectively.

The *Dhātu-Pāṭha* informs further on these sutras. The verb *as* meaning 'to be', which appears in the first and second persons singular of the present indicative as *–āsmi* and as *–asi* in the fourth and first of these *mahāvritti* respectively, is from *dhātu asa*,[1] which has *dhātvartha bhūvi*: after removal of the locative case ending *–vi*, it is *dhātvartha bhū*, meaning 'being'; *bhū* is both a *dhātvartha* and a *dhātu*, being the very first *dhātu* of all,[2] where its *dhātvartha* is *sattā* or 'goodness' or 'reality'. The clear meaning of *as* or 'to be' is that it is the very essence of 'isness', and in this context means 'that which you really are' which is found in 'reality, purity and in each existence' as a manifest expression of the *Brahman*. 'It Is' or *asti* means existence, and the explanatory term for the philosophical connotation is *avikṛita pariṇāma*, meaning 'unchangeable, changeable',[3] for that which is immutable and untransformable is nevertheless seen manifesting, expanding or procreating and continuously changing. This apparent paradox is resolved by the distinction between that which does not go through any substantial change and is ever Itself in the eternal present, and the forms, which are extensions and expansions of being which change within that which exists. The analogy is drawn in the Vedic tradition between gold and the ring: the ring is fashioned out of gold and assumes its circular form, but when melted down again it reverts to being gold; the form arises from the substance and returns to it.

The command *gnōthi*, as in the Delphic inscription *Gnōthi seauton*, is the second person singular of the aorist imperative of the Greek verb *gignōskō* meaning 'I know', which is from *dhātu jñā*,[4] as is *prajñānam* in the second *mahāvritti* of 'the *prajñānam* or consciousness is *Brahman*'. The root *jñā* has three *dhātvarthas*, including *avabodhane* and *niyoge*;[5] *avabodhana* means' informing, instructing' and 'knowledge, perception', and *niyoga* means 'injunction, order, command, appointed duty, necessity, obligation'. For as the Upanishad declares:

> All this Creation has consciousness as its impeller,
> In consciousness it is established,
> The World is revealed by consciousness,
> Consciousness is its support, consciousness is the *Brahman*.
>
> *Aitareya* Upanishad, 3,1,3

The indication of the meaning of the *dhātu jñā* and its *dhātvarthas* (from which root the Greek verb *gignōskō* is also derived), might imply that an extension of 'Know ThySelf' could be: 'Know Thyself as the consciousness which causes, pervades and upholds the Creation, which is *Brahman*'. Whereas there is no *dhātu* for personal pronouns such as Greek *se* (as in *se-auton*) or in any other language, the third person of the pronouns in many languages, including Sanskrit, Greek, Latin, French, German and English, are often from the same phonetic articulation, and in these languages a sibilant, such as *sva* in Sanskrit, is the sound of the Self; English even speaks of the 'swan song', when the Self is ready to quit the mortal coil, and *dhātu svana*[6] meaning 'to sing' has for its *dhātvartha śabda*,[7] meaning 'pure sound'.

'This *Ātman* is the *Brahman*' states that the indwelling Self is the Supreme Spirit. *Ātman* is variously derived from *an*, meaning 'to breathe', *at*, meaning 'to move' and *vā*, meaning 'to blow', and itself means 'the Soul, the principle of life, the individual Soul or Self' and 'the breath';[8] *dhātu an* also provides the Greek *autmē* or 'breath' and *aēmi* 'I breathe', and Latin *animus* or 'spirit' and *anima* or 'breath', for with the Soul comes the first breath and it departs with the last.[9] (Curtius maintains that the Greek *psukhē* for 'Soul' derives from *dhātu sphu*, shown as *sphuṭa* in the *Dhātu-Pāṭha*,[10] which has *dhātvartha vikasane* meaning 'developing, expanding, opening, blowing' and *bhedane* meaning 'breaking, dividing, separating, causing to flow',[11] but he points out that 'the original root *spu* returns with metathesis in *psukhē*'.) The *Brahman* is 'the one Self-existent impersonal Spirit, the one universal Soul or one divine essence and source from which all created things emanate and to which they return, the Self-existent, the Absolute, the Eternal'[12] and 'the Supreme Being, regarded as impersonal and divested of all quality and action'.[13] *Brahman* is from *dhātu bṛiñh* which means 'to roar'.[14] On account of a grammatical rule change,[15] it appears in the *Dhātu-Pāṭha* as *bṛiha*,[16] and has *dhātvartha* compound of *vṛiddhau śabde ca* meaning 'expansion and sound', with *vṛiddhi* also meaning 'the lengthening of vowels'[17] and *bhāshārthaḥ* meaning 'speech': so the activity of *bṛiha* is the spoken word manifesting as Creation, which is the projection of the indwelling Self of every *purusha* or 'individual Soul'.

The injunction 'Know Thyself' is the most famous inscription carried above the entrance to the temple of Apollo at Delphi, and is constantly invoked throughout Greek philosophy, usually accompanied by that other great dictum of 'Nothing in Excess'. In fact, there were many such sutras carved above the temple's entrance and several lists of these precepts exist. This list is an abstract from the third-century B.C. inscriptions from Miletopolis in Mysia:[18]

Gnōthi seauton	'Know Thyself'
Mēden agan	'Nothing in Excess'
Peras epitelei	'Observe the Limit'
Thumou kratei	'Subdue thy Spirit'
Hubrim meisei	'Despise Hubris'
Euphēmos ginou	'Keep a Reverent Tongue'
To kratoum phobou	'Fear Authority'
Proskhunei to theion	'Bow before God'

The concept of measure and proportion was fundamental to the whole of Greek philosophy. 'Nothing in Excess' and 'Observe the Limit' were the encapsulation of a philosophic concept that branched into practically every aspect of the fully formed Greek and Vedic traditions, whether it was measure in use of the senses, measure in the combination of the elements, measure in the mixture of pleasure and pain or proportion in mathematics and architecture. 'Subdue thy Spirit' is an approximate translation only of *thumou kratei*. The Greek word *thumos* defies exact translation into English, but the dictionary gives 'soul, spirit, the principle of life, feeling and thought',[19] which is very close to the Vedic concept of the *ahaṅkāra*, the *aham* in Creation, where the ego believes it is the doer and identifies with the action. *Thumos* and *thuō*, meaning 'I sacrifice' or 'I rage' (and Latin *fumus* or 'smoke' which is caused, for example, by the burnt offerings at sacrifices) come from the root *dhū*,[20] which has for its *dhātvartha* the word *vidhūnana*, meaning 'causing to move', and, as Plato stated, all movement comes from the Soul, the eternal unmoving. Of the remaining Apolline sutras that have been selected here, the concept of Hubris and its contradictory Nemesis stand out, meaning 'wanton violence, arising from the pride of strength or from passion'[21] and 'retribution, especially righteous anger',[22] respectively. This pair is a peculiarly Greek concept and is a sub-corollary of 'Nothing in Excess' and 'Subdue or Curb thy Spirit'. The remaining sutras speak for themselves, but the injunction '*Proskhunei to theion*' or 'Bow before God' is expressed in all great cultures and is a direct translation of the offering sounded at the start of all the Vedic hymns and texts, namely *paramātmane nama*, meaning 'to the Supreme *Ātman*, a bow'.

The relationship between 'Know Thyself' and 'Nothing in Excess' needs to be examined closely. 'Nothing in Excess' is a clear enough injunction in itself, pointing to the mean in all things as being the least likely to cause any harm. There is however a problem: man is full of appetites and these are entirely natural, but no appetitite or craving of the senses can ever be completely satisfied, for it is impossible to make use of each and every thing in Creation. An unrestrained tendency to pursue satisfaction inevitably leads to excess and excess causes misuse of energies, discrimination is weakened and the trend from finer to coarser is confirmed. The avoidance of excess as a philosophic discipline brings the relationship between senses and objects away from the coarse realm and back to the subtle realm.

The Vedic symbol for the subtle relationship between senses and objects is fire and butter: the more butter that is poured on the fire, the more the fire burns, 'as if increase of appetite had grown by what it fed on'. The aim is not, however, to put out the fire by depriving it of butter, for both senses and objects would then become useless. The point of this symbolism is that the relationship between senses and objects is not overtly either inward or outward-looking; the inner is eternal and is therefore independent, whereas the outer waits on time, space and the qualities and is therefore dependent. The philosopher appreciates this universal system and therefore works to become dependent on the Self, without which there is nothing, for in *prajñā* or 'consciousness' there is no division, no form, not even beauty, but only bliss. How is this journey to the Self to be accomplished? As the desire to know the Self strengthens and the enquirer feels the pull of the philosophic way, there is a natural reorchestration of energies towards the finer, and as the coarse begins to lose its hold, its strength becomes increasingly available instead to *buddhi* or to the 'organ of discrimination'.

Measure assumed a pivotal role in Plato's philosophy and became appreciation of the arts and the intuition which inspired the philosopher even in his most exactly regulated disciplines.[23] The main aim in the dialogue *Philēbos* is to discover what is 'a fair and perfect mixture' and what can best 'enable us to divine what is the essence of Good for man and for the whole universe'.[24] Now standing in the antechamber of the dwelling in which The Good is hidden, is seen first 'Measure', as a condition of the conservation of 'The Mixture' of pain and pleasure, then 'Beauty or Excellence' as an expression of the 'proportional fitness' by which 'The Mixture' is perfect, and lastly 'Truth', as the condition of ontological reality. These are the three Forms which are each related to the 'The Good', 'The Cause of the Mixture' and 'The Goodness of the Mixture'.[25] There will be a doorman, says Plato, who will admit only those pleasures which are both 'true and pure', that is not mixed with pain, for the essence of false pleasure is the 'absence of measure'.[26] The retreat from excess enables the enquirer to measure out the uses of the world and to evolve the unity within, which is the way of illumination, the dissolution of ignorance and the dawn of wisdom. Knowledge of the Self is a result of measure and provides knowledge of all things, which is why the sutras 'Know Thyself' and 'Nothing in Excess' inscribed on the temple of Apollo at Delphi are traditionally mentioned together and take pride of place before all others.

It is time to return to examine more closely a statement on the discovery of the Self from the first Chapter, namely: the 'Self discovering the Self through the Creation' when 'the ordinary mind's activity has stepped aside'. In the ordinary state of waking consciousness, the mind habitually divides Creation into subject and object, into 'I' and 'that', into the observer and the observed. This structure of automatic evaluation into subject and object becomes so embedded in psychological memory by force of habit that it continually presents what is past at the expense of the timeless present and also asserts itself as the natural working of what is loosely called the mind, when actually it is the enslaved and mechanical state.

This mind, being a living creature, struggles for psychological survival in the sense of strengthening its imagined independent existence by identifying, laying claims and building defensive barriers of conflicting ideas, of pleasure and pain, of good and bad, of right and wrong, of who and what is acceptable and unacceptable.

This collection of defensive habitual patterns is called the 'knots of the heart' in the *Veda*:

> When that Self, which is both cause and effect,
> Is realised, the knot of the heart gets untied,
> All doubts become resolved,
> And all one's actions become diminished.
>
> *Muṇḍaka* Upanishad, Ch.2, Canto 2, v.8

Śaṅkara's commentary on *Muṇḍaka* Upanishad says that the *granthi* or 'knots of the heart' are 'the host of tendencies and impressions of ignorance, in the form of desires that hang on to the intellect, which are based on the heart's desire and not on the Self'; the process of 'untying' is essentially one of elimination rather than accumulation, of undoing the doing.

> When all the knots of the heart are destroyed,
> Even while a man is alive,
> Then a mortal becomes immortal.
>
> *Kaṭha* Upanishad, Ch.11, Canto III, v.15

Just occasionally, but it seems all too rarely, there may be the experience of just observing, just listening and just being; in these conditions, the mind has been freed from the duality of subject and object and the attention is wholly in the activity of observing: this state of incipient unity can only arise when body and mind are still and at peace, when the being is content with whatever is presented and above all when attention is wide open, directionless, without any anticipation and innocent:

> Hence, he who knows this, who is at peace,
> calm, quiet, patient, sees the Self in Himself.
> He sees the Self everywhere.
>
> *Bṛihadāraṇyaka* Upanishad, Ch.4, Canto 4, v.23

Through grace, the observing or listening may in turn be seen as yet another object; then the Self is revealed as pure consciousness, which is the observer. As the knots of the heart dissolve, discrimination grows and passes through the five sheaths of body, mind, *buddhi*, *citta* and finally *ānanda māyā kośa*, the state of *ahaṅkāra* where the face of truth is covered by a golden glow. One after another the barriers of these sheaths are broken and the lover reaches the state where Creation, Creator and the Self seem to be One, that is *Ātman*, 'I Am'. This is a state of conscious activity, which has no subject and no object but is just the activity itself, remarkably similar to the activity of Aristotle's God, and is expressed in the Upanishads as follows:

> That which with the eyes he does not see;
> That through which with the eyes he does see,
> Thou should know that indeed is the *Brahman*,
> Not that which is worshipped [as an object of perception].
>
> *Kena* Upanishad, Ch.1, Canto 6, v.7

The Upanishad declares that seeing and hearing, and every other activity in Creation, are universal activities at the level of the Self. When the subtle mental activity is continuously at the level of 'I am seeing it' or 'I am hearing that', then it is the subject and not the Self that is seeing or hearing; the Self can only see and hear when 'I' and 'It' and 'that' are dissolved in the activity, when there is just seeing and just hearing brought about by attention when it is not directed by any subtle thought in the form of a desire or intention to a particular target or goal.

The attention is directionless when the seen or heard is dissolved in the seeing or hearing, thereby releasing the subject or observer from the action; the subject loses its separate identity when the seeing is also seen as an object, for the seen refers to the seeing, the heard refers to the hearing and likewise with tasting, touching and smelling. When these universal actions are all seen as objects, the observer stands in pure consciousness, which is its own substance and in which the idea of observer is finally dissolved.

This subjectless vision is only partly akin to the Platonic *hē noēsis* or 'pure perception', 'pure' in that it does not rely on the senses. In this state the Soul surveys the 'very being with which true knowledge is concerned: the colourless, formless, intangible essence, visible only to *nous*, the pilot of the Soul',[27] for Plato still preserves the individual Selfhood. The precise moment when the sense of the subject and object dissolve in an universal activity, when duality is banished and *Advaita* or 'Non-duality' is present, is not a mark that can be striven for or aimed at, nor is it a state that can be created, for it is the natural state that already subsists. This is set out in two further *mahāvritti* that complement the four already mentioned:

> I shall behold that blessed form of thine;
> For that person *aham* [am I].
>
> *Īśā* Upanishad, *śloka* 16

All this alone [*Idam*] is of the nature of the Self.

Chāndogya Upanishad, Ch.VII, Canto 26, v.1

Aham and *idam* are both *Brahman*, so every one and every thing in Creation is *Brahman*; so the inescapable corollary is that there is a universal fact of living, but there is no separate entity who lives, as is so fondly supposed and continuously assumed. This moment of insight appears, as the Upanishad declares, when the Self seeks out the enquirer and reveals its true nature.[28] This seeking without a seeker requires waiting without wanting, obeying the measures, allowing the knots in the heart to unfold, chanting the sacred hymns to dispel the darkness, gathering in good company, dying without death and being born without birth, until the Self comes in its own good time and is revealed by the Goddess of the Undifferentiated in its full majesty, power and glory.

Tomorrow, and tomorrow, and tomorrow
Creeps in this petty pace from day to day
To the last syllable of recorded time,
And all our yesterdays have lighted fools
The way to dusty death. Out, out, brief candle.
Life's but a walking shadow, a poor player
That struts and frets his hour upon the stage,
And then is heard no more. It is a tale
Told by an idiot, full of sound and fury,
Signifying nothing.

Shakespeare, *Macbeth*, Act 5, Scene 5

Epilogue

Veda is expressed by an oral tradition that was fully formed before being committed to writing; but *Veda* is a complete system of knowledge, that requires neither expression in speech nor in writing in order to be what it is. Being expressed as an oral tradition, however, it is neither possible to date it with any accuracy nor to ascribe authorship in the sense of naming an original author with any certainty that he was a particular man. The Greek and Judaeo-Christian civilisations do not share these two attributes, for precise authorship and accurate dating is very common. The fascination of the comparative approach is to have the fully formed picture of the *Veda* as a backcloth against which to study the development of the Greek culture over a short period of several hundred years, as the Hellenes developed their views of man and the universe towards an integrated philosophy that touched the *Veda* at many points and is indeed an expression of the *Veda* as regards many of its essential concepts. The joy of studying the evolving Greek philosophy from the Milesian Hylozoists through to Sokrates, Plato, Aristotle and Plotinos, who recombined Aristotelian noetics with the Platonic treatment of the sensible world as an image, is that there is a strong sense of watching the continuous development of 'one man in many embodiments' as he seeks out the truth about Creation and Himself.

The sheer number of concordances between the Indian and European traditions, whether in philology, linguistics, myths, epics, symbolism, polytheism, cosmologies, epistemology, philosophical systems and expressions of the way, the truth and the life is so astounding that it poses the question of how two apparently different civilisations could have shared so extensively in such commonality. If it is accepted, however, that the Vedic tradition is much older than the Greek, then the question becomes: how did the Greeks, pursuing the expression of their civilisation in an apparently unrelated development, incorporate or assume so much of the Vedic tradition into their own culture?

There is no doubt that the Indian and Vedic civilisation is the oldest in the Indo-European tradition, for the earliest date that can be ascribed to Homer is the ninth century B.C., nearly three thousand years ago, whereas the *Veda* is so old that it cannot even be dated;

historical research, in seeking precise dates, falls into the trap of looking for written texts, which may be derived from an oral tradition; but before them both exists that from which the oral tradition is derived, which is called *Veda*. Traditionally, *Veda* is said to have come with the Creation, in which case it could not possibly be dated unless an astronomer calculated how many *mahāyuga* or 'great ages' have passed in the reign of the current *Brahmā*, which is a very great number of years. That the oral tradition of India is ancient is also attested to by its great strength, in the sense that the *Veda* is complete and free of textual dispute. In short, it has withstood and passed the supreme test of time with consummate ease. However, the *Veda* declare that in the iron age, of which the current one has now run for over five thousand years, man's memory declines and the tradition has to be recorded in writing so that it can be remembered; by comparison, Homer's songs alone survived the eclipse of the rest of the Greek epic cycle, but for only two or three hundred years as an oral tradition before being committed to writing.

The Vedic tradition, although the oldest, has still survived intact in the Sanskrit language, which alone has the purity and refinement to express *Veda* fully. The fact that its vowels are pure, its consonants are divided into the five natural places of utterance, its alphabet is complete and its laws of grammar are the most articulate and fully refined of all languages, indicate that it is the forerunner of the other Indo-European languages which are derived from it, but in their derivation, these other languages suffer reduction in all these attributes of Sanskrit and do not have the same power to express *Veda*.

Nowhere is the role of Sanskrit in language clearer than in its expression of the root system; it is truly amazing how the key philosophic words in more recent languages are derived from roots expressed in Sanskrit. The fact that they are roots of the Indo-European system is indicative of their influence in the development of European civilisation, not just as roots of language, but as carriers of the ideas expressed in them. In fact, language and commerce were clearly the means by which Vedic ideas spread westwards to the Near East, *Magna Graecia* and on towards Western Europe and there is evidence of commercial exchanges between India and Greece during the second millennium B.C. (see Sedlar, especially ch. 1). For what other explanation could there be for the concordances discussed in this edition, such as the description of stringing the bow by both Vedic and Greek heroes; or the Upanishad's description of the Charioteer and the two horses, which reappears in Plato's *Phaidros*; or the myths of the dead, of Er and of *Yama*?

This whole universe is created by sound, which is causal throughout all aspects of Creation. Man is made in the image of God, for he alone amongst creatures has the gift of the power of speech. All communication, teaching, learning and knowledge depend on speech. And speech is the manifestation of the finest energies in man. In the Vedic tradition, the Goddess of Speech is *Sarasvatī*, meaning 'the ever-flowing utterance of creative speech', for she speaks Creation into existence and is the Goddess of this special medium for the communication of Truth, Knowledge and Experience, which are *Veda* for all mankind.

APPENDICES I-V

APPENDIX I

The Enneagram

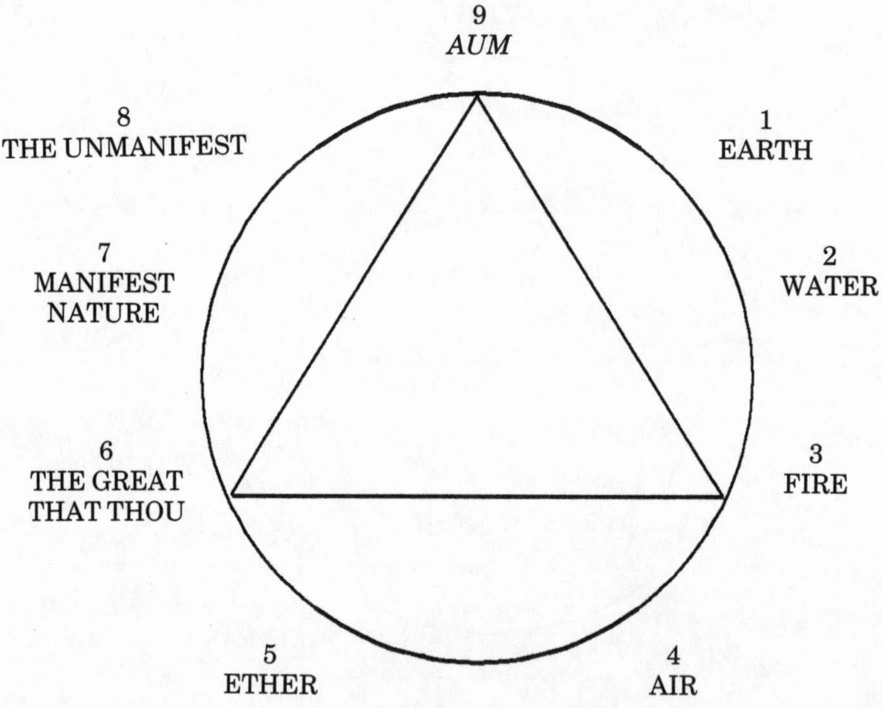

THE LAW OF THREE

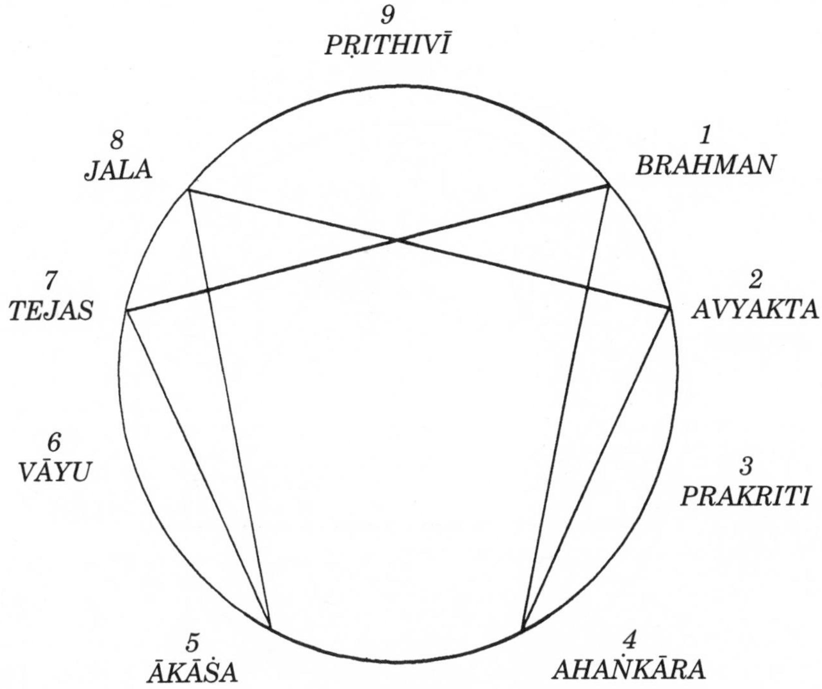

THE LAW OF SEVEN

APPENDIX II

The *Pañcīkaraṇa* System

Ether:	Ākāśa	=	1/2 Ether,	1/8 Air,	1/8 Fire,	1/8 Water,	1/8 Earth.
Air:	Vāyu	=	1/2 Air,	1/8 Ether,	1/8 Fire,	1/8 Water,	1/8 Earth.
Fire:	Tejas	=	1/2 Fire,	1/8 Ether,	1/8 Air,	1/8 Water,	1/8 Earth.
Water:	Jala	=	1/2 Water,	1/8 Ether,	1/8 Air,	1/8 Fire,	1/8 Earth.
Earth:	Pṛithivī	=	1/2 Earth,	1/8 Ether,	1/8 Air,	1/8 Fire,	1/8 Water.

APPENDIX III

Veda and *Vedāṅga*

Veda means 'knowledge', which in the Indian tradition was given with the beginning of Creation. *Veda* existed for millennia as an oral tradition and could be held in the mind of man. With the passing of the four *yuga*, however, the consciousness of mankind diminished, and it became necessary to record the *Veda* in writing in order to assist human memory. About five thousand years ago, at the beginning of the iron age, *Vyāsa* recorded the *Veda*; his name means 'compiler' and he is a celebrated mythical sage representing the *Ṛishi* and Seers who compiled the written testaments to the *Veda*. *Veda* is the eternal knowledge rather than these written testaments, though the latter embrace a well defined *corpus operum* within the greater Vedic tradition, beginning with the *Ṛigveda*. This does not imply, however, that *Veda* is limited to this *corpus*, for other works also carry the subtle sound of the Vedic systems of knowledge. Hence, certain works of Herakleitos, Plato, Plotinos, Boethius, Shakespeare, the Book of Common Prayer and the Authorised Version of the Bible can be considered as giving expression to *Veda*.

The four principal branches of the *Veda* are the *Ṛigveda*, a metric hymn of praise which sets out right conceptions, thoughts and interpretations, which are intended for loud recitation; the *Yajurveda*, which are prose hymns of praise dealing with worship of the Gods and rituals, are intended for chanting in lower tones at sacrifices; *Sāmaveda*, which are metric chants, dealing with unity and harmony, are intended for sounding with lower tones at *soma* and moon ceremonies; and *Atharvaveda*, which are hymns combining the essence of the other three *Veda* in a most subtle form, sing of *turīya*, a state of complete balance of the *Guṇāḥ*, in which consciousness has no desire and the idea of 'doing' is absent. (The common assertion that this last *Veda* was a later collection is probably an incorrect notion.)

The four principal *Veda* are *śruti*, meaning they are direct revelations of the *Brahman* or 'Supreme Being'. From the four *Veda* are sprung the *Brāhmaṇas* and *Āraṇyakas*, which are also *śruti*. The *Brāhmaṇas* are the ceremonial directions and are closely connected with the *Āraṇyakas*, meaning 'composed or studied in forests', and the one hundred and eight Upanishads are sprung from them. The Upanishads explain the *Vedaṅta* or six *darśanas* or systems of philosophy. All the works now mentioned constitute the *corpus operum* of the *Veda*.

The *Vedāṅga* or 'limb of the *Veda*' comprises six treatises which are designed to preserve the integrity of the *Vedas*. One of these, *Vyākaraṅa* or 'grammar', also includes two sutraic works, the *Ashṭādyāyī* or 'Eight Meditations' or grammatical aphorisms by *Pāṇini* and *Dhātu-Pāṭha* or 'a recital of roots' of language, which are both *smṛiti* or what is remembered by tradition and is treated as *Upadeśa*, or 'received wisdom' requiring no further qualification. These two works are the special keys to unlock the meaning of the *Veda*. Finally, there is *Upaveda* or 'Sub-Veda', which treats with certain important arts and practices.

VEDA

Ṛigveda

Sāmaveda *Yajurveda*

Atharvaveda

Brāhmaṇas *Āraṇyakas*

108 Upanishads

VEDĀṄGA

Ṡikshā	*Chandas*	*Nirukta*	*Vyākaraṇa*	*Jyotisha*	*Kalpa*
phonetics	rhythm	meaning	grammar	astronomy	ritual
			Ashṭādyāyī		
			Dhātu-Pāṭha		

UPAVEDA

Dhanurveda	*Āyurveda*	*Gāndharvaveda*	*Sthāpatyaveda*
archery & weapons	music	architecture	weapons

APPENDIX IV

The Divine Vedic Regents of the Directions

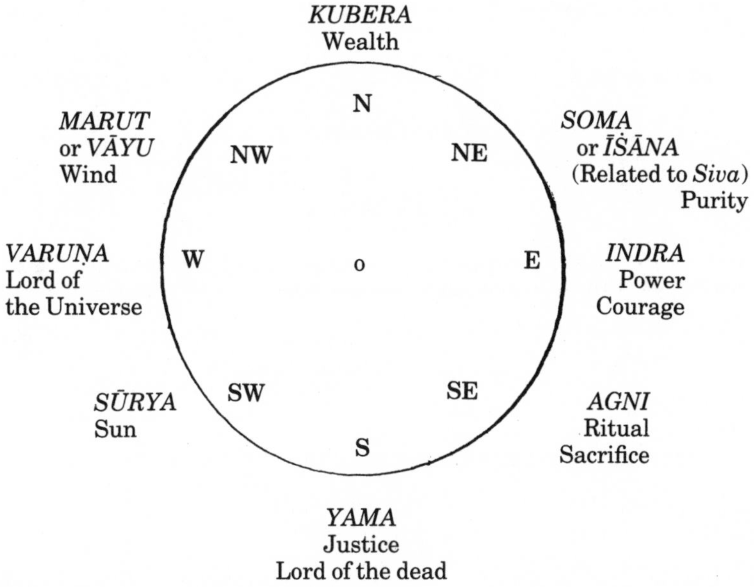

APPENDIX V

Plato's Divided Line

Condition of the Soul	The Line	The Ideas (1) and forms (2)(3) & (4)
Level One: *hē noēsis* – pure perception, leading to: *hē epistēmē* – true knowledge *hē phronēsis* – discrimination *hē sophia* – wisdom The test of knowledge: *logon dounai* – to give an account; to define	*ta* *nooumena*	1: *auto to agathon* – The Good Itself *auto kath' hauto* – Its own Self *ta eidē* – *kai*/and *hai ideai* – The Forms or Ideas known in their dependence on The Good *hē ousia* – Being; *to on* – Reality
The connection: *epistasthai to agathon hoti esti* to know The Good, what it is	The Intelligible World	*to kalon metekhei autou tou kalou* A beautiful object participates in Beauty Itself *homoion estin autoi toi kaloi* It is like Beauty Itself
Level Two: *hē dianoia* – intellect		2: *ta mathēmatika* – >< O [] [The universal forms are not known at this level in their dependence on The Good Itself]
Level Three: *hē pistis* – faith, comparable to: *hē doxa* – opinion *hē empeiria* – experience which are all known through *hai aisthēseis* – the senses	*ta* *phainomena*	3: *ta zoa* – the living creatures *pan to phuteuton* – the things that grow *pan to skeuaston* – all artefacts *ta tēn aisthēsin parekhonta* – the things producing sense impressions
Level Four: *hai eikasiai* – conjectures	Appearances	4: *ta en tois hudasi phantasmata* – things reflected in water. *hai skiai* – shadows

Notes

Abbreviations

VSA = V.S. Apte, *Practical Sanskrit – English Dictionary.*
M-W = Sir Monier Monier-Williams, *Sanskrit – English Dictionary.*
D-P = *Dhātu-Pāṭha: The Roots of Language*
AD = *Ashṭādyāyī* of *Pāṇini*
L&S = Liddell and Scott, *A Greek – English Lexicon*
D&K = Diels and Kranz, *Fragments*
Note: See the Bibliography for full publication details.

Chapter 1: The Birth of Creation

1 VSA, 643/3 and 907/2; M-W, 660/3 and 1052/2
2 VSA, 319/2; M-W, 235/3
3 VSA, 534/2 and 907/2; M-W, 526/1 and 1052/2
4 Genesis 1:2
5 *Fourth Ennead*, Seventh Tractate, l.10
6 D-P,1/1,1 p.17
7 *Śaṅkara's* commentary on *Aitareya* Upanishad, 3,1,3
8 M-W, 231/3; D-P, p.366
9 M-W, 1268/1 – see *spand*; D-P, p.372
10 *cf. Taittirīya* Upanishad, 11,9
11 *Gauḍapāda Kārikā*, 3,29, on *Māṇḍūkya* Upanishad
12 *Ibid*, v.47
13 VSA,41/1; M-W, 19/3
14 Variously ascribed to Epimenides
15 D-P, p.367
16 *Bṛihadāraṇyaka* Upanishad 1,5,21
17 *Ibid*, 1,3,1
18 *Laws*, 894A
19 L&S, 952/2
20 *Oxford English Dictionary*, 1971 ed. p.703/3
21 *Īśā* Upanishad, 1,8

Chapter 2: *Dhātu* and *Stoicheion*

1 M-W, 1270/3
2 D-P, pp.17, 329 and 366
3 D-P, Appendix 11, pp.366-75
4 L&S, 1057/1, but see earlier editions, *e.g.* 1883 ed., 901/2
5 D-P, p.350, 3/1, 46/1
6 M-W, 470/3
7 M-W, 755/3
8 D-P, p.358
9 Skeat, 244/1
10 D-P, p.392
11 M-W, 513/3
12 *Theogony*, l.728
13 *Ibid*, ll. 811-13
14 D&K, Fr.17, Fr.21
15 D-P, 26/2, and pp.265 and 279
16 *Timaeos*, 48B and 58C
17 *Metaphysics*, 5.3, 1014a26-1014b15
18 *Ibid.*
19 SVF, ii, 146

Chapter 3: 'Only the *Guṇāḥ* Act'

1 VSA, 406/2; M-W, 357/1
2 M-W, 1135/2
3 M-W, 863/2
4 VSA, 792/3
5 VSA, 468/3
6 M-W, 438/1
7 M-W, 1134/2
8 D-P, 25/1
9 M-W, 760/1

10 D-P, 19/2
11 M-W, 347/3, 481/3, 136/3
12 M-W, 861/2
13 D-P, 22/1
14 M-W, 872/1
15 M-W, 438/1
16 D-P, 30/2
17 M-W, 268/1
18 *Gītā*, 3,27
19 Simplicius *On Aristotle's Physics*, 1.2, 184b15
20 D-P, p.345 and 29/1
21 M-W, 707/1
22 D-P, 5/1
23 *Timaeos*, 53D
24 *Timaeos*, 54A
25 *Timaeos*, 54A-B
26 *Timaeos*, 53B

Chapter 4: The Traditional Indian and Vedic Gods

1 M-W, 1088/3
2 M-W, 25/1
3 *Manu-Smṛiti*, 1,10
4 M-W, 1182/2 and see *saras*
5 D-P, 14/2
6 M-W, 1246/1
7 M-W, 737/1
8 D-P, 1/1
9 M-W, 1107/3
10 D-P, 41/1, 44/2
11 M-W, 470/3, 7/1, 154/2
12 M-W, 1182/2
13 D-P, 20/2, 27/1
14 M-W, 347/3
15 D-P, 48/1
16 M-W, 898/3, 610/3
17 D-P, pp.350-1
18 D-P, p.351
19 VSA, 246/1 – 247/2
20 *Ibid.*
21 VSA, 345/1
22 VSA, 38/1
23 M-W, 477/3
24 M-W, 5/1; *cf.* Latin '*ignis*'
25 *cf.* Chapter 10 below
26 *cf.* Hesiod's Zeus in Chapter 5 below
27 VSA, 10/1
28 VSA, 761/1
29 VSA, 832/1
30 VSA, 843/3
31 M-W, 883/2
32 M-W, 1190/2
33 M-W, 343/2
34 D-P, 31/1
35 M-W, 336/2

Chapter 5: The Select Band of Olympian Gods

1 D-P, p.346 and 15/2; M-W, 481/3
2 D-P, p.347; M-W, 478/2
3 D-P, 28/1
4 *Iliad*, Book XIV, ll.1-152
5 *Ibid*, ll. 153-351
6 *Ibid*, ll.352-522
7 M-W, 321/3, *cf. Iliad*, Book XIV, ll.16-19
8 M-W, 1034/1, *cf.* ll.69-70
9 M-W, 835/3, *cf.* ll.169-74
10 M-W, 960/3, *cf.* ll.198-9
11 M-W, 270/3, *cf.* ll.214-17
12 M-W, 1259/1, *cf.* ll.315-18
13 M-W, 777/3, *cf.* ll.346-51
14 M-W, 1280/3, *cf.* ll.352-5, 247-8
15 D-P, 25/1
16 M-W, 1055/3
17 M-W, 500/1, *cf.* ll.383-7
18 M-W, 347/3, *cf.* ll.453-7
19 D&K, 64
20 D-P, 20/2, 24/2
21 M-W, 613/1
22 M-W, 859/1
23 *Gītā*, 10, 27
24 D-P, 47/1; p.344
25 M-W, 896/3
26 L&S, 21/1
27 D-P, 25/1, 29/1, 37/2, 44/2, 36/2
28 M-W, 426/1, 1134/3, 958/3, 397/3, 129/2, 559/1, 898/3
29 D-P, 24/2
30 M-W, 809/3
31 D-P, 37/1; p.343
32 M-W, 481/3
33 D-P, p.343

Chapter 6: The Five Vedic Elements and the Goddess *Māyā*

1 VSA, 195/1, *cf.* Shakespeare, Sonnet 62
2 VSA, 748/1
3 *Bṛihadāraṇyaka* Upanishad, 1,4,1
4 M-W, 578/3
5 *Protagoras*, 320C
6 *cf. Republic*, Book VII, where Sun : Fire :: Good : Sun and *Republic*, Book VI, 508 ff. in Chapter 15
7 M-W, 357/1
8 *e.g.* Shakespeare, Sonnet 15, p. xiii
9 M-W, 804/2

10 M-W, 804/3
11 M-W, 807/1
12 D-P, 24/2
13 D-P, p.296 and M-W, 809/3
14 D-P, p.351
15 *cf.* Shakespeare, Sonnet 53

Chapter 7: The Greek Creation Myths and the Four Elements

1 D-P, 19/1 and p.357; M-W, 99/2
2 According to G.S. Kirk's interpretation
3 *Metaphysics*, A3, 983b6
4 *Timaeos*, 52B-C
5 *Timaeos*, 32C
6 *Timaeos*, 58A-B
7 *Timaeos*, 30B

Chapter 8: The Gift of Language

1 *Kratylos*, 425D
2 VSA, 708/1
3 VSA, 865/1
4 A-D, 1,4,24
5 A-D, 1,4,32
6 A-D, 1,4,42
7 A-D, 1,4,45
8 A-D, 1,4,49
9 A-D, 1,4,54
10 M-W, 901/1
11 D-P, 34/2
12 M-W, 3/2
13 M-W, 972/3
14 *Manu*, 2,83
15 M-W, p.xi
16 M-W, p.xii
17 *cf.* Dr. R. Sharples, *The Criterion of Truth*, Liverpool, 1989; p.238 ff.
18 ap. Augustine *Civ. Dei* 7,28
19 Diogenes Laertius 1,21; Dillon 13
20 Ep. 65,8; Dillon 138
21 Diogenes Laertius, 1,21
22 *Adv. math.* 7,35 and 7,37
23 *De iudicandi facultate*, 2,3,8 ff

Chapter 9: The Great Ages, Conflagrations and Floods

1 See Chapter 13, n.2
2 *Works and Days*, ll.145-6
3 *Ibid*, l.184
4 M-W, 784/2
5 M-W, 761/1
6 M-W, 760/2
7 M-W, 1281/1
8 M-W, 258/2
9 M-W, 438/1
10 M-W, 765/1
11 M-W, 794/3
12 M-W, 410/2
13 See Theophrastus, Fr. 184; transl. by Fortenbaugh, Huby, Sharples, Gutas
14 M-W, 261/3
15 *Laws*, 676E
16 *Laws*, 677A

Chapter 10: The Seven *Ṛishi* of the *Veda* and of Delphi

1 M-W, 226/3; *cf.* VSA, 310/2
2 G.S. Kirk, *Homer and the Epic*, pp.197-201
3 *Ibid*, pp.208-17
4 *Nirukta*, *Yaśka*, Book 1, ch.xx.
5 M-W, 510/3
6 M-W, 785/3
7 Jeremiah 1:5
8 *Protagoras*, 343A; See Chapter 20, n.18
9 M-W, 786/3
10 *Apology*, 20E ff
11 *Republic*, Book IV, 427C
12 M-W, 1027/1
13 Hesiod, *Theogony*, l.280
14 M-W, 1249/3
15 M-W, 869/2; *cf.* Chapter 19

Chapter 11: The Epics as Spiritual Allegories

1 John 1:1,2
2 *Bhartrihari's Vākyapadīya*, Canto I, *Śloka* 1
3 *Mahābhārata*, *Ādi Parva*, CLXL; *Odyssey*, XXI l.404 ff.
4 *Rāmāyaṇa*, *Bāla kāṇḍa*, ch.67
5 M-W, 168/3
6 D-P, 28/2 and 40/2
7 M-W, 347/3
8 M-W, 145/3
9 D-P, 34/2
10 M-W, 169/1

Chapter 12: The *Iliad* and *Mahābhārata*

1 Herakleitos, D&K, 85
2 Book XVI, ll.781-822
3 *Mahābhārata*, *Drona Parva*, XLII-XLVII
4 L&S, 926/2 of 7th Edition, 1883; OUP

5 D-P, 40/1
6 D-P, 47/2
7 M-W, 985/3
8 M-W, 809/1
9 M-W, 99/1
10 Book 11, l.783

Chapter 13: The *Odyssey* and *Rāmāyaṇa*

1 Book I, l.60 and l.62
2 *Bṛihadāraṇyaka* Upanishad, 1,4,1; *cf.* Seneca, *De providentia*, 4,5 ff.
3 Book V, l.341
4 *Ibid*, ll.377-9
5 L&S, 1027/1
6 D-P, 23/1, 30/1
7 M-W, 506/3
8 M-W, 488/3
9 Book XVIII, ll.138-40
10 M-W, 59/2
11 M-W, 1020/2
12 L&S, 1401/2; Curtius, p.276
13 Book XX, l.355
14 Book IX, ll.89-97
15 Book X, l.305
16 *Kratylos*, 391D
17 Stanford, Vol. I, pp. 373-4
18 D-P, 42/2, 11/2
19 M-W, 890/1
20 *Aitareya* Upanishad 3,1,3 and *Śaṅkara's* commentary
21 Acts of the Apostles 28:3-5
22 Book. XI, l.330
23 *cf. Republic*, 618-20
24 Book XI, ll.601-4 and l.626
25 *cf. sarit* in Sanskrit: M-W, 1182/3
26 D&K, B.77. A and 118
27 *Republic*, 614C
28 *De Antro Nympharum*, 31
29 *Ibid*, 34, 36
30 Book XXIII, ll.247-53
31 Book XI, ll.100-37 and Book XXIII, ll.265-84
32 *Works and Days*, l.116
33 *Rāmāyaṇa*, *Ayodhyā Kāṇḍa*, Ch.XLI
34 *Rāmāyaṇa*, *Āraṇya Kāṇḍa*, Ch.XXVII
35 M-W, 1288/2, see 1288/1
36 M-W, 802/1
37 *Rāmāyaṇa*, *Sundara Kāṇḍa*, Ch.16; *cf. Kaṭha* Upanishad, II,111,17
38 M-W, 877/2 and 877/1
39 D-P, 18/2
40 D-P, p.246
41 M-W, 1218/2
42 M-W, 296/3 and 898/2

Chapter 14: Teacher and Student

1 W.K.C. Guthrie, *History of Greek Philosophy*, Vol.III, p.57
2 L&S, 971/2
3 *cf.* Aristotle, *Nicomachaean Ethics* (EN), 1127a9
4 *Gorgias*, 464B ff
5 *Phaidros*, 249E
6 *Kaṭha* Upanishad, 1,1,13
7 *Taittirīya* Upanishad, 1,3
8 M-W, 1140/2; VSA, 979/1
9 M-W, 836/1
10 *Muṇḍaka* Upanishad, 111,1,5
11 *Taittirīya* Upanishad, 11,1
12 *Kaṭha* Upanishad,1,2,9
13 M-W, 213/2
14 M-W, 422/2

Chapter 15: Knowledge and Nescience

1 *Republic*, Book VI, 509 ff
2 *Republic*, Book VII, 537E ff.
3 *Meno*, 72C
4 *Symposium*, 210
5 *Republic*, 476A
6 *Sophist*, 251E-252E
7 *Ibid*, 256E
8 *Philēbos*, 54A ff; *cf.* Chapter 1, n.6
9 *Metaphysics*, 1072b3
10 M-W, 1101/2
11 M-W, 1100/3
12 D-P, 20/2
13 M-W, 1274/2
14 M-W, 1272/2
15 D-P, 20/2
16 M-W, 398/1
17 D-P, p.351
18 *Phaidros*, 276A
19 D-P, p.10 gives a full analysis, with references
20 M-W, 43/1; VSA, 82/1
21 *Tattirīya* Upanishad, 2,1
22 See Chapter 18, final para., for full analysis with references
23 D-P, 18/2, 29/2
24 M-W, 97/2; VSA, 160/1
25 D-P, p.354
26 D-P, 29/2
27 *Taittirīya* Upanishad, 1,3,1

Chapter 16: Birth and Death

1 *Odyssey*, Book IX, ll.489-90

2 *Odyssey*, Book IV, ll.561-70; *Works and Days* ll.167-73
3 D&K, Fr. 55
4 *Theognis*, ll.243-44
5 Olympian Ode 2, ll.70ff.
6 Fr. 114, Bo.
7 Olympian Ode 2; *cf. Phaidros*, 249A
8 Fr. 127, Bo.
9 Empedokles, see D&K; Pythagoras, according to Porphyry
10 W.K.C. Guthrie, Vol.I, pp.199-212
11 D&K, Fr. 476
12 D&K, Fr. 113
13 *Phaido*, 81E ff.
14 *Ibid*, 84A
15 *Ibid*, 107C
16 *Republic*, Book IV, 435E ff.
17 *Republic*, Book VI, 490B
18 *De Generatione Animalium*, 736b28; *De Anima*, 430a22
19 *De Anima*, 408b24
20 M-W, 347/3
21 M-W, 947/3
22 *cf. Brahmāsūtrabhāshya*, IV,2,1-21

Chapter 17: Law and Justice

1 D-P, p.346; 33/1
2 M-W, 16/1; VSA, 34/1
3 D-P, 30/1
4 M-W, 1001/1
5 *Odyssey*, Book XIV, ll.83-4
6 *Iliad*, Book XVIII, ll.497 ff.
7 *Iliad*, Book XXIII
8 ll.213-47
9 ll.248-73
10 ll.274-85
11 ll.303 ff.
12 *Gorgias*, 475-77
13 *Gorgias*, 475A
14 *Gorgias*, 499
15 M-W, 510/3
16 *Mīmānśā Sūtra*, Ch.1, Canto 1, v.2
17 *Chāndogya* Upanishad, Ch.5, Canto 10, v.8
18 D-P, 32/1, 38/2
19 M-W, 1297/3; VSA, 1027/1
20 M-W, 254/1
21 M-W, 274/2
22 L&S, 1132/1; see W.H.D. Adkins, *Merit and Responsibility*, Ch. 5
23 VSA, 682/2
24 VSA, 380/3
25 For the dispute between *Vasishṭha* and *Viśvāmitra*, see *Rāmāyaṇa*, *Bāla Kāṇḍa*, ch 51-65
26 M-W, 1134/3
27 *Mahābhārata*, *Ādi Parva*, Ch.36
28 D-P, 26/2
29 M-W, 515/1, 650/2
30 D-P, 21/2
31 M-W, 204/3
32 D-P, 43/1
33 M-W, 601/1
34 *Republic*, Book X, 614B ff.
35 *Apology*, 41A; *Gorgias*, 524A
36 *Republic*, 617E ff.
37 *Ibid*, 619E
38 D-P, p.349; 40/1, 47/1
39 M-W, 1143/1
40 M-W, 721/1

Chapter 18: *Eudaimonia* and *Saccidānanda*

1 *Pol.* 1324a23 ff.
2 *EN* 1103a14 ff.
3 *EN* 1144a7 ff.
4 *EN* Book II, Ch.6
5 *EN* Book III, Ch.5
6 *EN* 1177a12 ff.
7 *EN* 1177b30 ff.
8 Corinthians 13:12; *cf. Phaidros*, 250B
9 D-P, 2/1, 7/1, 41/1, 44/1
10 M-W, 1133/2, 713/1, 1272/2, 397/3
11 D-P, 2/2
12 M-W, 1171/2
13 D-P, p.345; 13/1, 16/2
14 M-W, 1011/1
15 M-W, 1077/3
16 *Īśā* Upanishad, v.4
17 M-W, 347/3
18 M-W, 1297/3

Chapter 19: 'Madness in Great Ones'

1 *Phaidros*, 244C
2 D-P, p.350
3 D-P, 29/2
4 M-W, 426/1
5 *Taittirīya* Upanishad, 2,1,1
6 D-P, p.9
7 *Phaidros*, 245A
8 *Demokritos*, Frs. 17,18
9 L&S, 926/1
10 L&S, 882/2
11 L&S, 749/1 ff.
12 D-P, 20/1
13 M-W, 398/1; *cf.* M-W, 516/3
14 D-P, 6/2

15 VSA, 482/2
16 M.P. Pandit, p.31
17 *cf.* M-W, 869/2
18 D-P, 15/1, 49/2
19 M-W, 162/1, 1267/3
20 *Ṛigveda*,9,97,55

Chapter 20: 'That Thou Art' and 'Know Thyself'

1 D-P, 25/1
2 D-P, 1/1
3 M-W, 107/3 and 594/3
4 D-P, p.345
5 D-P, 40/1 and 45/1
6 M-W, 1280/1
7 D-P, 18/1
8 M-W, 135/1; VSA 209/1
9 D-P, pp.344 and 343
10 D-P, 6/1, 35/1, 45/1
11 M-W, 954/1, 766/2
12 M-W, 737/3
13 VSA, 705/1
14 M-W, 737/1
15 A-D, 7,1,58, and D-P, p.6, rule (iii)
16 D-P, 15/2, 46/1
17 M-W, 1011/1
18 *Sylloge Inscriptionem Graecorum*, Vol. III, 1268
19 L&S, 810/1
20 D-P, p.348 and 35/2
21 L&S, 1841/1
22 L&S, 1167/1
23 *Statesman*, 283E ff.
24 *Philēbos*, 63E
25 *Philēbos*, 61A ff.
26 *Philēbos*, 59E ff.
27 *Phaidros*, 247C; *c.f. Kaṭha* Upanishad, 1,3,15
28 *Kaṭha* Upanishad, 1,2,23

Bibliography

Sanskrit-English Dictionary, Sir Monier Monier-Williams, 1974 reprint of 1988 ed.; OUP.

The Practical Sanskrit-English Dictionary, 1985 reprint of 1965 4th edition; Vaman Shivram Apte; Motilal Banarsidass, Delhi.

Dhātu-Pāṭha: The Roots of Language, by S.R. Hill and P.G. Harrison; 1991; Gerald Duckworth & Co. Ltd., London.

Grundzüge der Griechischen Etymologie, Georg Curtius; transl. by A.S. Wilkins and E.B. England, Vth ed., 1886; John Murray, London.

Ṣṛīmad Bhāgavata Mahāpurāṇa, Part I, 1st Edition, 1971, transl. by C.L. Goswami; Motilal Jalan, Gorakhpur.

Māṇḍūkyopanishad with *Gauḍapāda's Kārikā* and *Ṡaṅkara*'s Commentary, transl. by Svami Nikhilananda, 6th ed., 1974; Ṡṛī – Ramakrishna Ashrama, Mysore.

Ten Principal Upanishads with Ṡaṅkarabhāshya, Vol.I, 1978 reprint of 1970 ed.; Motilal Banarsidass.

Bhagavadgītā with *Ṡaṅkarabhāshya*. Vol.II, 1978 reprint of 1929 ed.; Motilal Banarsidass.

Vishṇusahasranāma with the *Bhāshya* of *Ṡṛī Ṡaṅkarācārya*, R. Ananthakrishna Sastry, 1980 ed.; Adyar.

Vākyapadīya of *Bhartṛihari*, K. Raghavan Pillai. ed., 1971; Motilal Banarsidass.

Ṛigveda, Vols I-V, 1972 reprint of 1933 ed., Vaidika Samsodhana Mandala.

The Hymns of Ṡaṅkara, by T.M.P. Mahadevan, 1st ed. 1980; Motilal Banarsidass.

Sanātana Dharma by *Jagadguru Ṡaṅkarācārya Ṡṛī Bharati Kṛishṇa Tirthāji Mahārāj*, 1970; Bharatiya Vidya Bhavan, Bombay.

Manusmṛiti, ed. Gopala Sastri Nene, 3rd ed. 1982; Chaukhambha Sanskrit Sansthan, Varanasi.

The Laws of Manu, transl. by G. Buhler, OUP 1886, repr. 1979; Motilal Banarsidass.

Pañcīkaraṇam of *Ṡṛī Ṡaṅkarācārya*, 1971 ed.; Advaita Ashrama, Calcutta.

Brahmasūtra of *Ṡaṅkarācārya*, transl. by Gambhirananda, 2nd ed. 1972; Advaita Ashrama, Calcutta.

Mahābhārata of *Kṛishṇa-Dvaipayāṇa Vyāsa*, transl. by K.M. Ganguli, 4th ed. 1981; Munshiram Manoharlal Publishers Pvt. Ltd, New Delhi.

Rāmāyaṇa of *Vālmīki*, transl. by Makhanlal Sen, 1965 ed.; Rupa & Co., Calcutta.

Mystic Approach to the Veda and the Upanishad, M.P. Pandit, 3rd ed. 1974; Ganesh & Company.

Hindu Polytheism, Alain Danielou, 1964; Routledge & Kegan Paul Ltd, London.

India and the Greek World, Jean W. Sedlar, 1980; Rowman and Littlefield, Totowa, New Jersey.
A Greek-English Lexicon, Liddell and Scott, 9th ed. 1940; 1978 reprint; OUP.
The Iliad of Homer, Vols 1 and II, M.M. Willcock, 1978 and 1984; St Martin's Press, London.
The Odyssey of Homer, Vols I and II, W.B. Stanford. Vol.I: 1980 reprint of 1947 ed.; Vol. II: 1971 reprint of 1948 ed.; Macmillan, London.
Hesiod: Works & Days, by M.L. West, 1980 reprint of 1978 ed.; OUP.
Pindar, by C.M. Bowra, 1964; OUP.
Sylloge Inscriptionum Graecorum, Wilhelm Dittenberger, 3rd ed. 4 vols, 1915-1924; Leipzig.
Die Fragmente Der Vorsokratiker, Hermann Diels and Walther Kranz, 1960; Weidmannsche Verlagsbuchhandlung, Berlin.
The Presocratic Philosophers, G.S. Kirk, J.E. Raven and M. Schofield, 1988 reprint; CUP.
De Antro Nympharum, Porphyrius, transl. by the Dept. of Classics, State University of New York, at Buffalo, 1969; Arethusa Monographs.
Platōnis Opera, Vols I-V, various reprints 1976-79; OUP.
A Word Index to Plato, Leonard Brandwood, 1976; W.S. Maney & Son Ltd, Leeds.
Aristotēlis Politica, 1978 reprint of 1957 ed.; OUP.
Aristotēlis Metaphysica, 1978 reprint of 1957 ed.; OUP.
Aristotēlis Ethica Nicomachea, 1979 reprint of 1894 ed.; OUP.

Index